T0294780

Nine Months Is A Year

Nine

Months Is a Year

at Baboquívari School

Eulalia "Sister" Bourne

THE UNIVERSITY OF ARIZONA PRESS
Tucson, Arizona

About the Author

EULALIA BOURNE has "lived" the books she has authored. The intensity of the many years of her creative teaching in one-room rural schools is captured in this record of a matchless year at a ranch school in the Altar Valley. Incredibly the years of schoolteaching were the same years in which her homestead grew into a cattle ranch, established and thriving under one woman's care alone. Known as "Sister" to hundreds of her neighbors, friends, and former pupils, Sister wrote in her first book that she was wrapped up in "kids and cows." In WOMAN IN LEVI'S (UA Press, 1967), she told about the cows with affection, wit, and touches of poetry. Here she tells about the kids, and one of the best years of their lives — and hers too — at Baboquivari School.

ISBN 0-8165-0067-3 (pbk)

Copyright © 1968
The Arizona Board of Regents
Library of Congress Catalog
Card No. 68–57760
Manufactured in the U.S.A.

To us boys, school had its chief value, in fact its only value, in its games and sports. Of course, our parents and teachers were always urging us to work. In their efforts to make us study, they resorted to every sort of means — headmarks, presents, praise, flattery, Christmas cards, staying in at recess, staying after school, corporal punishment, all sorts of persuasion, threats, and even main force — to accomplish this result. No like rewards or punishments were required to make us play; which fact, it seems to me, should have shown our teachers and parents that play, exercise, activity, and change are the law of life. . . .

— Clarence Darrow, *Farmington*.

Contents

CHILDREN MAY NOT HAVE CHANGED but times and institutions have. This story of one year's experiences in a Pima County, Arizona, rural school, told by the teacher and pupils at Baboquívari all took place before World War II, before Sputnik, before "anti-poverty" measures. It happened in the Thirties when large ranches, mostly on public domain, were run like feudal estates; when top cowhands worked for $50 a month; when a schoolteacher's salary was $1125 a year; when country schools were supervised by county superintendents making two part-day visits per term; when the word "drop-out" had not been invented but dropping out was up to the pupils and the teacher's responsibility was to keep them coming.

It happened at a time and place when after all was said and done, a teacher and a bunch of children, assorted grades and ages, were happily, hopefully, enthusiastically on their own in the great and venturesome field of public education.

— E. B.

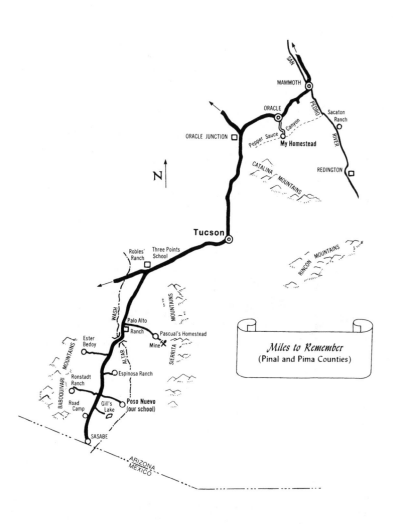

SAN

MAMMOTH

ORACLE

Sacaton
Ranch

ORACLE JUNCTION

Pepper Sauce Canyon

PEDRO

My Homestead

RIVER

CATALINA MOUNTAINS

REDINGTON

N

Tucson

Robles'
Ranch

Three Points
School

RINCON MOUNTAINS

MOUNTAINS

WASH

Palo Alto
Ranch

Pascual's Homestead

Mine

Ester
Bedoy

SIERRITA

ALTAR

Miles to Remember
(Pinal and Pima Counties)

MOUNTAINS

Espinosa Ranch

BABOQUIVARI MOUNTAINS

Ronstadt
Ranch

Road
Camp

Gill's
Lake

Poso Nuevo
(our school)

SASABE

ARIZONA
MEXICO

One Hundred Miles To School

IT OCCURRED TO ME all at once as I was driving down from my homestead this morning that at last I am contented here at this little school at a lonely "water" on a remote cattle ranch in Southern Arizona. The fact that it is one of the biggest ranches in the state makes its isolation complete, for there are no close neighbors.

When a new teacher and a group of country pupils of assorted ages and grades meet at the beginning of a term in a far-off one-room school there are many adjustments to make, and teacher will make most of them. There must be a long period of strenuous effort — not only to instruct the children, but to win them. It is not easy. Last year, and even into my second term with the same bunch, I used to cross off days on the calendar, rushing the week to Friday when I could shut the school-room door, and my door, and leave the noise and dust and contentions of Pozo Nuevo to go back to my home-stead in Pepper Sauce Canyon, two hours' drive from Tucson, in the San Pedro Valley.

Already it is March; time has rushed by — proof that the old homesickness and worry that troubled me for so long are past. This is my place now, and I am honestly glad that tomorrow is only Tuesday, for my interest in the kids and the school makes time fly. This Monday morning I left the cabin at Pepper Sauce at 4:30 a.m. and drove my old car at top speed the hundred miles down here — mostly over Arizona dirt roads — before 9 o'clock. After such a long day I am naturally tired, but not lonely or low-spirited I had a happy week-end working at the little ranch, and school will pleasantly fill the days until I can return.

My situation is out of the ordinary in several re-spects. There can't be many schools like this one left in America. Here it is — an organized county school, but there are no prospects for its development. It is located amid a scattering of ranch homes far from any settlement and there is no prospect of money for a school building. Sessions are held in whatever temporary quarters may be convenient for the two landholders in the six-town-ship district, neither of whom is a patron. The one-room school is maintained by Pima County and the state of Arizona for children of the vaqueros who work the cattle on these large ranches. Now and then there are part-time pupils from the camps of temporary prospectors or assess-ment workers, and occasionally some children from Las Carpas, the road camp.

My bus-riding pupils are worse off than I, for they
have to get up before daylight five days a week instead
of one, and travel over rough, unimproved roads in a
rickety, unheated beat-up old panel truck, never meant
for a schoolbus. Even in the Far West, still wild in its
rangelands, this is a strange situation for a county school.
And I am by no means a typical teacher.

I understood the curious stares of the dudes from
"La Osa," a guest ranch on the Mexican border twenty
miles south of us, as they passed me on the road this
morning. Probably no woman holding a teaching posi-
tion ever cut a stranger figure. I had got out to look at
the tires. The unscraped corduroy on the dirt road was
so bad that I was afraid I was driving on a flat. They
were in an open car and had a good look at me. They
saw a thin, leggy woman neither young nor old, dressed
in men's ranch wear. My brown Stetson was bought for
a larger head. My leather jacket needed cleaning. My
blue shirt and faded Levi's were freshly washed and
ironed and I had polished my boots before they were
covered by the dust.

To pioneer women, even at mid-twentieth-century,
clothes must be chiefly covering. When you sit alone in
a semi-desert wilderness to eat your evening meal it will
not help your morale to be clad in soiled Levi's. But if
the engine that runs the pump over the well down in the
canyon goes to popping and you must dash down a steep
rocky trail to wrestle with greasy machinery, it does help
your morale to know you aren't ruining good clothes.

The first months of school I did wear dresses. Hot
weather, as much as convention, demanded it. At the
beginning of each school year I buy a new dress to pep

up opening day and to be in style with the school girls whose new dresses are meant to impress me and the other pupils.

On a cold November morning my chance came as I'd hoped it would before winter set in. Ramón and Pancho, returning from their traps, came riding into the square in front of the long building just as I was passing from my room to the school. I admired Pancho's horse — a small chunky bay — and he jumped off and invited me to mount. I ran back into my room to don boots and Levi's for a dash up the road with Ramón, my oldest schoolboy. We galloped back to meet the school bus and there was no time to change. The ice was broken, my washing and ironing were reduced considerably, and my skinny frame protected from the chilling winds.

It was not personal appearance alone that caused the dudes to stare; they wear western clothes, but with a difference. My bug-splashed old car seemed to sit on its haunches with its heavy load, making a ramshackle introduction to the long line of trailing dust stirred up for miles behind. The ridiculous cargo could offer no explanation of my haste or destination. The car was piled hit or miss with bags and cartons of a week's provisions, personal stuff, library books, bedding, various odds and ends including a new broom; and it was topped off with Cherry and Honey, my two little dogs, poking their noses out to see what was going on. Immediately behind the seat perched the green cages housing the distressed canaries Tommy Tucker and Little Roy — always miserable while motoring. With every stop they cease clinging for their lives and start rapidly picking at their seeds. I must take these pets with me each Friday and Monday on the long, uncomfortable journey because they are my dependents. Once we arrive, they are assets. The children like them. The little birds hang in the south windows and sing when we sing, and when we don't. The children vie for a chance to give them drinking water and fill their baths. The small fry, apt to be neglected in a school of such varied activity, spend pleasant time watching the birds. Cherry, a fox terrier, usually lies under my desk. She barks at intruders, even personages, and sometimes growls when she thinks somebody may be giving me a bad time. Honey, a timid beige Chihuahua, stays curled up on my bed.

If the dudes meet Pascual of a morning they have no trouble figuring *him* out. He packs fourteen children, luckily thin ones, into his beat-up vehicle with the home-made sign, SCHOOL BUS. Pascual wakes up his son and three daughters at five every morning, gathers the other ten riders at stations miles apart along side roads, and makes seventy-two miles round trip a day over dirt roads. some of them perilous cuts in steep-sided canyons. Three groups he brings from the Sierritas, the long mountain range that forms the eastern rim of the wide Altar Valley; then he swings across sloping distances to the Babo-quívaris on the west to pick up another group, and turns back seven miles due east to the middle of the flatlands bordering the drainage arroyo.

As for me, I come from beyond the Catalina Moun-tains, the faint blue range far to the north, and on the far slopes, fifty miles the other side of Tucson, the bur-geoning city halfway between my home ranch and the ranch school. We meet here at Pozo Nuevo, an obscure "water" on the dusty plain along the banks of the long arroyo (dry except in flood time) that is a drainage spine for the vast area between the mountain ranges along the border of Mexico.

In the whole United States there may not be another school district as extensive as ours. From Pozo Nuevo you can go five miles north, seven west, ten south, and twenty east, without encountering a human habitation: an area encompassing about four hundred square miles, its residents just one family and me, for the bus riders live outside its fringes. But Prieto Aros' family is a small colony: himself, his wife, and their eighteen children, and a homeless young man they call cousin. Prieto is the vaquero in charge of the water and livestock in this wide corner of the Quarter-Circle DV Bar ranch which takes in about 300 sections. Prieto is a colorful individual who came to the U.S.A. from Chihuahua so long ago that no passport was necessary. He has been on this job for twelve years. In two marriages he has fathered sixteen children and stepfathered two, and has shouldered the responsibility of feeding and caring for them single-handed on a salary of $50 a month. From the state and county comes only schooling (which Prieto doesn't believe really necessary so the older boys are kept out now and then to help him with his work) and the services that go with it.

Pozo (or Poso as I'll spell it phonetically as we do here) Nuevo means New Well. This one is six hundred feet deep; it gives soft pure water via the power of a giant engine whose flywheel is taller than I. When it is running, the whole place vibrates with its deep steady throb. In desert regions any pump is a pleasure to hear for it means water, precious and rare, insuring life for many animals and a few trees and plants. But the well is no longer new, and maybe should be called Poso Bueno (Good Well) now. Everything here looks old except the little tamarisks and Doña Lupe's garden back of the kitchen. The patched roof, crumbling adobe walls, and gray shrunken corrals show the weathering of many years. Even the gates, made of heavy timbers, originally painted green, and hung on massive home-forged hinges, are faded and sagging. Five pastures corner at this water so there are three gates to open as you drive up. In day-time the Aros kids run out and swing on them at the sound of an approaching car. If it is the teacher they know she will hand out a candy sucker or stick of gum (not to be chewed during school) for this service. At night, in the cold weather, all the in-and-out of opening and closing gates is a hateful chore.

The building at Poso Nuevo is a long string of rooms like barracks, running east and west for over a hundred feet. The west room (originally two) is the school. Next is the teacher's room which joins the one where the ranch boys — seven of them at present — and their guests sleep. I've often wondered how they all crowd into so small a space. Once I peeked in and saw only two narrow iron cots. Bedding is scarce. In cold weather the door and small window remain closed, and the boys sleep in their jeans. There is a fireplace, the only one on the ranch, and I sometimes hear quarrels about the wood-getting. Usually the lot falls to Pancho who is bigger than the younger boys, and smaller than the older ones. The fire furnishes their evening light, just as it did for Abe Lincoln. Beyond the boys' room is the one where the girls sleep. It has no window, but connects with the floorless shed used as the kitchen and also with the "front" room which contains two or three chairs, a small shrine decorated with drawn-work runners and paper flowers, and a big white bed where the father and mother and baby sleep. After that comes the drafty space where they store hay and saddles. Then the biggest room of all, the pumphouse over the well, with its tall, peaked roof surmounted by a headframe, used when pulling the pipes. The saddle room and pumphouse form one side of the big corral used for horses and the milk cows. A vaquero asks little more of a dwelling than a roof and walls. He is not worried by having the horse corral backed up against his home. Flies and odors are looked upon as necessary evils. And water from six hundred feet underground is not likely to be polluted.

The only plumbing in the ranchhouse is the little sink under the half-window in my room. Bill, clerk of the board, put it in last year, and this year the small lavatory in the corner of the schoolroom because of all our messes with clay and water colors and printers ink. Our big water tanks, holding nearly thirty thousand gallons, are set on low cement platforms. Consequently the pressure is so poor that neither faucet will give water when any of the outside taps are open. But it is wonderful to have even part-time water indoors. And I am pleased with the new ceiling and cement baseboards that keep out all kinds of little pests. Last year I squashed a centipede on the little rug by my bed, and trapped forty-four mice in the six shelves that serve as pantry and dish cupboard. But the rats that scamper over the ceiling disturb my dogs and me only four nights a week. The other three we are at home at our ranch in the San Pedro Valley. The most disturbing thing there is the 3:30 a.m. rising on Monday mornings.

"You don't drive," Pascual said. "You fly" (he's thinking of the big clouds of dust that boil up under my wheels).

I have to go fast; that is, relatively. On these roads forty miles an hour is speeding and you can easily bounce into a dip and break a spring. The trouble is that Old Father Time hasn't noticed that I try to live in two places and hold down two jobs at once. The pressure on Monday morning comes from the hour I spend in the city doing errands. What a rush! Have the car serviced; leave the laundry; get the kerosene and the chunk of ice; and shop for five days' groceries for myself and the dogs and cat and birds, and the hot lunches for the school.

When I parked in front of the market this morning I could see the dark-eyed young man buttoning on his green smock and likely saying to himself: "Here is that lunatic wanting to buy twelve dozen oranges before daylight. On Monday, too; just when I'm ordering my vegetables."

"Two dozen beets," he called over his shoulder to the produce man. "And a crate of mustard greens."

When I leave the city just after dawn the road is mine alone and I really split the breeze. The eighteen miles of oiled road is easy, but for the cattle that hang about the highway and cross suddenly in front of the swerving car. Friday night I had a near disaster. It had been raining which made it hard to hurry on account of the mud and the wet dips on the dirt road. I had to turn on my lights before I hit the blacktop. At last relieved of bad roads, I stepped on it. Suddenly a few yards ahead I saw the bobbing rumps of a little bunch of cattle up the road. They had been drinking from the puddles made by the rain. I was not going over fifty-five, but the brakes were wet. In the wild careening I may have knocked the hair off a yearling or two, but no real harm was done. In the two years I have been burning up this road I have hit one. It was at 1:30 a.m. returning from a trip to Phoenix. All at once a big heifer popped up from a side ditch and stood broadside for the impact. I had almost stopped when I hit her, but she went down bawling piteously. How was I to put a quick end to her misery? That was the only time I have wished for a gun in spite of all the warnings about desperadoes and escaped convicts trying to get across the border. When I forced myself to get out I could see that she was lying flat, the bumper pushing into her belly. I got back into the car and reversed and was happy to see her jump up and trot slowly but capably out of sight.

After daybreak I can see far enough ahead to take precautions. This morning I was ten minutes late at Robles, where the road right-angles toward Sasabe. With disregard for nervous tension and damaging dips (off the pavement now), I was only seven minutes late at King's cattleguard, and four minutes late at Palo Alto in spite of the momentary pause when I met the dudes.

At the bridge I was right on schedule, banging over the iron runways with the dogs clinging to me in fright. With minutes to spare I swirled up to the gates — Pancho waiting at the first, Pili at the second, Víctor at the third — and had time to revive the birds and wash my hands while the boys were unloading the car, which they like to do because it gives them a chance to see what I've bought. And I spoil them by handling out bits of cookies, or crackerjack. It will make it harder on their next teacher, but their pleasure is my pleasure.

When the kids come hurrying in at the jangle of the bell — a small brass one meant to hang on the neck of a *caponera* (boss mare of the remuda) — it is a satisfaction to see their friendly eager faces and their fresh Monday clothes as they line up, salute the flag, and pass by my desk — their hands spread out for fingernail inspection, grins on their faces to show they have washed their teeth with the brushes the school gave them. Individual charts are kept, and annual prizes awarded, courtesy of the teacher.

Herlinda and Lolita, pale delicate sisters, twelve and eight, have a shining spotless look every morning. Dainty Francisca has a perfect record, too, but she has the advantage of being the only child in the house of an adoring aunt. The snaggle-toothed, chopped-nailed smaller ones give proof that cleanliness is not a natural human attribute. Allowances must be made. I wrote a note about a little girl's habit of biting her nails. The grandmother in charge of the home sent me word to light a match and burn the culprit's fingers. This was effective. It cured me of writing notes.

My baby girl Teresa, now half past six, can seldom pass muster in personal neatness. Her light brown hair won't lie in place unless her mother has time to curl it with the iron heated over a kerosene lamp. Her nails are long and short, clean and otherwise. Her stockings are wrinkled, one often slumped over her untied shoe. Her little red sweater is likely to be wrong side out for she dresses in the dark.

"Teddy," I said, "there is breakfast on your teeth."

She smiled good-naturedly. "The toot' brush lost," she piped in her baby voice.

"Too bad. Make me remember after school to give you another."

"All right."

She sighed contentedly, skipped around my desk, snatched a piece of prized white drawing paper as she passed, humped up in her uncomfortable old desk, and began to draw. She is a happy little girl, a joy to be around.

Being plump, she doesn't have to line up at the call "Cod liver oil" (made tolerable by a chaser of half an orange). Many of the young drylanders that come unwrapping spoons for their morning doses seem to like the taste of the gooey mess of vitamins that smells up the room, splashes the floor, and smears my Levi's.

"Dr. Bourne," they call me, particularly if I am wearing sun glasses. Indeed it is a rare day that I don't have to treat cuts, sores, vaccinations, impetigo, or infections, along with headaches and stomach aches. I keep a young drugstore in my room.

A country school, exerting the only social, hygenic,

and moral influences outside the home on young people who might be content to be barbarians, cannot set schedules that are inviolate. Our morning session on Monday, at least up to recess, is an orientation and organization period; we catch up on what has happened, and survey what is ahead. Today we had new library books (causing a noisy stampede for choices) to list and distribute, the weekend to talk over, and the mail, which Socorro had saved from Saturday when Arturo and Víctor rode four miles to the highway mailbox. Our rural free delivery functions on Tuesdays and Saturdays. This morning there were two fan letters for *Little Cowpuncher,* the school monthly magazine we put out by means of a used mimeograph donated by Constance Smith, our county school superintendent.

There was a letter from a Tucson subscriber asking us to send a copy to the president of the National Federation of Women's Clubs in Washington, D.C. The other letter was from a lady in Illinois enclosing a dollar to help with expenses, and wanting us to send her a copy of the September issue so that her set for the year might be complete. When Socorro, in charge of back files, brought out the September number we looked it over and were amused to see how slight it was: only four pages. Now we print eight. It has no fiction, poems, jokes, or book reviews. Its stories make us laugh — already part of our outgrown past. They do give graphic ideas of our locality and personalities.

Of all the innovations school has made in the lives of these back country children, *Little Cowpuncher* is best. It has brought direct contact with the wonderful world the other side of the mountains. *Little Cowpuncher* did not originate in this community. It began with the Valdez, Moreno, and Bingham children at Redington — away off in the San Pedro River Valley. I brought it with me here so that this group of isolated Mexican-American children could be presented to readers gracious enough to help bridge the chasm dividing these youngsters from their heritage of citizenship of America and of the world. Closer at hand, publishing *Little Cowpuncher* is a group enterprise binding us together in a common purpose, and sometimes thrilling us with tokens of success. Also, it gives immediate reasons for studying spelling, punctuation, and English, although I print the children's stories as they are finally turned in, for they make better reading in original forms, true and uncorrected.

People laughed at Víctor's story about our new equipment in the September issue because he said the clock could "walk" eight days without winding. Literally, in Spanish, a clock *walks* instead of *runs*.

Ramón's story telling how he helped his father and brothers round up thirty-four bulls to be tested was striking. He said: "The bulls have to be seen by a doctor to see if they are all right. They vaccinate them by the government to prove that they don't get t.b."

Edward's story was a bit of local color:

Yesterday Father and I killed a large snake. She took two hours to die and was strong and healthy at the very last. It even made my father nervous because she was so hard to kill. People said she was the biggest rattlesnake they ever saw. She was six feet from head to rattle and when I skinned her after taking off the head she measured eight inches wide.

Ysidra, in the title story "School Begins Again at Baboquívari," was inspired to summarize our social function in one line: "We have a few pupils — not very many as we had last year. And now we have seen each other."

Far off here where loneliness flourishes in the isolation of space, school's choicest lure is the opportunity for fellowship. Just to see each other is something!

THE AROSES

This father, another mother	This mother, another father	This father & this mother
José (Joe)	Socorro	Arturo
Concepción (Chato)	Francisco (Franqui)	Víctor
		Consuelo (Chelo)
Catalina (Katie)		Pedro (Pili)
Ramón		María (Meli)
Pancho		Mercedes (Mercy)
Ysidra		Evangelina (Eva)

A Family of Vaqueros

BY THE MIDDLE of the second year you get used to living cheek by jowl with seven brothers. And the noise, if it isn't contentious, seems as natural as wind or rain. Tonight they are singing. Every night from supper till bedtime they sing. They sing in harmonies or thirds, and Frank knows how to accompany them, *moda mejicana,* on his guitar. Usually the music is not gay, but in its strange wild melancholy it is effective. Of course most of their songs (except those strictly for my benefit and learned in school) are in their native tongue; since it is not my language I am less likely to be bored by the banal repetitions of the verses.

Now they are singing *Delgadina,* a terrible ballad probably based on fact as is the way with ballads, but

pleasing for its hypnotic tune. It is easy to harmonize and
they make the most of it — big and little boys all singing out together, happily indifferent (I hope) to the
horrible implication behind the words (a girl wronged
by her father). They sing to be singing, caring nothing
for themes but taking pride, as far as the text goes, in
memorizing the words.

The Aros children are all talented singers. Their
father is a good singer. His voice is worn by *muchos años,*
but I have heard him, when on a *parranda,* sing all night
long — while all the rest of us under his roof pretended
to sleep — accompanying himself on the guitar when
Frank gave out.

Although they fear their father and sometimes feel
the weight of his hand or quirt, his children are proud
of him. They imitate him in work and play. Even when
he behaves his worst, they make excuses for him, or take
his peccadillos with amused tolerance. Socorro said:
"When my little sister died My-father got drunk and took
his gun and was going to shoot God because he killed
my little sister."

They never say "Father" — always "My-Father."
His name is Pedro but he is called Prieto because he is
very dark. He is a genuine vaquero. Besides being a
master with ropes and spurs, he knows the habits of cattle
and horses, knows hundreds of them by fleshmarks, and
knows how to make them do what he expects of them,
however harsh his methods. He is a typical old-time
Chihuahueño, not above medium height but so thin that
he appears tall. With his long, concave figure, hatchet
face, drooping mustache, sagging pants-seat creased from

many days in the saddle, and his wilted old black hat with the peaked crown, he would make fine material for a cartoonist.

He likes my little dogs, particularly Cherry because she is smart and he says she is cleaner to have in the house and car than his babies. This doesn't mean that he objects to babies. At first his reserve and sternness toward his school-age children deceived me into thinking that his large family was a burden. As I came to know him I knew better. Late one afternoon I was hunting for Cherry who had returned from our walk ahead of me and I came upon Prieto and his wife seated on the ground in the corral on the sunny side of the pumphouse. The baby, his fifteenth, was bouncing on her mother's lap, waving her arms in the air. Prieto was cooing at her, and leaned down to kiss her small full lips.

In the tradition of paternal authority he has complete rule over all his offspring and apparently wants to keep them under the family roof forever. The two oldest boys are young men past twenty, yet they remain around the family board, picking up whatever temporary jobs Prieto can get for them. When Catalina, twenty-two — considered well along in years for an uneducated, unmarried girl — was preparing for matrimony he took measures to prevent it. He told her that her suitor was a rogue who wanted her only to make tortillas for him, and he forbade her to leave the house. Finally he and her stepmother promised her that if she would give up this marriage they would buy her anything she asked for and would take her to any dances and fiestas she wanted to attend. This promise they attempted to keep for months. And Socorro told me that the reason Prieto drank so much last spring was because he was sad when Catalina moved to town to get a job and to contact her romance. He doesn't talk to her now when by chance they meet, and he vows, I am told, that he will never take her and her homeless infant under his protection. This I consider a pose that time will undermine. Doting parent that he is, his whim is law. If he says Ramón cannot go to town with the teacher and the others of his class to visit an art exhibit and watch a magician do his tricks, Ramón, seventeen, stays to pick beans without a word of protest.

Last spring there was a dance at Las Carpas. The Aros car was in its usual state of disrepair. Alfredo, a young bus driver from the Road Camp, took the mother and the baby and the girls. The three oldest schoolboys were to go with me. The younger children had to stay at home under Ysidra's care. She, twelve, is not old enough to be out socially, but is old enough to take responsibility for the kitchen and her young brothers and sisters.

Prieto, squatting on his heels in ambush out by the water tanks that evening, watched me get in and back the car out into the road. The boys, in clean shirts, their hair slicked down, ran to climb in, giggling and pushing for choice seats. Suddenly Prieto called an order, and they stopped in consternation.

"You did not ask my permission to go," he said peremptorily.

"We asked *her,*" said Ramón, indicating his stepmother who had gone.

"Pero no me dijiste a mí," his father stated angrily, and the boys immediately crawled out of the car and went to take off their good clothes.

I did not dare intercede, but I knew he had no objection to dancing. Once he had danced with me! It was at the last Halloween party, held at night in the decorated schoolroom. It doesn't take much to make a party gala in the far outlying settlements. We had worked at this one — the whole school and the district mothers — so it was especially gay. The teenage pupils were loathe to see it end. When the *gente de razón* and other distant neighbors and guests had gone, Socorro kept the phonograph going. She put on a rollicking piece and took my hand to step out and dance with her. We did jig steps, separately. Yielding to the rhythm I began to improvise. She picked up a big Mexican hat from a desktop and fanned my feet. The watching children yelled in delight. Suddenly I had a partner. Prieto, who had been squatting on his heels in the shadows back of the stove talking with other vaqueros, jumped out in front of me, half bent over, an intent look on his face, dancing furiously. His boots rose knee high and dashed jauntily forward and back and sideways, scarcely touching the floor. Without once looking at me, he led me, outdanced me. The gleeful kids went wild. When the music ceased he slouched back into his corner and turned to speak to his neighbors as he wiped his face with his colored handkerchief.

It is plain to see that Señora Aros is gradually getting the upper hand in the everlasting man vs. wife contest for family authority. They tell me she used to

have to take all her own youngsters and go away to stay
with friends or relatives. Last year she went so far as to
ask me for report cards for her own children. But this
year she is secure. Her oldest stepdaughter, Catalina, is
the one that moved to town. She and Prieto's second son,
Chato, have been the resenters of stepmother authority.
Chato even struck "My-Mother" in a quarrel last spring.
Now he is away for weeks at a time. And Prieto, whose
long years of long days as a vaquero are at last getting
the best of him, is taming down. This spring his wife
dared to hide a bottle that he brought home with him.
And at the first hint of danger she sends Arturo to hide
the pistol in the little arroyo back of the house where we
throw our rubbish.

Much of the good singing now sounding across the
partition comes from her side of the family. She has a
high-pitched voice that easily carries. Víctor, her third
son, has a voice like hers. It is fun to see him, at a program, stand up in front and sing a high soprano above
all the others. Bill Ronstadt, our clerk of the board and
mentor, particularly enjoys his singing. "Did you hear
that high voice?" he asks a guest. "That was Víctor."
And he pushes the little guy up to the limelight where
he puts on a knockout grin and brings down the house.
Víctor has a wide mouth. For two years he has won the
pie-eating contest at the Altar Valley Annual School
Meet.

Prieto's wife is called Doña Lupe, but I think of her
as "My-Mother." "My-Mother says do you have a bottle?
The baby threw hers on the cement and broke it." "My-
Mother says if you can send her an aspirin." "My-Mother

says please give her a soap." "My-Mother says she is going to Tucson with you Friday because she needs to buy some things for us." "My-Mother says she will make Inez's skirt and any of the costumes you want."

"My-Mother" astonishes me. Suppose I had to feed and clothe all these children on fifty dollars a month? Could I ever be so placid, so self-contained in the confusion of so big a family, most of them self-assertive boys? At first I misjudged her. She seemed to sit all the time with a baby on her lap and let the stepdaughters do the work. I was hasty. She guards her strength and favors her own, but she is a good manager and loves life with a gusto that all around her must feel. Her children find her equal to any occasion. If an ant stings Meli she runs to My-Mother for some *cuajo* (saved from the stomach of the last cow killed) to ease the pain; when Chelo has a fever, My-Mother stews some dried tapiro blossoms and makes a tea that sweats out the poisons. When Frank — her first son and the apple of her eye — has a sore throat she has the teacher take him to town to the county school doctor; and when one of the girls is stricken with romance, she can handle that, too.

Not only does she spend the family check, she usually collects it. Whoever is handy and has a car in running order is commandeered to drive her to town where she trails down the *patrón* and "settles" with him — or draws money in advance to make her purchases. She tries to feed her family well. They raise their own beans, corn, and squash by dry-farming a level patch of ground a mile east of Poso Nuevo, and My-Mother seems to have an inside track with the rain gods. And sometimes they butcher a cow *con permiso del patrón*. They use even the bones. While Cousin Manuel is making jerky (*carne seca*), he splits and sun-dries the bones and saves them for soup and to give flavor to frijoles. They have a few chickens and turkeys but the small number of eggs are eaten by My-Father or any member of the family who happens to be sick.

Manuel is chief farmer as well as houseboy and handy man. He has lived with the Aroses for years; and if he earns any money at outside jobs he turns it over to My-Mother who buys him what he needs. The school children laughingly tell me Manuel believes the earth is flat, and that someday he will find a buried treasure. At times he sees ghost lights flitting in faraway places where some money is buried.

With Manuel and a passing guest or two they are always eighteen or twenty for meals. Yet they have a limited supply of dishes and cutlery and their table seats only eight. They eat in relays — three tables for each meal. First the girls serve the father and the oldest boys and guests; then the school children; then they sit down and eat with My-Mother who has been present all the while, sitting at a little cook table feeding a baby and overseeing the kitchen and provisions. The food is served directly on the plates from the pots on the stove and each child gets only what is placed before him. I sometimes hear complaints about this. One says the reason he does not grow faster is that the girls do not give him enough to eat.

This three-table routine means many hours of work each day, and a continual round of dishwashing which Ysidra escapes only during school hours.

Although none of the Aros children have had to work really hard compared to the labors suffered by children of the poor in other parts of the world or in the early history of our country, My-Mother has taught domestic tasks to her girls so successfully that any of them after the age of ten can run the household while she is in town two to six weeks for a confinement. And the boys know that living means toiling.

Ramón and Pancho shoulder the biggest jobs. They milk five cows, tend the horses, work in the field before and after school in crop season, help their father with the cattle, and keep up the eternal round of wood-getting. This year Frank and Arturo have also entered the ranks of woodmen. Even Víctor and Pili sometimes go out for an armful. At special times when a fiesta or roundup is coming, they harness the big-footed horses to their rickety wagon — made from pieces of abandoned ones — and bring in a regular load of good dried mesquite limbs. Such a load lasts this populous family only a few days. Most of the time the kids go afoot to the *montes* (thickets) and carry fuel, a boyload at a time. Only Ramón is allowed to use the axe, and this by express permission each time. The others go out barehanded, wrench dry branches from the gnarled tough mesquite trunks and break them into stove lengths by hitting them on the ground. In good weather getting wood is something of a lark. A boy has a chance to be free of supervision so that he can loiter a while, hunt for *chucata* (tree gum) and enjoy life.

But on cold mornings when the wind is sharp and frost covers the ground, when Ysidra (whose task it is to be first up each morning to start the kitchen fire) comes to the boys' room and in no gentle manner routs Pancho out to go bring wood to cook the mush and heat the beans, I hear him coughing and sniffling and muttering bad words as he takes out into the cold. He owns no gloves, socks, or underwear, sometimes no hat, and his shoes are seldom what they should be. I shiver to think of him braving the icy dawn in a sweatshirt with Mickey Mouse stenciled on the front.

Pancho is resentful because they never make Frank or Arturo (My-Mother's boys) go out in the cold. Most winter mornings those two stay wrapped in their quilts until after eight o'clock. Occasionally his bitterness flares into revolt so violent it is hard to take his part. Frank admits to being lazy, but he is good-natured, never insolent. Arturo, half-brother to both Frank and Pancho, has a winning disposition. It is impossible not to love him. Pancho, fifteen, sturdy, dark, with straight black hair, is the only one of the school boys in the family with a terrible temper. Usually My-Mother's commands are obeyed. Her disciplinary methods, I understand, are old-fashioned. Frank, her favorite son, became a problem at school for a while. One afternoon I lost my head and scolded him sharply before the whole school. His sister Socorro said, with indignation, "I have told My-Mother, Mrs. Bourne, how he is behaving in school and she says she is going to whip him."

A stifled giggle swept over the room. Frank looked down and said nothing. He towers six inches over My-Mother. But there did result improvement in his conduct.

The singers across the partition have come to the end of poor "Delgadina." She has died of thirst. Her room is full of angels.

Immediately the wrestling, giggling, and bantering begin. Pancho starts it by calling Víctor "La Victoria." Víctor retaliates by calling Pancho "La Panchita"; and Arturo, who has just been called Artureña, giggles of "La Panchurea"; and the fight is on. It is not yet a serious altercation — merely a commotion of noise and wrestling. Boy giggling is so vexatious that at times it is a relief when they go to battling in earnest and end with bellowing shrieks I cannot pretend to ignore.

"Mrs. Bourne!" shrieks Víctor, probably on the floor with Pancho sitting on him.

My function as school policeman is not legally in force at nine o'clock at night, but I am pleased that the young rascals respect my authority.

"Pancho! What are you doing to him?"

"Nothing."

"You boys stop that *barullo*. I'm trying to read. Sing another song."

During the romp Frank has been strumming chords persistently, calling out "¡No, hombre! ¡No, Hombre!" when jostled in the fray. Now he asks, with an adolescent break in his voice: "What do you want us to sing?"

"Mi Primer Amor," I say, that being the first thing I think of.

At once they are off, pleasantly singing in the dark. There is no lamp for the boys' room. Sometimes they have a candle, but usually, until warm weather, only the light of the small fire in the chimney. When the nights are hot, they sit in the dark until they feel sleepy, then take off their shoes and turn in.

There are two iron cots in the room. Singles. I imagine the older boys, José and Chato — past school age and now in the kitchen playing cards with the girls — sleep in them. The younger ones roll up in a quilt each on the floor.

When they rounded up the mares and colts for branding this spring an electric charge went through the schoolroom the minute the lively beasts rushed into the high wooden corral across the courtyard.

"I suppose we might as well declare a recess," I said.

With whoops — "Thank you, Mrs. Bourne! ¡Qué maestra tan buena!" out they all went and to the corral in a split second. Before I could get my hat, trot over and climb the fence, Ramón, rope in hand, had joined the men in the midst of dust and smoke, and flying hooves. As I settled on the top pole of the enclosure beside Edward, José missed a loop and Ramón leaped out and forefooted a beautiful little sorrel filly. He glanced up wondering if I had seen his neat catch. Pancho was on the colt's head as she hit the ground. Arturo was putting wood on the branding fire.

"They are a family of vaqueros," Edward said, in envious admiration.

Little cowpunchers they are, born to the saddle and spurs and ropes. But right now they are pouring out their voices in a love song.

> *¿Sabes, vida mía, por qué lloro?*
> *Porque te quiero, porque te adoro —*

Sometimes they listen to my battery radio when I bring it down from the ranchito for a special program.

No use trying to get them to read at night. The household affords only two kerosene lamps. One is in the kitchen-living room. There the visiting and card-playing is done. There Socorro does what she can of her eighth-grade homework and reads her library books amid the hubbub. There are so many crowded around the poor light that the younger boys must be sent away. Don Prieto, unless on a *parranda* (fortunately not often), succumbs to labor's demands and relaxes in the white bed in My-Mother's room immediately after supper. Only an emergency will get him out. The other lamp is the small one burning before a picture of a *santo,* also in My-Mother's room. It is useful when the baby needs attention as it burns all night when there is oil enough.

On pleasant evenings everybody gathers under the little trees out in front of the Aros quarters and the girls join in the singing. The girls never go into the boys' room which is separated from them by an unbroken adobe wall, although there is a thin nailed-up door between my room and the boys' — except on bath days. Then the bather, girl or boy, takes a turn at the washtub filled from the tap outside under my little window, locks himself in, hangs a blanket over the small north window, and splashes and sings. The waiting line is like a barber shop on Saturday afternoon.

Eloísa and Socorro, the biggest girls since Katie left, sing second; Ysidra and Chelo are sopranos, although Ysidra can sing second if she wants to. Meli, two and a half, can sing and knows words to many verses. Even Mercedes, a year old last fall, hums tunes. It's a good thing there are no monotones in the family, for singing is their daily activity, and they make fun in the rudest manner of anyone who cannot sing.

This musical talent made it hard for me to break into their good graces. The teacher before me was a musician, had a piano, and made life for these nightingales one grand sweet song. Bill warned me, and bought a portable phonograph. I had many records, and bought more. But what is the best phonograph in the world compared to a piano right in the room? I had two advantages: I could teach dancing, and I knew their language. And before long I discovered Frank could play a guitar. Nobody taught him, although I suppose the fellow who left one here for several weeks during the roundup showed him some chords. "Franqui" is gifted with innate knowledge of key and pitch and harmony. He was captivated by the instrument, spending all his time out of school with it. And when the fellow came to get it, My-Mother persuaded Prieto to give him a horse for the guitar. It took patience and tact to get Frank to bring the guitar into the schoolroom and accompany all of us in the Mexican songs that fascinated everyone. Then one day the man brought back the horse and took his guitar. None of us had money to buy another. School was sad. The whole place was sad.

Luckily I was able to trade a gold wedding ring no longer in use for a second-hand instrument which, according to the dealer, had made a radio performer a living for six years. Certainly the pleasure it brought to Poso Nuevo was worth both sentiment and old gold. Besides, then the Aros family accepted me as a member of the tribe.

At first I couldn't understand why one family should

have two boys with the same name. "Franqui" and "Pancho" are both nicknames for Francisco. One afternoon before I knew the kids well enough to demand privacy, I took Cherry for a walk. Before I got out the gate there was a stairstep line of followers, from Ysidra with the baby on her hip, on down. As I walked along watching Cherry, they ran races, picked flowers, and tumbled in the sand in the little arroyo in the big pasture, becoming chummy enough to discuss their family on our way back. They had lived at Poso Nuevo for four years. Before that they were at Calabasas where their parents had married twelve years ago. It was a second marriage for both. Ysidra said: "My mother had me and Eloisa and Pancho and Ramón and Katie and Joe and Chato."

Arturo said: "My-Mother had me and Socorro and Franqui and Víctor and Chelo and Pili and Meli and Mercedes and two little babies that died."

My-Mother is still a young woman. This year Eva was born.

It seems little trouble to have a large family if there are big girls to be nurses and housemaids. Catalina, Eloisa, and Ysidra, within the limits of their experience, are experts. Socorro is capable, too. They make tortillas every day, sometimes twice a day — seventy-five or ninety at a batch — the big thin ones so much more tedious to make than the little fat ones (*gorditas*). The necessary skill is beyond the comprehension of most gringos. It means two to three hours over a hot stove for each batch, not including the mixing and shaping. Socorro offered to teach me to make tortillas. I was fascinated by her clever manipulations when she came into my room to give me instructions. The younger boys took advantage of the opportunity and climbed up to sit on the water pipes outside my window — usually forbidden territory. They shrieked with laughter at my fumbling mistakes, and yelled advice and encouragement, having a wonderful time. But I shall never learn. If you are going to make really good tortillas, you almost have to make a career of it. No woman who feeds her good-sized family tortillas ever works outside the home steadily. Her life is spent in the kitchen. Bill and I were discussing our pupils one night when I drove up to get him to sign my voucher. I remarked about the imperviousness to learning of one of them. He cried: "But I have seen her single-handed cook a meal for twelve people *with tortillas!*"

Bill takes proud, intimate interest in the Aros kids. Perhaps it is for their singing. He knows and loves music. He has a strong attachment to the native people of this sunny land and appreciates their artistic skills. Furthermore they have been Baboquívari pupils ever since he has been clerk of the school board. When I am telling him something that happened in school he is likely to interrupt with: "I like old Ramón." Or "Arturo is a good kid."

Bill is the perfect board member. He says, "Sister, that's swell," and signs the vouchers. There is no squabbling in our district. Pascual is the other board member (the law requires at least two members to sign the vouchers) and he adores Bill, and looks up to him. The children used to call him "Weelie" which is absurd. He is not fat but weighs two hundred pounds and bears the dignity of great vitality and a fine handsome physique.

When his six-feet-two blocks the doorway you feel a part of the big outdoors is coming into the room. In a way it is incongruous for such a big man to be so clever with pencils, colored chalk, and musical instruments.

> *¿Sabes, por qué nunca te he olvidado?*
> *Porque tú fuistes mi primer amor.*

Another song is finished in my nightly serenade. Ramón, probably to please me, leads into *Mi Viejo Amor,* an oldtime song that Bill sang for us the day he brought his guitarita and we all sang together. We have practiced it often, for we want to sing it for Bill's bride, Sally, that he is bringing from the "East" (Illinois in this case).

We ran an *Extra* of *Little Cowpuncher* when Bill and Sally returned from their honeymoon to "Las Delicias," the lovely ranch at the foot of the tall Baboquívari Mountains. Mary wrote the lead story:

Monday morning we were very busy at our school subjects when we heard a car at the gates. We shouted: "It's Bill!" for we were anxious to see him. We all went out to greet him and his companion, Mr. Hill. He looked happy and gay as always. I thought he was going to be serious not happy and gay as he used to be because he is now married to a nice girl but he looked just the same as always. He brought us our big new wall maps — World, U.S., Europe, and our state. — Mary Hernández.

Marcela, at a later time, asked why we call him "Beel" when his name is "Weelliam." That brought on a lesson in nicknames and she was assigned to write this story for *Little Cowpuncher*:

There is a funny strange custom of nicknaming which we Mexicans call them *sobrenombres*. Nearly everybody in our school has one that he knows better than his name. Here are some: Herlinda, Linda; Dolores, Loli or Lolita; Pedro, Pili; Edward, Lalo; Teresa, Teddy; Ramón, Monchi; Consuelo, Chelo. I don't know the real reason of nicknaming but I imagine it is because nearly all Spanish names are long and hard. That makes it difficult to holler to someone. That is my opinion. We Mexicans have lots of queer customs.

Now we have received three new pupils. They are Americans. Th teacher calls them Nordics. They have easy names. Inez, Bill, Jack. Yet we Mexicans on the third day were calling the boys Hoover and Roosevelt and the girl Princess because she has beautiful yellow hair.

That story amused Bill when he came by my quarters one evening to check on some school business. He found me correcting quiz papers and picked up one that made him rock with laughter. It was a geography test paper. I had typed some unfinished sentences to be completed by writing in the answers:

1. A great circle drawn around the middle of the globe —
                              is the equarter.
2. The most northern point on the earth —
                              is the north pole.
3. The cold northern ocean —
                              is the Arctic.
4. The island from which come the icebergs —
                              is the Frigid Zone.
5. The cold current which carries the icebergs southward —
                              is the moon.
6. The warm current which melts the icebergs —
                              is the sun.
                    Víctor Aros, Third Grade

Pancho Celebrating Christmas with a burro.
By Edward H.

Pancho Behaved

PANCHO WAVED TO ME just now as he dashed past my
window on Ramón's little speckled mare. So there are
no hard feelings over the fight we had in school today.
No blows were given (his weight is 117 and mine 107)
but we were both angry. The outcome was that I sent him
home — two doors down the line. He pretended not to
care. But he missed hearing *The Call Of The Wild* read
during literature period, and I imagine My-Mother found
plenty for him to do.

The extent of her cooperation in my disciplinary
measures makes me feel guilty. I think of the time I failed
her last year when she called for help. She appeared at
my window, peering in one morning when I was dressing.
Annoyed, I kept her waiting while I stepped behind the
oilcloth drape to finish putting on my clothes.

"I don't want you to give Pancho recess today," she said in Spanish. "Or noon hour. Because," she explained when I stared at her coldly, "he refuses to milk the cows this morning. You know that Ramón and he milk the cows every morning. But Ramón is sick today and Pancho does not want to milk them."

I didn't give her the sympathetic cooperation she wanted; I thought she was unjust to Pancho. Some of the others should have been made to help him. Besides, I resented her shifting her home problems to my already overloaded shoulder.

I kept Pancho at recess and asked him, in what I hope was a friendly manner, to tell me why his mother had made such a strange request. He was so mad that he sobbed and sputtered as he answered. He said she always made him work like a horse and never made Frank and Arturo do anything. It was impossible not to pity him, and not to be a little scared at the furious resentment he displayed. I praised him for being a good worker and gave him a screwdriver and ten cents and told him to take some of the desks off the old runners. The desks, outmoded, uncomfortable, too big for most of my pupils, were hard to move out of the way when we wanted to practice dancing or rehearse our plays or give a program. The larger ones sat directly on the floor. Most of the others were perched on long thin boards, hard to sweep around and easy to stumble over.

Pancho's black eyes flashed at me when I gave him the dime and he mumbled thanks (so seldom do these children have any pocket money!). And he got down on the floor and went to work, dragging his long legs around the desks and sniffling with hurt pride. I went out to the ball game. At noon I kept him, as his mother had asked. But I also kept all the other Aros boys and gave them a talking-to about justice and fair play among members of the family. Ramón was detained only as a witness. I publicly gave him credit for taking his share of the work. Frank hung his head and pretended to be interested in a book on his desk. Tears filled Arturo's lovely brown eyes as he starcd at me appealingly. Víctor cried: "Aren't we going to eat?" My-Mother did not call on me again.

My battle with Pancho this morning was over his conduct on the playground when we went to practice baseball. He was mad because he was not chosen on Ramón's side. In spite of my entreaties and the good nature of the other boys, he never wants to play unless he can win. It was foolish of me to try to force him to be a good sport. Since there were no spectators and we have been together in this school so long that we are *como una familia,* he talked back to me.

Often I have wondered about the tendency of my school children, taken in groups, to know when to be loyal and respectful. I am only *la maestra,* their servant, in a way, and they are not really afraid of me. But they will not be disloyal publicly. I remember the lively little ones — Mexicans all, six and seven years old who spoke no English — that I had in groups of thirty-five, forty, or more than forty, each semester when I taught in the city. We would be very busy (teaching is a noisy business) and probably using some Spanish words (taboo in tax-supported schools), when a quick eye near the window would spy the superintendent coming across to our building.

"*¡Viene el panzón!*" (Here comes Fatty!) the lookout would cry, and the roomful of chatterers would scurry to their seats frozen into decorum like baby quails. I don't know why — I've always wondered about it — but the identical warning developed spontaneously in group after group. We showed a united front.

Now, far from any higher authority, teacher and pupils together have developed into a social unit. In private we sometimes have noisy altercations. The children, as a rule, let me know what they think and feel, taking a defensive stand about their impulses as grown-ups do. But let outsiders come in, and the kids' loyalty is so firm that the county superintendent thinks I never have any discipline problems.

Pupil loyalty is gratifying, but a lone teacher cannot always count on it. Therefore I shall always be grateful to Pancho for behaving, that black afternoon in October when Three Points School came and not only gave us a walloping defeat at baseball, but bragged rudely and jeered at us on our own ground. I overlook much in Pancho when I think of how narrowly we missed having a disgraceful riot that day. He pitched for us. On two occasions when the razzing got rough I saw him tempted to sock an enemy with the ball. It is surprising that he did not yelp out coarse answers to the bad words hurled at him. His self-control was a special victory because it happened before our school had any real interest in baseball.

There are good reasons why baseball ranks high in country schools so limited in enrollment that few of the pupils are of the same size. First, it is inexpensive. If necessary the players can make their own diamond, gloves, bats, and balls (many a game I have taken part in using balls made from ravelled stockings!). Another thing: it is just hard enough and easy enough to appeal to moderately active boys and very energetic girls. And because it's our national sport young Americans are almost obligated to learn it.

My first year here I failed to do my duty by the game. I had taught primary children so long I had forgotten the rules. For years my small pupils had played King's Base, and Run, Sheep, Run, and singing games such as "Florendish y Florendá. "Florendish," believe it or not, is "London Bridge" as garbled by tiny Mexican children who have learned the game from older brothers and sisters privileged to go to school. I've had fun watching the little ones, like animated dolls, stamping around gustily singing:

> Florendish y florendá,
> Florendá, florendá,
> Florendish y Florendá,
> Mai-fe-le-di-O.

Word corruptions among non-English-speaking little ones are no cause for worry. I once knew a dyed-in-the-wool U.S. patriot who sang "My Country Teas" until she was in the fourth grade.

Although I confess I did not do my duty by baseball that first year, in the beginning I did try. Bill had bought a new ball and bat and we had no other playground equipment. Ramón and Edward were the only pupils interested. Las Moras School and Sasabe School had organized teams. And two years ago our Baboquívari

School even won a game at the intra-school Altar Valley Track Meet held here that year. Our school won by running in a bus driver and a cowboy or two to fill out the nine. When I came, the children told me they didn't want to play baseball because there were not enough boys. Many of their former schoolmates had moved into Las Moras District, thereby becoming rivals. We had three big girls, but they begged off. I tried, half-heartedly, until one morning I caught a ball thrown by a 130-pound boy on the end of my right thumb. I gave up.

But in the spring there was another track meet, held at Las Moras. We won respectable scores at running and jumping, for we had practiced for those events. And Víctor took the pie-eating contest. After lunch we had to sit on the sidelines and watch Sasabe and Las Moras play a thrilling ball game. My kids were left out. That wouldn't do!

It was Otto's initiative that got the track meet organized. He is a true baseball enthusiast, having played on his college team and in the state league. This year he and his wife — who teaches primary grades in the school where he is principal — moved to Three Points at Robles, halfway between here and Tucson. In September I met them at teachers' meeting and asked Otto to come down and organize a baseball team for us. He agreed. We both spoke in good faith, but each with a different meaning. I thought he would go to the board and give us a kind of chalk talk, tell us the fundamental rules; then take us out on the field and demonstrate and give try-outs and figure us out a team. His was a more effective way: the old sink-or-swim method. (After all, what did I suppose his pupils would be doing while he was coaching mine?)

Our slow mail service kept us from receiving his letter saying that he was going to bring his school to play ball until the very day he was coming. Happy with excitement, we hurried to get ready. Ramón, Luis, and Pancho crossed the big arroyo with Pascual, carrying ashes to mark the lines, shovels and hoes for the weed eradication, and gunny sacks to fill with sand for bases. They measured off a diamond which turned out to be too small. Edward drafted Mary and Arturo to help him decorate our schoolroom. They cleaned the boards, tacked up water color paintings, and found flowers for the green jars. Socorro, Ysidra, and Herlinda swept and sprinkled the floor, dusted the room, and put out new paper towels and drinking cups. The little children emptied waste baskets and dust pans, arranged the books on the shelves, and picked up litter in the yard.

We met our visitors — a surprising gang who filled two buses and two cars, and overflowed our whole yard — with sincere pleasure. The teachers were cordial. But their pupils held aloof, ganging together, looking at us coldly as antagonists. To my amazement I realized that they had come down as competitors. Wasn't Otto going to demonstrate and coach and organize? He wasn't. He brought out score sheets, already blocked and labelled, and handed me one to fill in with names of my team. My team? I was stunned.

"Who is your catcher?" he demanded when I stood in shock.

"We don't have any," I faltered. "We have no team. We've never played."

Disappointed, but determined to make the best of it, he called my boys, and they, in ignorance of what they were in for, compiled eagerly. At his urging, the six biggest boys chose positions. Our girls were smart enough to decline, so Three Points loaned us three players who were not on their regular first team, but, as we soon learned, were well imbued with school spirit.

Their top nine had been working for three weeks and this was their initial game. They were madly excited. When they ran out on the field to warm up they whizzed around like professionals, throwing and catching the ball so that it never touched the ground. They not only played with skill and enthusiasm; they had rooters — bunches of girls and boys grouped around under the mesquites to cheer their triumphs and razz our inefficiency.

After the first inning, in spite of Otto's generous umpiring and advice, my little cowpunchers were stricken with shame. And they were outraged. These loud-mouthed strangers were not our friends, as the Sasabe and Las Moras pupils had always been; they were scornful opponents come to crush us with smashing defeat and brag about it. Their score rose like the dust; the desert resounded with their rude shouts and insults. Later my girls told me that they were sure Otto and his wife couldn't understand what their youngsters were saying in Spanish — a language rich in invective and obscenities. The three boys they had lent us made "outs" each time up to bat: one out, two outs, three outs. Their schoolmates rushed out of the field without having to unbend. The rooters bellowed with pleasure.

"*¡Verás!*" shouted their first baseman as he put Frank out. "This boy don't know his rules!"

The only thing in our favor was that it went fast.

Our big boys caught the flies and grounders often enough to make their half-innings not too long. Our halves were saved from complete farces by Ramón. He had had some experience and caught on fast. He played catcher. His face was dark with heat and shame, his shirt was wet with sweat, and streams of perspiration ran off his nose. But his saddle-bowed legs flew over the ground with incredible speed as he caught every ball thrown to home-plate. When he went to bat he cracked the ball over their heads far out into the brush so the little children had to hunt it. So we did get some runs.

The heat of early October beat down. But I was cold with anger. Instead of the happy visit we had looked forward to we were challenged to take overwhelming odds; and were constantly insulted from the players and the sidelines. I began to worry about how my kids would react.

"See," I called to Arturo, "you have to touch the boy with the ball — not just touch the base." I wanted everybody to know we were learners only.

"Now you know what a tip is," I shouted. "Look, boys, you can only take one base when the ball is thrown straight over first."

I no longer hoped to put across any hints to our barbarous attackers. My aim was to influence my own boys and keep them in hand. Pancho was the one I worried most about. Arturo would complain at injustice, then laugh. Edward was certain to talk back in protest. His tongue was never still, but he is a courteous boy and there wasn't much chance of his starting a fight against such big odds. Our big boy — Ramón — as spunky a young fellow as I ever had in a schoolroom, was lost in battle. He played ball. In an emergency Frank withdraws into a world of his own and comes up unhurt. But Pancho is a fighter and tough as a Spanish pony. Sensitive, high-tempered, stubborn, resentful of ill treatment, he will take big odds. The teacher who preceded Helen considered him hopeless and so wrote in the school register. This appraisal I took with a grain of doubt. From what the children told me I knew that she was out of her milieu in a ranch school of Mexican-Americans. She scolded them, saying that they were lazy, ignorant, and dirty. She was quick with a blow and once struck Edward across the nose with the sharp edge of a ruler when he turned to speak to his neighbor in back of him. I imagine it was her undoing when she took on the Aros family with whom she had to live in isolation. Bill had told me that he heard she took a shot at one of the boys who was peeking in her window. After I got well acquainted with them I asked which boy it was. They told me she didn't shoot at them. She threw hot water on them when they hung about her window, and they retaliated with a shower of rocks. She brought out the gun, they said, only to hold Katie at bay when she was about to storm the fort. And Pancho took an active part in this war.

Pancho is strictly a country fellow. He had lived within a two hour journey of the city all his life, yet he told me: "I don't know Tucson." I took him with the group one night to see the motion picture *Anne of Green Gables*. It was done as a reward for those who had read the book, among whom he wasn't one. But I hoped it might have a good effect on him. He showed interest in everything — the pretty show, the crowded streets, the bright lights, and the refreshment stand where I treated my guests to hot dogs and sodas. But I saw him shrink with awareness of his own deficiencies. He has never asked to go to town again. He remains in the background when our school attracts attention, and he hates to have his picture taken. Here in the remote rangeland where life is unruffled by the scarcity of trifles so common in the city, he can work and fight and respect himself. On his own ground he is quick to take offense. During that dreadful game he wouldn't look at me. I looked at him often enough. He was our pitcher and there was a chance that any minute he might sock somebody with a hard ball, or throw down his glove and start a riot. But, no. For once he smoldered in wrath without exploding. He behaved.

As Otto was putting his players into the bus I heard him say: "I'll get you some harder games."

That was the lick-that-killed-grandpa as far as my decorum was concerned. Without a wave or a smile I strode back into the schoolroom and rang the bell. My beaten, abused young ones filed in and slumped into their seats. They looked up at me. Now what?

"Boys and girls," I said, "*Let's get'm!* Let's work until we are *good* ball players and go to their school and beat the socks off them. And with none of the rudeness and insults they gave us. Let's show them how to play ball and be civilized about it. All who will help, stand!"

They arose as one with a great noise of shuffling feet and clattering deskseats that startled Pascual who was getting the bus ready to go.

"It won't be easy," I warned, walking back and forth

before them. "We can't neglect our lessons. We owe the state that. Besides the achievement tests are coming up. And we have this big project of practicing our play and dances for the Halloween party our guests and friends are coming to see. And to play *winning* ball we have to have *time* to practice. But somehow we'll *make* time! Are you with me?"

They were with me. I had to tap the bell for order.

"Now while I give the little children *two* days' lessons, you sit down and get *two* good lessons in spelling and arithmetic, and write your hearts out about what happened this afternoon. You know that tomorrow we are going to make that "Extra" of the *Little Cowpuncher* for Bill's wedding."

I used Víctor's story for its brevity and mildness.

THE BASEBALL GAME

Tuesday the Three Points came to play us ball.
All the children in the school came in 4 cars to the ball game.
They came and beat us. 17 to 6.
Because we hadn't practiced.
Mary said to those girls We congratulate you for your game but not for your manners. — V. A., *Third Grade.*

We worked, we overworked, and the children stayed with me because we had a goal. Pascual held the bus as long as he dared each afternoon; after he left, with special permission from their parents, I kept Ramón and Pancho and Frank warming up in the bullpen. I truly believe that no school ever put more activity into short, fall days. Baseball was Otto's forte. It wasn't mine. But I had asked for it. And, surprisingly, it turned out to be true that practice makes perfect. After several days of intensive training we took an afternoon off and went to our friends at Las Moras for a trial game. Emma Townsend, their teacher, was an outdoor type who liked games. Unlike me, she was up on the rules. We knew it didn't matter which side won; we wanted the kids to learn. Socorro wrote this story for *Little Cowpuncher*:

AT LAS MORAS YESTERDAY

Thursday we went to play ball with Santa Margarita School at Las Moras Ranch. Everybody was glad to receive us and they treated us politely all the time. We were lucky because in our last inning we raised our score. We hope next time they will have a chance to win for they are surely good sports. S. A. — *Eighth Grade*

The next week they came to our school and took their revenge. We printed these stories in *Little Cowpuncher*:

THE BALL GAME

Friday we played a ball game with Las Moras.
We let them strike first because they came.
I was without shoes and I had to run and get
the balls in the stickers.
They laughed at me when I grunted to hit the ball.
And we had a very good time. —V. A. *Third Grade*

WHAT HAPPENED TO OUR DIAMOND

We cleaned up a place near the school to play baseball with Las Moras. Weeds were dry and as high as our knees and full of stickers. We dragged an old gate over the weeds with the teacher's car. Every big boy got on the gate to hold it.

This place had not been used by the cattle for a year. They were gathering and holding cattle in the City Hall Pasture where we used to play baseball with Three Points. That is why we had to make a new place. And what do you think happened? That day the Las Moras were coming to play with us the cowboys turned all the cattle into the pasture where we cleaned. We had marked between the bases. We used a gallon of the teacher's gasoline and then we weren't allowed to play there.

When they turned the cattle into our new diamond and the cows began to tramp it and lick the salt we had to work as quick as we could to get a diamond ready back in City Hall Pasture. And after all that work we had they beat us with one run.

—Ramón Aros, *Eighth Grade*

And so one quiet sunny day in November we drove to Three Points School for a return match. We hadn't warned them and Otto was somewhat taken aback. He said they had quit playing baseball and were now playing soccer; and that some of their team had moved away.

"Oh, well," I said, "You know how we play baseball."

A game was arranged. Socorro reported the event for our paper.

LITTLE COWPUNCHERS WIN A BASEBALL GAME

Tuesday we took the pleasure of redeeming ourselves playing ball with Three Points. They were not expecting us but they came out to greet us with kindly manners. Everybody was full of joy and had lots of enthusiasm in playing them ball. We played politely.

We thought of going at recess that morning to take advantage of the nice warm day which was not windy or harmful to our game. We felt sorry because one couple of their boys was gone from their district. But they seemed to match us better. It would have been more fair if everybody had been there who came to play us here.

Anyway we defeated them just as they did us when they came down here. The score was seventeen to six. Which surprised us and we were afraid we were going to fail. We had two girls, Ysidra and I on our team, and Víctor was the smallest player on both sides. We know that Ramón and Luis our pitcher and catcher were the ones who won the game but we all enjoyed ourselves and we were very polite to the losers. — S. A., *Eighth Grade*

Edward Hernandez

The Fourth "R" - Riding the Bus

OUR FRIEND, Mrs. King (wife of author-editor Frank M. King), when we met her during the rodeo at Tucson mentioned the story in *Little Cowpuncher* about our "Gringos." She was so glad we published it because most people today have no idea that there are places in the United States where children still have to go through so much, just to go to school. Referring to the little Emerys who live far up in the mountains, she said "To think that young as they are they must get up so early every school morning, get their own breakfasts, and walk a mile over rocks and cactus before 6 a.m., then ride two hours more on the bus. Why it isn't even daylight at 6 o'clock this time of year!"

I told her that even at school these three have

Commuters on Pascual's Regular Line

Edward Hernández

Mary Hernández

Marcela Hernández

Teresa Hernández

Ester Bedoy

Frances Salazar

Cruz Sánchez

Prudencia Sánchez

Luis Badilla

Herlinda Badilla

Dolores Badilla

Guadalupe Badilla

Inez Jane Emery

Bill Emery

Jack Emery

Alfredo Mendoza

burdens to bear. They are blondes among dark-skinned contemporaries who outnumber them. And they are small. One noon hour while I was writing afternoon lessons on the board I noticed Bill Emery hunting through the *Book of Knowledge*. I asked what he was looking for.

"I'm trying to find *gringo,*" he said worriedly. "That's who they call me and I don't know what it means."

One day I heard Jack Emery addressed by one of the big boys in this manner: "Hello, Jackass."

It is surprising the extent to which children bear hardships without protest, even in America — where protest is not an unusual mode of communication. One morning I scolded Teddy because she was inattentive in class and didn't keep her marker on the place in her reading book. Mary, her oldest sister, came quietly to tell me that Teddy had been sick in the night. She had earache. She couldn't eat her breakfast, so they wanted her to stay at home. But when she began to cry and said she wasn't sick any more they let her come. She had not known how to defend herself, so she remained stoically calm — except to jump, startled, when I raised my voice the third time she missed her turn.

Our western ranch children are used to hardships. Once, at Redington School, the Valdez six forgot to bring their lunch. When one of the older pupils told me about it I went out to round them up and take them to the teacherage for something to eat. Manuel, embarrassed, and annoyed, said: "I can stay two days without eating." He was nine years old.

The Baboquívari School bus riders have astonishing fortitude. Tonight I know how uncomfortable their daily journeys are, for I took them home this afternoon, and my car has more easy-riding gadgets than their old, rickety bus.

Pascual, our bus driver, broke his drive shaft this morning coming down from Las Delicias. When I turned off the highway toward Poso Nuevo I overtook Edward and Bill Emery walking for help. We went back to Las Delicias to get Bill Ronstadt to tow Pascual into Tucson for repairs, and I brought the children, clinging all over the car, inside and out, to school. This evening, after the seventy-two-mile jog to deliver them and return, I am convinced that these children are paying high for their education.

It hadn't occurred to me that their endurance was extraordinary until, after a taste of their daily routine, I told them to write a "Complaint" column for *Little Cowpuncher*.

Indirectly, the idea came from Víctor. We were recording weights, and noting the good results from the troublesome school lunches. Troublesome indeed. Some trouble to Pascual who fires up my little cook stove and makes the cocoa each day, and trouble to me. I must do the shopping, advance the cash, make out accounts, and wait weeks for school officials to okay the triplicate invoices and authorize reimbursement. This, besides having my room crowded with groceries, and having to find time to make the sandwiches.

I reminded the ones on the underweight list that they must not let the extra food — sandwiches, cookies, cocoa, and fruit — take the place of their regular meals, for we wanted them to gain.

Ysidra, barred from the extra lunches by overweight, angrily told on Víctor. She said he starved himself at home to get the good things at school.

"What about that, Víctor?" I asked sternly.

His high-pitched voice could be heard all over the yard as he arose to say he did not eat the beans at home because Ysidra did not cook them "good." She didn't put salt! And when he protested, she put too much salt. For spite! The children all burst into laughter, except Ysidra. I held my composure, but the idea came to me that a page of "complaints" might go over well in *Little Cowpuncher*.

Mary, sweet Mary, couldn't think of anything in her life to complain about. When I suggested that few people would want to ride over her bus route twice a day sitting on a tin lunch pail, she was finally inspired.

At the end of our "gripe" pages, after all the pupils from the second grade through the eighth had expressed themselves on tattling, writing notes, teasing, unfair playing, daily rations, and anything else they wanted changed, Mary and Edward presented the plight of the bus riders.

Every morning I get up at 5 A.M. and ride from 6 till nearly nine. And in the afternoon from 3:30 till 6:00 P.M. on a 8 lbs. lard pail which sits between the front seats of my father's bus. Can you imagine how it feels?

Then I read in the car all the time as I ride. Nobody makes me do that but it is the only chance I have to read outside of school and I can't write lessons in the car because it wiggles and bumps. And as hard as it is for me I always read whole books, not skipping through them, and I never tell the teacher I have read a library book until I have read it through. Then there is always somebody who cheats and gets credit for books not read all the way through. I have complaints about these cheaters that wouldn't be fair to say in public. — M. H., *Eighth Grade*

My reasons for complaints about coming to school so far and early are something that nobody knows except the ones who are traveling. People think we have a good time riding. But it is a mistake. You feel sleepy, miserable, and cross. You get up at 5 o'clock every morning with hardly any appetite and still you have to eat because about after 10 o'clock you feel hungry. If anyone wants to get tired of school let him try it. But even though we have a miserable life still I don't miss school. I always try to have a perfect attendance. . . .

I wish one of these days the Government which is doing so much for some people would make all these roads better and the lives of some of us easier. It may be wrong to complain but never the less I give my opinion and have my freedom of speech. I know the Pima County School System is paying for a bus to take us who live far away to school to help us become educated citizens. But we do also suffer for our education. — E. H.

Sometimes the little ones can't stay awake on the bus or during the long school day. When they put their heads down on their desks and sleep I won't let them be disturbed. Many afternoons when the first two grades are dismissed at two-thirty, I bed down seven-year-old Jack Emery in the back of my car. Once the bus left without him. He awoke in dismay to find me at the wheel dashing to catch them. But they had already missed him and were returning. His nine-year-old brother Bill was absent one day. It began to rain while they were standing out in the dawn waiting to be picked up. He ran back to the mining camp where his father had left the three of them about a mile above Pascual's little ranch. Jack and Inez Jane stood and took the rain until the bus came rather than miss school.

When these young people come every day, in all kinds of weather, sick or well, it shows real interest. In this case I think it may be a feeling that they might miss something. With so many plans and projects our schedule is often variable. It depends on the weather and the general state of our health just what day we'll plunge into pottery-making, landscape painting, playwriting, dance practice, or track-meet drills. We never know when the county superintendent will arrive with a moving picture (powered by the motor of her car with a rear wheel jacked up) or a set of achievement tests. We always have a book going, and nobody wants to miss a chapter. I read aloud (dramatic readings with theatrics) immediately after lunch, an arrangement that gets the pupils promptly into their seats. And often there are grand projects such as the Halloween Party, the Rodeo Parade, or the May Festival. Our attendance record is excellent.

Hardships notwithstanding, the older bus riders, especially, have outgrown their homes and need contacts that only school can give. I think, in particular, of Edward and Mary, two gifted young teenagers. It is not accurate to tag them "Mexican ranch children." When in the primary grades, they attended school in Los Angeles and in Tucson. Their ethnic distinction is that their mother's father was an Irishman from the Old Sod. But they subsist chiefly on frijoles and tortillas, live in a floor-less shack on their father's homestead, and are attending their fourth year in this isolated country school. The benefits they get from their present activities are appreciated. Mary said: "Edward and I are learning lots this year. My father asks us questions about the weather and the clouds and things like that when we are coming on the bus and he can see that we are learning very much."

At this, Socorro, who is shy about making mistakes when she wants to express herself in English, had a problem to present. "You know, Mrs. Bourne," she said, "My father does not believe that the rain comes from the ocean and the wind blows the clouds over here to us. He says he sees the clouds grow on the tops of mountains here. On the Santa Ritas he sees them grow."

We went into the matter as well as we could with the reference books at hand, using up our allotted time for history and physiology that day. In ranch country nothing is as important as rain.

Edward is our *Little Cowpuncher* artist. He is talented and ambitious. He is dark-skinned, black-haired, slight of stature. I wondered about his name. Neighbors call him "Eduardo," his family call him "Lalo" (which the Aros boys sometimes reverse to "Lola" to tease him), but he wants to be called Edward.

I have seen Edward develop from a clever-fingered boy who could make delicate wire baskets and cut freehand silhouettes to a self-confident artist sure of his ideas and their execution. To Edward as a developing artist school has meant above all *opportunity* — such as Bill Ronstadt's being brought in to give art lessons.

Edward has been a joyous surprise, for at first I didn't take to him. He seemed unruly because he never could keep quiet. Bill told me about the teacher who hit him across the nose with the sharp edge of a ruler. It could have put his eye out. I couldn't believe a teacher would hit a child in the face for nothing — later I heard that he had turned around to talk to the boy behind him. He was fourteen when I met him and could no more be still than could a weathervane in a breeze. I accepted his compulsion to talk; it is seldom life's business to be still and quiet.

Plagued by his chatter the first day of school, I put him to figuring everybody's height and weight. It made a noise, but a legitimate noise. For several days I kept plying him with busy tasks. But I didn't suppress him. After the second week he began writing notes to me on the blackboard, usually, to my irritation, leaving out punctuation marks. In the morning when I turned to my special panel to put up the daily chart, I might find scrawled in a nice clean place: *when are we going to have art.* After lunch, *may we draw today* would stare at me from the back board. I ignored these suggestions. I was struggling with the hardest task I'd ever had. No pupil except Mary could read. The school books might as well have been printed in Greek. Now let this impertinent boy *try* to read and learn history dates and fractions — and high time!

But Edward didn't have long to wait to get his desire. For my five primary children, one morning I drew on the board with colored chalk a crude illustration of Little Boy Blue. I saw Edward quit his arithmetic and watch me as I struggled with the haystack and cornfield. At noon he slipped in and expertly worked over my picture.

"Edward, did you do that?"

"Yes, Ma'am."

"All right. Thank you. We're going to have art in this school."

This was a year before Bill Ronstadt married. But

bachelors are generally hungry. When I invited Bill to dinner I asked him to come early and teach drawing and painting while I made the casserole and the pie (our establishment had no icebox or refrigerator). Bill had never had young children under his direction. When I sat in on his classes I felt as if I were auditing a university lecture. He was wonderful with chalk and pencil, fluent with Spanish — and a big success as a teacher. Edward, Mary, and Socorro did so well he thrilled to teach them.

And Edward was a problem no more. How versatile he is! Besides drawing and painting, he plays the piano by ear, sings tenor, writes stories, drives a car, rides a horse, is a good marksman, is student enough to do two grades in one year, and at home his father calls him his "right-handed man" (so what if he isn't still and quiet!). He gathers and cuts firewood, changes tires, and is the water-carrier up a steep slippery sixty-foot climb from the well in the canyon to the house on the hillside.

Even so, his father and the vaqueros tease him about his interest in art and his passion for nature study. He told me indignantly one morning as he handed me about a hundred long-stemmed pale violet *covenas* (picked while he kept the bus waiting) that Pascual called him "sissy" because he liked flowers. I told him about Wordsworth, Thoreau, and Burbank. He went right to the *Book of Knowledge* and looked them up.

Mary is younger than he, but ahead of him because he has had pneumonia twice. She is a short, plump girl with a pretty face and lovely hair which she hates without a permanent. Worried about her figure, she often starts her long, hard day without breakfast, and is careful to eat lightly at lunch. I tell her that the reason she has headaches often is because of hunger. But I cannot deny that beans and tortillas are not slenderizing foods. She maintains that her headaches are caused by reading while the bus jiggles over the rough roads.

When can she read? At school she is busy all day. At home they make her go to bed early because she must get up at five o'clock. But she *will* read. I believe she is the only pupil I ever had who plodded through every page of *Little Women*. Last year she won our prize for reading the most library books. I am proud of the reader she has grown to be, and I like her stories, too. When she told how she spent her Thanksgiving vacation, for our December *Little Cowpuncher,* she divided the material into five parts. Part I was about Wednesday, the afternoon she went to town, always a thrill for her; Part II was Thursday when she attended her cousin's early morning church wedding and ate two Thanksgiving dinners. Then she wrote graphically of a ranch girl's experiences.

Part. III. *Friday*

That morning, in cleaning my cousin's house where we stayed, and packing to go back to the ranch, I went to sleep everything I did. So I took my baby niece and put her to sleep and slept with her. When I awoke my aunt came with the exciting news my cousin from Los Angeles had come.

After that visit we went to two houses to say goodby, and so it was dark when we came to the ranch. Then I had to make a fire and get supper and make tortillas. Imagine how I felt. I said to myself, I won't go to town any more because when I feel so tired from the long bumpy road, then I have to make a fire and make tortillas.

Part. IV. *Saturday*

We had to get up early again. Alas, the only days we might have slept a little late. For now on our holidays we had to go make a new road. Our neighbor closed the road we had been using. He told us he was going to use the land.

So we had to pick and shovel and rake and roll big rocks. On that land there are rocks as high as our bus tires. We cut cactus, paloverdes, mesquites, and *yerba del burro*. It was hard work. I had some Levi's and put on an old hat so to not get burned. The next day my body felt just as if I had been riding a bronco horse.

Part. V. *Sunday*
Our last holiday passed also with the hard rough road work. I heartily wished it had been a schoolday even if I had to do arithmetic all day. It was the hardest work I have ever done in my life for we have been on the ranch not much over three years. But I did enjoy the two days in Tucson. — M. H., *Eighth Grade*

During the fall months we had for a few weeks (while their father did some assessment work on mining claims) the little Sánchez children. Prudencia, the oldest, in the third grade, wrote this account of her Thanksgiving celebration: "I stayed at home. I ate bread and potatoes and candy."

Contrast with that the feast at Palo Alto where Frances Salazar lives with her aunt and uncle who adore her, and indulge her: "I ate turkey in the night of Thanksgiving. Lots of people came to my house and I invited Marcela to stay 2 days."

Frances is a happy little girl whose popularity and gaiety may stem partly from the fact that she is a natural honey blonde. The bus picks her up about seven-thirty in front of the big house where her uncle is stationed as cowboy. Ysidra, fourth grade, who was a guest at the party wrote it up in this manner:

I went to Palo Alto with my mother and the girls. And the big boys. Socorro and Frank christened Frances doll in the afternoon. When we got there Charli, the uncle of Frances, killed the turkey and they took the feathers from it and cooked it. At 11:30 in the night we had supper and we drank cocoa. But they didn't have lots of cocoa. It was not enough for all the audience.
— Y. A. *Fourth Grade*

Nobody was left at Poso Nuevo that holiday but Pancho and the three youngest boys. Arturo wrote of their activities:

Wednesday we had a Thanksgiving party at school. We were thankful because we had a perfect attendance for a whole month. We ate pickles and carrots and buns with weinies and pumpkin pie and candy. But Thursday on the day of Thanksgiving we did not have a good time because the girls and my mother and the big boys went to Palo Alto and left Pancho, Victor, Pili, and me alone at the ranch. We were not afraid of anybody that would harm us. To eat we made a sugar candy and ate many prunes. A. A., *Fifth Grade*

The four Badilla children entered Baboquívari School this year, so they still seem like new pupils. But they gladly entered into our work and play, and shared our enthusiasm for baseball, singing, parading, making pottery, and publishing *Little Cowpuncher*.

The aim is to have at least one story from each little cowpuncher every month. But when we were ready to go to press Herlinda had been left out. In last-minute panic I gave her a piece of scratch paper and said: "Write a story."

"What shall I write about?"

"Oh, write about yourself." She did.

MY OWN STORY

I am a little cowpuncher girl. I live in the Ronstadt Ranch near the Baboquívari Mountains. It is the Las Delicias Ranch. I eat Mexican food. Beans and tortillas and bread and milk because I am a Mexican girl. This week at our school Mrs. Ewing from Illinois and Mr. and Mrs. Ronstadt came to visit our school and we sang them many songs. H. B., *Sixth Grade*

Her sister Dolores, called Lolita or Loli, is a special child. In school she seems like something from dream heaven, so I call her my angel. This amuses the other little girls. We sing a lullaby the last line of which is "Angels will watch my darling." At that line Teddy and Chelo smile and point to Loli. She is a demure child with pale skin, dainty features, and soft waving hair shoulder length worn looped back with a ribbon. I like to hear her read, for the sweet throaty quality in her voice. I can't imagine scolding her. Perhaps her frail loveliness has something to do with valvular trouble in her heart; we have to be careful that she does not overdo. She won a prize for getting a hundred perfect lessons before any-one else in school. She is eight years old and has caught up, in school work, with her brother Lupe who is nine.

Lupe is a funny boy. Funny, without being rude or smarty. Everybody likes him and the children laugh at his antics without teasing him. In lessons he is slow but sure. He will not quit an assignment just because it is closing time.

"Come on, Lupe! The bus is going!"

"Wait me. I no feenish my test."

There he stays, half-sitting, half-standing, writing in his big, clear letters until he answers all the questions that have been given him, and mostly with correct answers.

Luis, the oldest Badilla, is a slight boy of fourteen — also a victim of chest trouble. But there is no occasion to call him angelic. I lose patience trying to get him to read the required number of library books. I scold him for his annoying habit of inciting giggling spasms among the Aros boys. Ramón has to move across the room from him to keep his composure. When the boys have their unsupervised baseball at noon, Luis, now forbidden by doctor's orders to be catcher (which he plays expertly), is umpire. Though thinly dressed, he never complains of the cold. He likes to ride the bus since he doesn't have to get up so early — he lives only seven miles from school — and insists on taking his share of opening gates and changing tires.

Bus riding, in spite of hardships, has its pleasant side in good weather. The children from lonely ranches enjoy the chance to gossip and play. Many times Mary or Herlinda reads aloud or tells stories to the younger ones; and Frances amuses them by translating into Spanish the stories they have heard at school. In warm weather Pascual leaves part of his load in charge of Mary and Edward in some pleasant spot along the road while he goes up a sideroad to Las Delicias, or to Peyron's for little Ester. Poor child. She is too frail and undernourished to bear up under school and bus riding. Every year she falls ill before attending school long enough to pass, so she is still in the first grade, although eight years old. While Pascual is gone, the waiting children pick flowers, eat *covena* bulbs, or practice for track meet or dances. Sometimes they have seen snakes or coyotes or skunks, but nothing bad has happened to them. And once in a while they get a thrill such as Edward described:

A RARE THING THAT HAPPENED

We were waiting by Cerro Prieto for the bus when right before our eyes stood a herd of blacktailed deer. They were about thirty — does, fawns, and bucks. They stood very tame looking at us. All the kids were excited, yelling "Deer! Deer! Deer!" That frightened them and they ran away leaving a cloud of dust. — E. H.

[Author's note: Edward hesitated to publish this story. He was afraid some heartless hunters with no respect for lawful seasons might

*come and kill them. We waited until the deer had time to change
ranges before printing it.]*

Pascual, our bus driver, has a sunny disposition despite his chronic parental grumblings and ceaseless chatter. A clerk in the county superintendent's office calls him *Señor Muchas Palabras* — Mr. Many Words. His services to the school are not limited to driving the bus and signing vouchers as a trustee. He fires up the teacher's stove about 11 a.m. and makes the cocoa. He mends broken windows and screen doors, and at times takes a hand at yard duty. But his most valued service to the school and community is that of barber. He cuts hair for any and all and is in great demand before fiestas. One by one, after the grownup cowboys are shorn, my boys, and some of the girls, get excused from the schoolroom and run out to the backless chair under the tamarisk tree in the rear where Pascual talks and jokes and snips off locks all day long.

Happy merry Christmas Pancho.

Same to you, Ramon. Let us ride our broncos for our celabration!

Edward Hernandez

Christmas or Halloween

THE LENGTHENING March day lingers. Its warmth has an enlivening effect on the young Aroses, glad to overflow into the yard once more. Poso Nuevo, tight and lonely after winter sunset, is pleasantly at play this evening. In the corral the little calves bawl now and then to check on where their mothers are. The chickens that roost at the corner of the pumphouse are loitering and gossiping. There are sounds of yapping dogs, Frank's guitar, and the children playing on both sides of the building.

Ramón and Chato are vigorously pitching horse-shoes in the back yard outside my little window, and showing enviable skill. Eloísa and Socorro, amateurs, are their partners. The air rings with clang of iron, girlish cries, and lusty male shouts. They jangle over scores goodnaturedly, then suddenly their voices all sound at once, shrill with passion, as they call each other *chapuzero* and *bribón.* The side yelling the loudest wins the argument. They glance at my window and see me smiling at their contest and omit saying the usual *palabras malas.*

The smaller kids are whooping and yelling out front. Arturo forgets that I can hear him and lets loose the wild laughter I try to suppress. He and Pili and Víctor are tormenting the little burro that the vaqueros brought for Víctor because he had made a vow to be the best cowboy in the world when he "is a man." Sullenly Víctor sits on the stubborn, confused little beast, heels digging vigorously, sawing on the bridle. Arturo and Pili attack from the rear. When the *tranchito* balks, they rush at his heels with a rattling old iron wheelbarrow, and blows from sticks and Pili's rawhide rope. The *tranchito* kicks up as he dashes forward and pitches Víctor over his head. Arturo and Pili shriek with laughter. In true cowboy fashion, Víctor jumps up and assaults his mount.

As I opened the screen a moment ago to try some referee work, Pancho came out of the hayroom and gave Víctor a good wallop for hitting the burro on the head. Pancho, I notice, has more sympathy for animals than any of the other boys. Capitán and Guardián, the two old ranch dogs, come over to him as he squats on his heels, back to wall, to watch the donkey training.

Frank has heard Pancho come, and calls to him. But Pancho shouts: "No, *hombre.*" He wants his supper first. He knows that Frank, who does not have to do chores, has already eaten, and that when the singing starts it will be hard to break away.

The little girls are playing over by the arroyo. Chelo and Meli have been taking care of Mercedes, pulling her around in a battered little wagon. Now they have left her and are running across the iron pipe that bridges the little gully, yelling and waving their arms to keep balance. Mercedes wails in protest of abandonment.

All these sounds blending in the mild evening breeze make the place alive with human clatter. By contrast I think of the lonely quiet of Los Alisos, the homestead I left yesterday at daybreak. In that remote canyon the far side of the Catalina Mountains is the quality of melancholy that haunts any isolated, impoverished habitation. It seems to be waiting, like an empty stage.

Friends who struggle up the deep sand in the rough box canyon say: "Why did you pick such a faraway, hard-to-get-to place for a homestead?"

Yet they must know that stockraising requires grass and water rather that accessibility. And the little place has enticing beauty.

Last fall, the day before I came down to make ready to open school, Buddy, my horse, and I helped drive the south canyons of the upper water to gather the weaner heifers. When we reached the head of Trail Canyon and rimmed out on the high rise that overlooks not only the little ranch but the whole twenty-mile length of Pepper Sauce Canyon and about a hundred miles of the San Pedro River Valley, I stopped the bunch and held them there while The Cowboy scouted a draw for some we had missed.

The summer of tending my garden, helping with

the cattle, and hardening myself again to the saddle had gone too swiftly. I looked long at the dramatically picturesque little homeplace on the shelving slope above the two great trees in the canyon, noticing the pink roadway up the narrow side gulch where I had done so much pick and shovel work; the red adobes and gray roof of the cabin I had helped construct; the stout brown poles of the new corrals I had sweated over; the bright corrugated iron hay barn; the gray cement water tank and the shining round *pila* where the animals drink. Looking, I felt a stout pride of ownership. Sparklingly green at the back of the house was the garden enclosed by a green ocotillo fence whose fifteen hundred thorny branches I had helped weave through the barbed wire, watering them until they began to grow in place. The flowers and squash vines (one forty feet long!) weren't visible from that distance, but my eyes rested pleasurably on the bunchy green of the young trees and the tall corn stalks soon to turn yellow with frost.

I gazed deliberately to mark the scene well in memory. In the months since, I have treasured it while living in cramped quarters in the midst of a large family with little chance of privacy. The loneliness in the canyon is peaceful, broken most often by the wind in the branches, the call of night birds, mourning doves and hunted quails, the evening yipping of coyotes and hooting of owls, the bawling of lost calves and worried cows, and — so rare that it scarcely seems worth mentioning — by thunder and violent winds and rain showers.

I fit into the landscape there as our pioneer forebears fitted into the Far-West frontier — enjoying the liberating quiet, finding time to read and work and create a chance for a life with meaning. It is a place of hardship — with now and then precious contentment.

Since I must work abroad to keep things going, I appreciate the noisy vigor of Poso Nuevo where I hope to create, by school activities (in addition to school routines) an environment of stimulation, to develop resourcefulness and social responsibility in individuals whose lives are short on opportunities.

When I drove up to see Sally Ronstadt recently after school she asked for copies of *Little Cowpuncher* for October and November, and mentioned that the December issue was sad. Others have said the same. But I am sure we were not sad when we wrote it, although I do not discount the dreariness of being left out of the world's festivities.

Even if it didn't work I still think my idea of trying to skip a big Christmas was good under the circumstances. But I've learned my lesson. Never again — where children are involved — will I try to rationalize the social calendar to fit into budget or income. It is useless to claim that I didn't have the money for a Christmas celebration *this* year. In all my years of schoolteaching I never have had the money. This time I was trying to be sensible. In October I told the children that I could afford only one big party before the rodeo parade in February, and asked them to decide on the date: should the celebration be for Christmas or for Halloween? The decision was made by secret ballot. Slips of paper were distributed to all members of the school (myself included) and the two holiday names were printed on the board to be copied by the voters. Of course Halloween won. It came first! Also, in Arizona October is one of the best months. Weather was an important factor for us as our program could be more elaborate if held outdoors. Also the participants in the program would be healthier before the cold weather set in. Then too there are few distractions in the fall so we might hope for a bigger audience, especially as the roundup — with about twenty cowboys — was due near the end of the month. Finally, what counted most with me, we had given a wonderful Christmas party the year before, one we couldn't hope to surpass or even equal.

Until that Christmas there had never been a night program or a community Christmas party in Baboquívari School District. There was our chance! The whole great field of a traditional Christmas Eve in the grand American manner was open — including a crowning surprise to all, even the grownups, when — just as the children were lined up in front of the Christmas tree singing "We wish you a Merry Christmas" the door was shoved open and in came Old Santy Claus, red suit, white beard, and all, carrying a sack full of green net bags filled with goodies for all the children present including preschoolers. The gasp of astonished delight that filled the room could never be repeated.

And if we had another indoor party we would have a smaller audience for last year there were more transients in the vicinity. This wide valley-plain between rough, treeless mountain ranges seems to tempt those adventurous enough to want to come in and take a chance on making a stake. There are dreams of prospects that might develop into gold mines or copper mines; of dry farms or small ranches; of temporary jobs on the big established ranches. In a few months most of the new settlers fold their tents. Even many of the vaqueros — those less typical than Prieto — hear the call of shorter hours and bigger wages over the mountains. Last year we had an extensive road camp which brought more families into the neighborhood to crowd the school and give us two bus routes.

So our twelve-by-twenty-four foot space was packed that clear cold *Nochebuena,* and our program wasn't the only attraction. The Aroses killed their pig, and their guests were making a double party of it. They attended our show the first part of the night — until 11 o'clock — and then spent the remaining hours until daylight visiting and eating tamales in relays. Two dozen tamales made, four or five guests sat down to eat them and drink coffee. Their dishes removed and washed, two dozen more tamales cooked, another handful of guests sat down to eat and drink coffee. So it was on through the night, the smaller children sleeping bundled up in clothes and quilts, the older ones playing around the big fire out in the yard, the women gossiping and holding fretful babies, the men mobilizing against monotony and the stinging cold with wine or mescal from across the border.

Our entertainment was not the usual bashful half-prepared children's performance for an audience to smile at and applaud politely. It was a real play in three acts with costumes and make-up, and it was a smash hit! It was the first time in the community that players had worn elaborate costumes and spoken their lines with vigorous feeling. It was several "firsts" in the annals of our school. Frank, miserable when conspicuous, made his debut as a guitarist — so made-up and dressed-up that he forgot most of his self-consciousness. The actors were herded into the teacher's room and prohibited by main force from circulating among the crowd in their exciting get-ups before curtain time. Greatest novelty of all: the comedy was in Spanish. Excepting a very few (and they all understood the language), all our visitors were Mexican-Americans. For their pleasure, and our own, we wrote and produced a play in the only tongue the entire audience could comprehend. Never was an audience more entertained. Never did actors receive more spontaneous applause.

Among the characters we had such fun creating and naming (how Edward roared aloud with laughter as he dashed off page after page of dialogue for them) were a charming widow, a timid bride, a solemn priest, a swashbuckling sheriff, a heroic horseman wrongly accused of banditry, and the hit of the play — Don Cacahuate (Mr. Peanut), Edward of course, a rich old bachelor, foppish, fastidious, excessively romantic and courteous. The house literally shook with laughter from the moment the curtains (sheets strung on a clothes line) parted. From the first scene to the last the performers were urged on by stamping and hand-clapping and hearty *vivas*. Two of the fathers now and then yelled at me in English: "That's fine, Mrs. Bourne!" "That's all right!"

As the first scene was ending Pascual sneaked up to where I was hidden in the folds of the makeshift curtains and loudly whispered: "Say, Teacher, begin it over! Some people have come in late and that first act is too good to be missed!"

The enthusiastic reception to our play I felt justified my risk in using Spanish in a county school program. Had there been a chauvinistic critic present I might have been "defrocked," as the law insisted all Arizona schools be taught in the English language. This wasn't exactly school, and yet in a way it was. We had composed this play and studied the parts and rehearsed it during school sessions. Yet I felt that honoring their language would help parents to be more interested in their community school and cause them to cooperate in its aims and programs. I knew that the parents present who had attended public schools in our state during their youth had been snubbed and scolded and even punished for speaking the melodious tongue of the padres and conquistadores. Some of them were even trying to bring up their children with no knowledge of their "native" language — but it is good to know two languages; it is a fine thing for little children to accept both languages as their heritage. It has been my observation that teachers who come out hard against speaking any Spanish at all are themselves monolinguistic.

After I retired at 2 a.m. I lay listening through the thin plank door to the boys and the girls (allowed in the boys' room while the all-night festival went on) repeating our songs and scenes at the request of their visitors, and it made my heart glad.

What a wonderful Christmas program! I wanted to retire on my laurels in that particular department. I planned to have this year's first show an outdoor festival that would depend on the visual effect of bright costumes and lively dances. I was leary about trying another all-Spanish program — for this time, as our acquaintance and reputation spread, our audience would not be a hundred per cent Spanish-speaking. So I made my bid for Halloween rather than Christmas for the first semester grand blow-out, and the children — for the time being — were with me all the way.

As it happened we had another triumph. The weather was perfect. Sparks from the huge bonfire rose high and straight in the still, moderately cool night air. The audience was jolly and responsive. To cap our success five teachers from other rural schools took the time and trouble to come. When they crowded into my room after the show to drink coffee and eat the tacos that Pascual's wife and mother had made for my personal guests, they overwhelmed me with compliments.

"The hours and hours it took to teach those dances!"

"And to do them with such finish!"

"The mothers made those costumes? Now if I gave anything like that I'd not only have to buy all the costumes, I'd have to make every one of them myself."

One teacher said frankly: "I'll never again have my pupils give recitations and readings on a school program."

That it turned out so well was a big relief for I was worried. Our last rehearsal was terrible. The children must have been inspired by their costumes. They went through lines and steps so perfectly that I was ashamed of the shouting tantrums I'd had during rehearsal. That very day I had kicked Ramón out of the show. Not until I was dressing the dancers in my room did he come with apologies. I gladly let him take his part which I'd thought I'd have to do myself.

It took a lot of sewing to make all those costumes. My-Mother made nine different outfits. And Amadita (Pascual's wife) sat up until midnight the two nights preceding the show sewing by a kerosene lamp. After her own four children's costumes were made, she found material and made another for a little girl in a family of five children whose mother tries to run a household on fifteen dollars a month.

The star of the show — which was probably as much of a surprise to her as to the rest of us — was Ysidra. It was her first favorable impression on the public. I could scarcely believe my eyes — after the nerve-wracking time I'd gone through trying to train her. At an ungainly age, she sulks because she isn't allowed permanents and cosmetics like her sisters. Stubborn, if she can't get a step the first time or two, she balks. "I can't," she says flatly. "I can't do that." She was unhappy about her part. Mary was a Spanish dancer. Socorro was a colonial dame. Both had lovely costumes. Ysidra had to be an old witch, and hers was the last dress to be made. I bought several yards of black cambric and sent it home with her. When My-Mother got ready to make it (after dark the night before the party) she sent Ysidra to my room to ask how I wanted it. Frantically busy, I sketched roughly a long uneven skirt, tight bodice, and big sleeves. My-Mother improved on that. She sewed into the neckline at the back a long jagged-edged cape that swirled gorgeously in the dance, and made a tall cap with bells on it. The day of the party she made a special trip to town to buy her nine masks and got one for Ysidra so ugly that it was grand. Thus motivated, Ysidra turned into a vigorous old witch with a bloody whip in her hand driving the spirits of mischief, winning laughter and applause with her amazing leaps and fantastic postures.

All the children wrote accounts of the performance; Socorro's was chosen for the news story in *Little Cow-puncher.*

Friday evening Baboquívari School had a real show here at Poso Nuevo which cost our parents and our teacher a lot of money to have it really nice. We tried to help Mrs. Bourne in everything we could to have our dances as cute as possible on account of many people coming from far away to make our big audience. Everybody was doing his best and felt merrily all through the show. It was a little play with many dances and all with costumes. Some were cats' dances, a witch's dance which was the hit of the whole play, and some other dances.

After the performance we bubbled for apples, toasted marshmallows on the big fire in the yard, and had songs with the guitar, and went into the school and danced for awhile for fun.

The main thing to make it nice was everybody and the teacher were dressed in different costumes. Another interesting thing was that we dressed our stage with corn stalks and strips of colored paper. It was outside with the car lamps for lights and everybody said it looked gay and pretty.

At the party we had distinguished guests. Some came from Three Points, some from Sahuarita School, some from Tucson, the whole school from Las Moras, and a woman from the 7X Ranch. Two came from Las Delicias, our clerk Bill Ronstadt and a sailor boy by the name of John Hill from the *U.S.S. Pennsylvania* who for our pleasure he wore his beautiful sailor suit and he looked very nice in it. All enjoyed the show, the players and the audience, too, and some seemed to have a joyous time. I know I did. It was lots of trouble and work and expense and a long way to come for our audience most of them. But it was a fine good party. — S.A.

After that exciting triumph I thought we could let up and hit our lessons hard until February. Then came December. And all the children in the nation and all the schools in the county began getting ready for Christmas. We were going to skip it. Oh, of course there'd be a quiet family-like party in school the afternoon before the beginning of the holidays. Teacher would give each pupil a small gift, and the girls were making handkerchiefs and pincushions for teacher. But we had already had our big celebration. We would stick to our agreement and take Christmas lightly. But the December *Little Cowpuncher* was coming up. For language lessons one morning the pupils were asked to write a few words on this subject: "Do You Honestly Like Christmas the Way It is Now?"

They were given a brief history of the origin and practices of the ancient Christmas festival; and a propaganda talk about its modern transformation into a commercial enterprise by which merchants hook people into buying more than they can afford of things they could do without. Emphasis was made on the expense, the trouble, the disappointment, the sacrifices, and the heartaches. They listened attentively, searching their editor's words for a cue that might plunge them into the deeps of literary composition. There was a silent period of earnest struggle, then one by one they came up and turned in their papers and took up something simple, noncontroversial, and rational: arithmetic.

Examining their sincere and touching efforts that evening, I knew I had lost. I had made a stand against tradition and custom and, alas, the longing in young hearts, and I had not prevailed. Like it or not, ready for it or not, Christmas would roll right on around and come to Poso Nuevo and our impoverished school. Without a hint of disappointment and dismay, next morning in a calm teacher's attitude of directing learners, I handed back several papers saying: "Put periods and capital letters to your sentences;" "Arrange your ideas into paragraphs." "Look up correct spelling of words marked." Then I cut the stencils that evening and printed the stories verbatim. And took to heart my own lesson: Christmas is overwhelming; there is no escape from it.

Here are excerpts from each grade's contribution:

CHRISTMAS THOUGHTS

Second and Third Grades:
I like Christmas because Santa Claus bring me lots of things. But big children dont like Christmas. — D. B.

I like Christmas because my Santa Claus bring me toys and all the children are in bed and the Santa Claus put toys in a stocking and some candies. — F. S.

I like Christmas becuase my Dear Santa Claus brings me some candies and a pair of shoes. — M. H.

I like Christmas because in Christmas time all the children are asleep and Santa Claus brings some toys. — P. S.

Fourth, Fifth, and *Sixth Grades:*
I like Christmas. I like Santa Claus. And I like the Christmas tree. I like the turkey and I like the dance. — V.A.

I like Christmas because we make tamales. And I like it because Santa Claus comes at night and leaves the toys for my little brothers and sisters. I like Christmas. — Y. A.

I like Christmas because we give some Christmas presents and because it is fun too. — L. B.

I like Christmas because we have a holiday and a good time playing and running and jumping free. And I like Christmas because our mothers and fathers and some other people give us presents and we eat good things. Yours sincerely, A. A.

I like Christmas because it is a great holiday. And because we go to sleep and dream that Santa Claus brings us toys and other things, and sometimes is true. — H. B.

I like Christmas when I go to other places to pass the night. When I stay here at the ranch sleeping I don't like it so well. I used to like Christmas when I used to be a little boy because Santa Claus used to bring me toys. — F. A.

Eighth Grade:

That is the holiday I enjoy most when I have money. Without money Christmas is nothing for me. — R. A.

I honestly love Christmas for being the a memory of Christ when he first came to earth. One reason I like it is because we have some vacation to refresh our minds and to go and see our faraway parents [she meant relatives] and friends. And have enough time to go to parties in the middle of the week. And the main thing I like, and this is the truth, is I like Christmas because in Christmas my mother and father do their best to give us clothes. In Christmas I receive more clothes than any other time. — S. A.

I usually like Christmas because there is some excitement at home every year. This year my married sister is coming from Los Angeles and it is a long time since we have seen her.

And nearly everybody is happy at Christmas, especially little children. They always get something even if they are very poor and they are easy to satisfy.

There is much to think about Christmas. It is true that the merchants win because you have to buy from them as Mrs. Bourne says. It is a commercial holiday. But I do like Christmas. — M. H.

Do I like Christmas? The answer is Yes and No. Yes is because it is a custom of the family to have a little candy and something new. That is if our parents can afford it.

Sometimes we are invited to parties *(Nochebuena* we call it in Spanish) to have tamales, tacos, enchiladas, and so on. Now these are good things to have while you are awake all night dancing, singing, shouting, and laughing. Friends all meet together and have a good time and sometimes make new friends.

My other answer is No, because it is the custom to give presents and postcards. When somebody gives you something it is your part to give something in return. But if you can't afford it, as our teacher says? You feel cheap and even stingy. It sometimes gives you headaches to think of it. And some Christmases are worse than others. So it is hard to judge from both sides. —E. H.

There it was. The little ones still believed in Santa Claus and the older ones were good sports. We had a Christmas Party. It was not a grand affair with community participation as on Halloween. It was a simple, unrehearsed, noisy, raise-the-roof, costly frolic with three gifts to each child distributed by the old but new-to-them

"Fishing Game." And there were candy, nuts, and fruit — enough for everybody to take some to the ones at home. And there was a Santa Claus. In fact, three of them. They were kind readers so touched by the *Little Cowpuncher* stories that they went to the trouble to beg and buy materials for a nice Christmas box for the school.

Perhaps the story that touched them most was that written by Antonio, a short-time pupil who was with us a few days while his father worked on a mining claim assessment in the Sierritas. His Christmas story was:

Santa Claus is going to give me nothing.
I dont like Santa Claus because every year she bring me nothing.
My mother one time she gave me shoes and a toy.
But Santa Claus has never bring me nothings.

100% Attendance

Dog-gone it — Missed again!

Baboquivari School

arturo

A.D.A.

WHILE BILL WAS HERE this afternoon he asked about our Average Daily Attendance. This means he is figuring out the budget for next year. I know he is wondering if they can afford to keep up the teacher's salary as it is at present. By careful management he eked out a five-dollar raise last spring. Other years the question is how to avoid a cut. A school district is allotted state and county funds on the basis of daily attendance. Our attendance has been high for the number of pupils, but there has been a big falling off in our enrollment. Through no fault of the school or the district, our floating population is in exodus. That means a lower figure on my check; but since it means a better chance to teach and learn for me and the pupils that are left, I am not sorry. In any case, money, like time, flies away.

What does a rural teacher know about economics? Hard times and good times seem pretty much the same to people who manage to keep going on small salaries but never quite make ends meet. When I was teaching for $720 a year I contrived to run along within hailing distance of current expenses. When I earned $1800, no improvement showed up. After my five-dollar raise last fall, the price of groceries jumped. In sad foreboding I looked at the cans of milk marked for a rise of more that a cent each and realized I couldn't win. That night I got satisfaction reading a paragraph from Oliver Wendell Holmes' *The Autocrat of the Breakfast Table:*

The natural end of a tutor is to perish by starvation. . . . I don't mean that you will see in the registry of deaths that this or that particular tutor died of well-marked, uncomplicated starvation . . . they fade and waste away under various pretexts — calling it dyspepsia, consumption, and so on to put a decent appearance upon the case and keep up the credit of the family and the institution where they have passed through the successive stages of inanition.

If there were more pupils I'd get a little more money but I'd spend more, buying them extra workbooks, art supplies, prizes, and materials for parties and treats to keep up pleasant teacher-pupil relationships and in general pep up educational processes. The little booklets of exercises in silent reading, language, and arithmetic I buy for the forced, unnatural activity I must carry on in singlehanded effort to keep six or eight grades going at once. I concede that if I were compelled to furnish such supplies and devices I would seethe with rebellion. As it is, I accept it as part of my job. In the beginning I do it in self-defense. Circumstances force me to be shut up with rowdy young creatures a large portion of each day, so I take measures to rationalize them. As time passes I develop an affectionate interest in each individual and am motivated by nobler aims. The parties, treats, and prizes cost more than a teacher can afford — true enough; but such a use of money is bread cast upon the waters. Father Kino, who so gloriously spent a lifetime civilizing the forerunners of us Southwesterners, made lavish, judicious use of fiestas, pageants, ribbons, and trinkets.

My predecessor, the year before I came, had thirty-nine young people corraled in a space that is crowded with twenty. For a time she had to seat some of them on the window ledges. The outcome of her suffering was a five-dollar raise for me.

As clerk of the board, it is Bill's part to make the budget fit the money, not the need. So I told him that up to the present, our average daily attendance would be at least twenty. He was relieved, but clearly he wished it were twenty more.

As of the budget he was projecting if a district has an ADA (Average Daily Attendance) of twenty or above, it is allowed $65 per capita from state and county educational funds. Any lower figure means a flat apportionment of only $1250. This must cover a year's expenditures for instruction, operation (wood, janitor, supplies, maintenance — broken windows, sagging doors, new flagpole, stovepipes, and so forth), and other fixed charges such as insurance, county library, and school nurse.

After Bill left I went to the register and made sure that we were safely over the twenty mark with an enrollment of twenty-three. Not much room for many absences, but we don't have many. There have been two months of perfect attendance and no month has fallen below ninety-five per cent. If we didn't have the new children this semester — the little *gringos* from the mining claims — it would be above ninety-eight per cent every month. The three little Americans can't come in bad weather because they have to walk a mile before they take the bus, and it has been a wet winter and spring; besides, they are small and delicate — thin little blondes of seven, nine, and eleven. But few little *gringos* could show more gallant pluck. They get up at about four-thirty every morning, walk a mile in the cold dawn, ride for hours in the rattling old bus, and spend a long day at school before another long ride.

Our fine attendance — right up to minimum requirements — has its regrettable side. The children have experienced hardships to keep it up, but they haven't complained. In a sense they've been brain-washed, propagandized, sold on the idea of being here every day. And it's teacher that has sold them.

Cautiously, with their eye on the cash register, legislators in Arizona — much of it still thinly settled in the back country — apportion money to school districts according to Average Daily Attendance. In a county where the population varies widely, more than half of the schools by the time of World War II were classified as rural, one-room. That meant an insignificant number of votes to politically minded legislators who allotted them little more than enough to pay a teacher of modest requirements. Could they think that country school teaching is easier or needs less training and experience than city school teaching? It might be considered eight times as hard, for there are eight times as many grades in each room. There is something in the argument that outdoor people can live cheaper than urbanites. Clothes, for instance, are cheaper as long as they stay in the country. When they have occasion to mingle with town folks they need whole new outfits — top to toe. As a rule they don't have much expense for rent, telephone, electricity, and water bills. But these can be offset by transportation expenses. Even for a teacher who lives *near* the country school, every loaf of bread or pound of butter, every pencil or Band-Aid, must be brought from town in a car. There is not likely to be any delivery service, and the more remote the area, the less likely there are to be adequate means for keeping large supplies of food. And in an "undeveloped" area, anybody with an operating automobile will turn up running errands and doing shopping for the neighbors.

Of course, you won't hear anybody maintain that schools are run for the benefit of teachers, although you do, in country districts, hear such remarks as: "She's a good teacher, but she's had it long enough. Give some other girl a chance." Or, "She's got a husband who draws compensation. Why not give it to somebody who really needs the job?"

Totaling up my monthly mileage, the county superintendent once said: "You are just teaching for fun." "No," I said, "for love."

What would happen if country teachers, or all teachers, were paid enough to live on comfortably? For one thing they could buy necessary materials that country districts and parents can't afford. Bill told me that H. used to buy things out of her own pocket, and suggested that I let him know when I wanted little extras. When school opened my eight grades included five beginners who had to be kept busy and amused for hours while other classes were taught. On my first trip to town I bought paint books and alphabet blocks for each kiddie. There wasn't a chance to write out formal requisitions and wait for the processing of same; besides, you can't make school vouchers to the dime stores.

An unfortunate consequence of the Average Daily Attendance system of budgeting country schools is that it calls for frantically determined effort on the part of the teacher to keep the children coming. And it sometimes calls for astonishing fortitude and a man-sized sense of obligation on the part of rural children.

I congratulate a boy for devotion to duty when he comes to school with a temperature of a hundred and two degrees rather than spoil his record and ruin the monthly report. But as a sensible adult I also feel rather foolish for having influenced him to take this risk just to keep a clean page on the school register. Often, when by hook or crook I have kept up a high ADA record, I have been positively embarrassed by commendation from the officials.

For three years at Redington, on the San Pedro River, we had won the county prize for attendance percentage. The discomfort and vigilance it took would fill a book. Times when floods were roaring down Redfield Canyon, Tacho — our bus driver — carried the kids across on his back, wading the dirty waters fourteen times, twice a day, when the swift current was too deep for his little old pickup to navigate.

When the roads were passable and a child was too sick to come on the bus, or under his own power if within walking distance, Lavita Bingham, my neighbor, mother of little cowpunchers, wife of the clerk of the board, brought her baby and sat with the children — shoulder to shoulder with me in plans and maneuvers to save the little school — while I got in my car and went after the absentee. If he were laid up with a bad cold or stomach ache, I bedded him down in the back seat so I could watch over him and dose him, and drove him back to roll call. If too sick to take part in routine activities, he lay wrapped up in the car until Lavita and I figured we could count him present. Luck was with us for nobody was ever any worse for the makeshift ambulance trip.

Licha and Tita even came to school every day while they had measles. It was seventy-five miles over bad roads (which were impassable in wet weather) to the doctor. Until they broke out, Lavita and I, doing our best with her big doctor book, didn't know what they had. Tita was miserable with fever. I took her to the teacherage and gave her cold drinks and aspirin and a liquid diet. At noon I read to her and gave her an oral spelling lesson with a dark cloth covering her eyes. Licha was the next to come down.

She was twelve then. Her father, our bus-driver, carried her in to her desk from the pickup — so sick she could not hold up her head. We both begged her to go home and go to bed. But she was a victim of my attendance propaganda and endured torment to keep from being counted absent. I doctored the two little girls, protected their eyes, and heard them answer "present" each day so that they both might be on the silver-dollar list at the close of the year. On Friday afternoon I made the hard journey to town for medicine and doctor's advice and got permission to shut down the school until the disease ceased ravaging. The girls recovered without permanent damage — and what a prize day we had at the end of the term!

For the grand finale I had eight silver dollars (our enrollment was ten) polished with an eraser till they shone like new. I called up the eight candidates, with appropriate flourish, and flung the handful of silver down on my desk with a mighty tinkle. The light on the children's faces was reward — and exoneration.

Rosario was another notable award winner at that assembly. He was a retarded boy who had been in the first grade three years, so his motive may not have been eagerness for knowledge. But he took off his shoes and broke the ice in the wide river with bare feet every school morning that bitter January. I appreciated that, because I had to do it myself sometimes to make sure the little car could get across the treacherous sand.

Lavita brought her sick son to the school door in her car and sat with him there, as determined as he and I that his long record of perfect attendance should not be destroyed by a wicked virus.

Extreme measures, yes, but we felt they were necessary. We had only ten registered pupils and our ADA had to be eight. When the county records were compiled our names appeared in the Tucson papers and we received, for top attendance percentage in the county, a beautiful state flag that cost $7.50. Only Vera, the county nurse who came out to see us once or twice a year, had the good sense to say plainly that the place for sick children was at home in bed. I tried to hush my conscience with the thought that I probably gave the sick children more effective care than they would have at home. Their shoes, in most cases, were saved for school even in winter. Busy mothers let them run outside in the wet and cold without wraps; or kept them under cover in poorly ventilated rooms. Furthermore, the school medicine chest, supplemented by the teacher's, is always better supplied than any found in isolated ranch homes. It is a wonder, though, that there was no instance of a sick child's having grown worse for hospitalization at the Redington little adobe "knowledge box" on the mesa above the river bed.

At Poso Nuevo we have no river. No pupils walk to school. And (knock on wood) we have been free of epidemics. We have a considerable amount of indigestion, and we have lots of headaches, earaches, toothaches, infections, impetigo, and malnutrition. These maladies interrupt school work but seldom cripple the ADA. Bad colds, trips to town, and stormy weather are most often the causes of our absences. Edward and Teddy are subject to "flu" which threatens to go into pneumonia. The first of the month is cowboy payday and the Badillas go to town for provisions. If they intend to stay overnight they take the children with them. The Emerys, our little

Americanos, can't come if it storms. So we don't win honors for attendance records.

Under the circumstances we have done well to keep in the "twenty" class. Our worst obstacles are caused by transient population and great distances from school. If the children of a community are permanent residents they can be traditionalized into sacrificing for their school's ADA. But if they know they are here for only a few weeks or months, what can it matter to them?

In the interest of child health perhaps it is an advantage that we are so situated geographically that the teacher can't send tracers after absentees, or go to get-them-or-know-the-reason-why. If a child doesn't arrive on the bus, he is safely absent that day. But if the bus doesn't show up it means a breakdown, and teacher must go to the rescue.

The second month I was out here, while I was still trying to fit Baboquívari School into Redington patterns, I went looking for the bus one morning and trailed it to its very lair up in the wild, rough Sierritas. The Aros kids went with me. They had cleaned themselves up and appeared at the appointed hour, so I hated to cheat them out of any time. We had "classes" as we rode along — the "times tables," "states and capitals," and history dates. Over the thirteen miles to Palo Alto Ranch we expected to see the bus at every turn, but, no. From there we went seven miles, all rough, homemade roads, to Escondido, another little ranch. There we met Pascual and Edward walking for help. The bus had a broken axle. It couldn't have picked a worse place. It was far off in a steep rocky canyon which could be reached only over rock outcrops that chewed up tires and let loose all the squeaks in my car. To climax my misfortune, Pascual's car, which I was attempting to push and bump along in front of mine, ran backwards as we tried to make a sharp crest and knocked six dollars worth of dents in mine. Of course he didn't have six dollars and neither did I. When we finally got the bus to the highway at Palo Alto — the badly corrugated dirt highway — I had to drive the Aros children to Poso Nuevo and go back and tow the bus to Tucson. In such fashion the ADA is constantly vulnerable to Acts-of-Crises. A story in *Little Cowpuncher* for a year ago illustrates the point:

OUR ATTENDANCE STORY

This month we have had lots of trouble with our attendance. The eighth day of Feb. Socorro was sick with appendicitis. They took her to town to be examined and the doctor said she must go to the hospital to cut her side. She did not come again to school until the 25 of Feb.

The next absence was Ramón. In Feb. 12 he had a sore knee. He could not walk well on it. Mrs. Bourne sent him in a school bus to Bill Ronstadt, our school board, and told Bill in a letter to take him to town with the doctor. The doctor said his knee had to be cut and he could not come back to school that week.

The third to be missed was Frances Salazar. Her little nephew the baby was sick and they took her to town when they took Licha. Because she was going to be alone at the ranch. She has 8 years. So that keeps us from having a perfect attendance and from going to the picnic at San Xavier Mission. — Alfredo Leivas, *7th Grade*

Our most common enemies, bad colds and stomach aches, can be battled here on our own ground. Seldom a day passes that I don't dish out bicarbonate, aspirin, nose-drops, and milk of magnesia. (The school cupboard contains a full pint of castor oil, but the children stubbornly consider it punishment.) Our clinic has been so successful that the little cowpunchers don't miss school except in emergencies. There has been only one day's absence in the eighth grade (four pupils) all year. Mary missed one Monday through no fault of her own. She had gone to town with her parents on a payday weekend for gasoline and provisions. On the way home Sunday evening their car broke down and had to be towed back to Tucson. It was late Monday before it was ready to travel, and Tuesday morning before it returned the bus riders to school.

Edward saved the day for the rest of the riders. He had stayed at the ranch with his grandmother and two youngest sisters. When his father had not arrived by six o'clock (still dark) Monday morning, he walked over the hills and got a neighbor to bring the children to school. (I took dispensational authority and counted nobody tardy).

Edward is dependable beyond the call of duty. One cold morning I was victimized by sinusitis and did not come out of my room until nine o'clock. All the pupils except Edward were crowded around the stove.

"Edward is sick," Mary announced.

This was distressing news. It was a pity to spoil his record when the term had less than three months to go. In spring weather, too. But he had kept his fingers crossed for three weeks, March being his pneumonia-prone month. Despondently I touched the bell and faced a gloomy day without the stimulation of his bright face there by the south window. About ten o'clock he walked in. I stopped my lesson. All of us watched him as he walked down the aisle and slumped into his seat in time for literature.

"Where did you come from?"

"The car."

"You were sitting out there in the cold as sick as you are!"

"I wasn't cold."

He could barely speak. His eyes watered. His face was dark with fever. But his interest in what was going on was unconquerable.

"Don't you want to go in and lie down on my couch while your father makes the cocoa?" I wanted to fuss over him like a mother.

"No," he answered shortly. He wanted to be let alone. I was humbled before his staunch spirit.

We dosed him all day. He seemed better at dismissal time, but I suggested that if he did not feel *much* better, he had better stay at home in bed next day. But he came. And seemed much better. And Inez Jane, who had been threatened with something like "flu" was better. The weather was better, too. It was such a fine day — no wind for a change — we decided to celebrate our attendance triumph by taking our lunches and going for an outing about eleven o'clock. We had tried to keep up our school work during illness and now we walked out on it on purpose — much more fun.

It was an inspiring day to be outdoors. With March changeability, suddenly it was warm sunny spring. Long housebound, we met the bright sunshine with a burst of enthusiasm that was richer because we all shared it. Our picnic by the man-made lake will be long remembered. And we managed to get some educational profit from the day by crossing the border into Mexico and visiting the

94

little grade school at Mesquíte where practically all they
had was plenty of ADA. Of the "themes" handed in next
day, Frank's was chosen for our paper.

OUR SCHOOL PICNIC

Yesterday was a nice warm sunshiny day and we made a plan
to go to a picnic at Gill's Lake which is a mile long and a beautiful
one, too. When we got there all the children were jumping around
very happy, and most of them went into the water wading. After we
played and warmed our beans and tortillas and ate, we decided to
go to Mesquite, a little pueblito on the other side of the border of
Mexico. It was in Sonora.

Mrs. Bourne and Mr. Hernández, our bus driver, asked the
young man who was the professor if we could visit their school.
When we went in Mrs. Bourne told them if they could sing some
songs for us. They said No. Then she said if they wanted us to
sing for them, and they did.

Then a bad thing happened. Just as I was tuning the guitar
one of the strings broke. And I could not help the children to sing.
So we had to sing without the guitar which didn't sound so good.
After we sang then they wanted to sing too. They sang four songs
for us, and they sang very pretty. They are good singers.

Those Mexican schools are not as good to have things for their
children as our schools in America. They don't have but only a
few books of which we have thousands of them here. They don't
have a victrola, globes, maps, and lots of paper of different kinds
and pencils and crayolas and water colors. I think the schools of
America are the best in the world.   —Frank Aros, *Sixth Grade*

All nine Aros children, living right here in the building, have answered rollcall every school day this year.
Barring serious setbacks, each will receive a certificate of
perfect attendance from the county school superintendent,
and a silver dollar from teacher at the honor assembly
held the last day of school. Bill has no sympathy for me
when I spend twenty dollars to close a term. "It's your
own fault," he says.

It is. It's my credo. In fact, it's what I can do to
express my conviction *that children ought to be paid for*

going to school. This opinion is purely personal. I would like to tell it to the world, but it would be spitting in the ocean — a moment's shocking impact, then the powerful rush of the incredulous world smoothly closing over the thought to give it obliteration.

No, World! Listen! Children are people. School is their work. It should be paid for — at a time and in a measure comprehensible to the child mind — in medium of exchange, not intangibles too far away and uncertain to have meaning. School is a slow, seemingly endless grind that demands tiresome application and curtailment of liberty. What a pity that its personnel, from both sides of the desks, cannot have the dignity and satisfaction of monetary rewards in reasonable proportion. I wish parents could start the ball rolling by paying their children regular cash sums — say ten cents a day for attendance and bonuses for achievement — money that they might consider that they had earned in their own right.

Children will work for gold stars and certificates of honor and a dollar for a whole year's perfect attendance; and most of them finally catch on that eventually — if they live and do well for an ever-increasing number of years — they will receive the benefits of well-paying jobs and, let us hope, cultivated minds and personalities.

But they would work harder and with better spirit if, in addition to these far distant rewards, their school days would accumulate into pay days periodically from the very start of "dear old golden-rule days." Long ago I heard that children who are good for nothing, are good-for-nothing; and oh, 'tis true.

But nobody is about to pay children for going to

school, so what can teacher do about all this? She can spend her money, such as it is, arrange schedules and materials to cultivate the habit of attendance, and she can *motivate* and keep on motivating, until every child who misses school without a good cause will have all his peers down on him. Meanwhile, teacher can hope that the day will come when the needs rather than the number of children in the schoolroom on any given day will inspire and guide the calculations of the law-makers.

EDWARD D. HERNANDEZ

In the Far Southwest

IT IS A LOVELY spring evening and strangely quiet for March now that the wind has stopped blowing. When I went around back of the building a few minutes ago to throw the day's tin cans into the arroyo, I stopped under the mesquite at the south corner of the schoolroom and looked at the Baboquívari Mountains wrapped in the serene vagueness of moonlight. There is a compulsion to stare long at things that are beautiful, a yearning to remember them forever; not accepting the universal law that all must pass, but trying to immortalize the fleeting moment. Tonight's enchantment is double because to-morrow will be Friday — the gift of calendar-makers to school people.

Tonight there is a flurry of expectation about Poso

Nuevo. Pancho Badilla, vaquero from another "water" on this vast ranch, is visiting the Aros family. They are singing "Las Gaviotas" in the kitchen and it sounds very pretty at this distance. I can imagine how they are grouped. The girls are crowded together around Eloisa, with her little hand-written book of song verses, in the corner by the sewing machine; and the boys are sitting on the benches around the table, all freely singing and taking care not to look at each other.

I could sense excitement even before Arturo came to my window to say that Joe (his oldest brother, José) and Chato (his next oldest brother, Concepción) are going to the roundup in the morning, Badilla having been sent to recruit them. They will make camp for three or four weeks the other side of the Sierrita Mountains, several days at Batamote up on the divide, a day at San Juan, two days at Palo Alto, then here at Poso Nuevo the last stand of the Quarter-Circle D V Bar *corrida.*

We have the roundup twice a year — spring and fall at branding time. For the family here it is a great event — as certainly it is for the school — outranking all legal holidays, saint days, Christmas, and even the Tucson rodeo. The children are carried away by all the excitement. They will eat with the chuck wagon. The outfit will kill a fat cow. There will be cars of company driving up to see the cowboys and hear the news. The girls will dance in the front room with the younger vaqueros. The boys will hunker around the campfire or sprawl on the bedrolls listening to the insolent, inconsequential, profane gossip of the cowhands. And every night there will be singing until late bedtime. If there is anything *para quemar la garganta,* the singing may last most of the night. Pancho Brown will play the guitar. Our Franqui will sit near him as long as he plays no matter how late it gets. He will seem inattentive, just sitting there, never singing. But when the cowboys have gone he will take the guitar and practice all the tricks that Frank Brown performed on it, and teach the new songs to his brothers and sisters.

Our roundup is probably the most pretentious "works" in Southern Arizona for it covers so much territory. Tons of hay are hauled in ahead of time. The DV chuck wagon is a big truck loaded down with grub and about two dozen bedrolls. The twenty-odd cowboys, most of them regular employees of the ranch, are all Mexicans. You hear nothing but Spanish even if the big boss comes out from town. And the cattle work is done in the ancient vaquero manner, as is the horse breaking.

Last spring there was a *gringo* with the outfit. I was curious about the tall blond man squatting alone by the fire while the Mexicans were spending the late evening with the Aros family — singing and dancing (*paseándose*). On the third evening I ventured out to talk with him. He was a bank representative (sent out to take count of the cattle), a man of experience in relatively cultured environments. During our conversation he said, in a sincere and kindly way, that it was foolish to try to educate these children or encourage them to go to high school.

"They are happy now," he said, sure of his opinion, "because they don't know any other way of living. If you educate them up to American standards, then what have they got to look forward to? There aren't enough white-collar jobs for them, and they won't be satisfied with frijoles and tortillas and a *parranda* once in a while. Leave them as they are. It is better for all concerned. We need this class of labor."

For the moment, as we sat listening to their songs and chatter and laughter, it appeared that he was right. They seemed completely satisfied, wanting no modern civilization with its eternal worries over finances, diets, sanitation, and economic advancement. Their ancestors have lived like this for hundreds of years. Their customs and manners are securely fixed by traditions. They know what to expect and what to prepare for; how to train their young to fit into recurring patterns. Few of them are ever restless with discontent or fear of insecurity. They accept the vaquero life of freedom and bondage.

Conceding all that, I had another viewpoint. I knew that the glamorous simple life on the range could not bear close inspection. Many of the men lounging about in a carefree manner — after twelve or fifteen hours in the saddle — were wearing the same clothes they began the roundup in. They carried no toothbrushes or antiseptic lotions. Most of them used a common towel and comb. None were making any provisions for themselves or their families beyond the daily food. Practically all of them were doomed to painful and destitute years of old age.

They had killed a cow the evening before, right in the courtyard between the corrals and the house. I covered my head with a pillow and yelled to shut out her death cries, for they cut her throat and let her die lingeringly "to make the meat more tender." They took out her ribs to roast and eat before she was entirely skinned. A piece of meat they sent to me on a plate was still twitching with muscular life. The kids standing around watching the whole butchering process were given a rib or two each. Arturo and Víctor made a fire of chips in the back yard to char theirs before eating them. Little Mercedes screamed in terror when they immersed her in the *panza* while its contents were still warm with animal heat in an effort to cure her rickets. The offal was kicked aside a few feet before the dogs tore into it and dragged it over the yard. One piece was under my car by my door.

As we sat talking by the red hot coals the cowboys were singing and laughing, their songs monotonously crude, their jokes coarse and cruel. Some of them, odorously unwashed, were dancing with the patient romantic girls, their boot heels clopping on the cement floor raising a sinister gray dust.

In a way perhaps they were satisfied with their ill-paid work and immature play, accepting their destiny. But they all, even the children, looked tired and bewildered — as if sensing that their destiny was defeat. I wondered if they feared intuitively the hard road to improvement, beset, as it surely is, by unknown miseries, roughened by man's savage inhumanities.

"Teach them to read and write a little," the bank man said, "and figure enough for their simple accounts so they won't get cheated. Then leave them alone. Somebody has got to do their work, and they like it."

I told him that his words reminded me of the time that a city school principal said to me: "Don't kill yourself over these children. They'll only be somebody's washwomen and ditchdiggers."

And I had answered her, "Well, let them be washwomen and ditchdiggers who love literature and good music and have trained imaginations to make them feel compassion for other living creatures."

It seemed courteous to grant him his side of the discussion. But I did tell him some of the interesting things my pupils were doing to widen their experiences and enrich their lives. They might be "these Mexicans" to the bank man; to me they are individuals — my Arturo, Edward, Pili, Teddy — every one of them. And I know and share their thoughts, their pleasures, their pains, their worries. I want to help them.

Of course I can't give them jobs or money. I can't prepare them in any definite way for "this changing world." I am not even sure what changes they will encounter. What I want to do right now is to influence their attitudes and outlooks. Perhaps, in a small group such as this, it is impossible — except in rare cases — to teach them to think for themselves. I can only hope to infect them with a taste for literature because it epitomizes all we know of human life. I want to arouse in them respect and desire for liberty, justice, and tolerance — within reason. I want them to believe in germs, sensible hygiene, reasonable ambition, fair play. These things have been done for the ancestors of the banker and me, and for most (I hope) of American citizens. They were done by education. And often by the direct influence of dedicated sympathetic individuals such as Horace Mann and, perhaps, Jane Addams.

Ysidra has just knocked on my door and asked to borrow the school clock. The alarm will ring fifteen feet from my head about three o'clock in the morning to arouse the boys who are to ride off to the "work." Too bad I can't share their enthusiasm, for, like it or not, I shall have to endure another roundup about the last of April or first week in May. I hate the dust, the racket, the infringement of what privacy I have — since my only door opens right on their camp a few yards away — the suffering of the animals, and the brutalizing influence on my boys.

The little cowpunchers watch the branding with keen pleasure. Sometimes they are called upon to help. Branding is necessary. But in practice it is deliberate mayhem and done in the grossest cruelty. Boys in this region do not object to cruelty. They like outdoing a living creature that tries to get away. It excites their imaginations so that there is always the troublesome aftermath of games at school recesses. After the roundup the kids play rodeo. If they are ropers they have lots of fun. Every fellow who has a rope is a vaquero; the others have to be cattle. It is bound to end disastrously for the weaker ones for, as in actual cowboy practice, it's a battle of brute force with all the odds on one side. I let it go on for awhile because I know the young rascals are learning to *lazar*. But as soon as one of the small boys gets his feet jerked out from under him and his face skinned, I ban the game during school hours.

So the spring roundup (*corrida*) is under way. All I can do about it is try to emphasize the skills of roping and riding, the importance of well-trained and well-kept horses, and — to the best of my knowledge, the types and good points of the cattle. And it does make good live material for *Little Cowpuncher*. The young ranch children like to write about cattle work better than anything else. Their favorite subjects for drawing are horses and cowboys.

THE HOLD-UP

While we are in school this morning we hear the thundering hoofs of the cattle coming on the plain. We hear the cowboys hollering their Indian war whoops. The cows are bawling as hard as they can for their little *orejanos* (long-eared ones).

The vaqueros are having a hold up or a rodeo as we call it in Spanish about fifteen feet from our schoolroom at the corner of the pasture west of us.

There are about fourteen cowboys. The boss, or the *mayordomo,* and a helper are separating the cattle such as the calves that are not branded. You can see the horses so calmly among the sharp horns of the cattle.

This cattle belongs to a rich man whose home ranch is far over the mountains to the east of us. He has a very fine herd of Herefords. Twice a year he has a roundup on account of so much cattle. Today in the afternoon they are going to brand the little long ears. The school kids all like to see them brand.   — E. H.

BREAKFAST AT THE CHUCK WAGON

Every morning we get up very early to have breakfast with the roundup cook and help him wash dishes.

He makes a very good breakfast and gives it to the cowboys and some to us. His name is Reynaldo Salcido.

Today they took the chuck truck to bring some hay for the horses.

We have supper with Reynaldo too every night.

Day after tomorrow they are going, and we must thank the cook for his kindness in giving us the good food.   — Arturo Aros

MY WEEK END AT PALO ALTO

Saturday morning I rode to Palo Alto with Mrs. Bourne as she went to town. The roundup was camped there. So I enjoyed myself looking at the cattle they had in the big corrals.

When the cowboys rode away I had nothing to entertain myself so I went to Frances's house and played with her and Chelo, my little sister who was visiting her.

Afternoon I went with Frank Brown to Las Delicias Ranch to buy a wrench to fix a pipe that was broken by the cows.

So I had a good time during the week end. — Frank Aros

ROUNDING UP THE MARES

Saturday and Sunday we gathered all the mares again because the boss told my father that they would come and help him drive them to Palo Alto. We got them ready Saturday and fed them. We are still feeding them as the men have not come yet.

Those two days were very windy and rainy. We all got wet. Just for nothing for I think my father is going to turn them loose again because they have been three days in the corral without enough to eat. My father is angry for this is two times he has gathered the mares, because they told him they were coming to take them and then they haven't come. And we can only help him on Saturday and Sunday because we have to go to school. — Ramón A.

THE ROUND-UP

When the Round Up truck came to Poso Nuevo I peeped through the school window and saw some of the cowboys taking our wood which I brought for our family to use and I felt bad. But when they left they left a pile of wood for us.

They are coming back again in a few days. This wasn't a real round up — only a few came this time. There are going to be lots more when they come again because they are going to gather all the cattle. This time they got only the steers. They didn't brand the calves because they were in a hurry to deliver the steers. — R. A.

CUTTING HORNS TO STEERS

The boss came from Canoa, the big ranch, and said to gather all the cattle so as to get the little steers and cut off their horns. We were eight in all that went to get steers Saturday. We brought twenty-eight that belong to the water at Buenos Aires and only eighteen for Poso Nuevo to cut their horns off.

I think my father is going to keep getting them. We don't get to help him very much because we come to school. We have time only on Saturday and Sunday. On those days we are a family of vaqueros. — Frank Aros

In writing stories about our way of living the little cowpunchers are likely to assume that everyone knows ranch work. They know it so well. In most cases it is about all they do know. Mary and Edward are exceptions. They have read more books and have understood better what they have read. They have seen many moving pictures so that they have romantic notions of the big world outside, and dream of idealistic success for themselves over the mountains. Most of the others have a stubborn satisfaction with the ranch and don't want to know anything else. They submit to the school corral since they must, but their hearts are out *campeando* (riding the range). Ramón, Pancho, Luis, Arturo, Víctor, and Lupe can already make hands at ranch work. They serve apprenticeship during vacations and weekends. Frank, unable to exert the needed energy, is a problem to his environment.

"I don't pay much attention to horses," he told me one day, baring his soul. He seemed to be trying to say "You see I can't be a vaquero — the only future my family can offer me. Can you do something about it?"

There is a fearful gap to bridge between isolated children such as these and the confusing, roaring, rushing, smashing, industrialized, smart-know-how world of our modern civilization. Independence costs so much effort, when it is up to the individual, so much time and endurance, that it may never seem worthwhile to many little cowpunchers. The bank representative need not worry for another half century. Personally, I pin my hopes on the next generation. My little cowpunchers' children must go out into the changing world and change with it.

Tomorrow they will talk excitedly about the roundup. As they hear of its gradual approach their interest will increase. Nobody can remain indifferent to it. I like to see the horses. Early in the morning from my half-window over the sink (my only window) I watch the wrangler drive the *caballada* to the corrals across the courtyard out front. They come boldly, just a little bit faster than their driver would like, heads up, manes and tails swinging, still free in the cool, brisk air, not yet submitting to the brutal control of men.

There is a dusty clattering interval in the corral as mounts are roped out. I cannot see the lassoing except in snatches as I go in and out my door. The saddling up takes place in the yard. The schoolboys hang around with the greatest interest. Backs are humped, stinging ropes lash out, and salty steeds are topped off under whip and spur in a tumult of shouting, swearing, wild laughter, and facetious pranks.

It is amusing to hear the nicknames the vaqueros tie to each other. They are apt, but sometimes unkind. There are the Spanish equivalents of the everpresent Shorty and Curley — Chapo and Chino. Pancho and Chico serve for Francisco as Rich and Dick do for Richard. But our vaqueros are more personal, even cruel. Whatever is peculiar about a man becomes his label. He is called *Prieto* because he is dark-skinned; *Mocho,* because he is lame, or one-armed; *Gordo,* because he is fat; *Jorochi,* if he is inclined to be humpbacked; *Zurdo,* if left-handed. One of our roundup hands is called *Borreguito* (Lamb); another is *Ojo de Liebre* (Jack-Rabbit's Eye); then we have *Cara de Papa* (Potato-face); *Coyote; Huero* (Blondy); *El Viche de Tubutama* — because he is always going around looking for a good time — something like our *Playboy.* One is *Zopilote* (Buzzard), because he is so dirty; another is *Duque* (pronounced Doo-qui) because he is always feeling good. The cook is dubbed *La Madre* as he performs the lowly tasks of feeding, washing up, and generally making the boys comfortable. He is not always successful on his own behalf. Last time he was here Arturo came to me twice to get bicarbonate for the uncomfortable "Madre."

The roundup detracts from school interest and school spirit. I must share my children with the *corrida* excitement. Partly to offset the interruptions and get their minds back at school I tried to put them to writing stories for *Little Cowpuncher* about other subjects in our environment — perhaps the weather or the great outdoors round about us. They came up with stories on what the cowhands were doing for diversion, judging cattle, beans as the "salvation of the west," and horse-racing, a festive event at roundup time. I was forced to conclude that their minds had not really been diverted from the roundup at all. Here is what they wrote:

THE LITTLE WILD PIG

Thursday the cowboys brought a wild pig. A *javalina.* It was a little one. It bit one of the cowboy's fingers with her little sharp teeth. We gave her some pumpkin to eat. At night we put her in a pen of chicken wire and she ran away. We could not find her.
— Víctor Aros, *Third Grade*

THE STORY OF GOOD CATTLE

The difference between good cattle and common cattle is that good cattle have a straight back, short legs, a kind of flat face, and a bushy tail at the end. They are dark red with white faces. Their horns are different too. They don't have them long and high like the common cattle. They go down toward their faces a little.

We saw some at the Livestock Show at the Tucson rodeo that are worth thousands of dollars. We all here know good cattle.
— R. A.

FRIJOLES — A SUBJECT OF GREAT IMPORTANCE

Beans are the salvation of the west. If we didn't have beans to eat some of us would starve to death. We have been discovering that most Americans from nowdays are enjoying our best food: beans and tortillas. Beans to ranchers are the staff of life.

When we fry beans the lard has to be well burned so the beans will taste good. Not all of the Mexicans know how to cook beans. Each family cooks them a different way. Most of the people who live in the West eat beans. Each day is our Thanksgiving day for beans.

— S. A.

THE STORY ABOUT THE RACES

There were three races. Concepción Aros won two and P. S. Hernández won the other. The first race was run by Brownie and Cottontail. Brownie started first but at half of the ground Cottontail was ahead. Two brothers rode the horses, Ramón and Chato Aros. The second race was between Alberto Leivas and Chato. Chato won that too. And then there was another race which P. S. Hernández won with Brownie. He is not a bad horse. He runs pretty fast, but he is too small.

This happened at Poso Nuevo Ranch. Everything ended happily.

— Ramón Aros

Mr. Kinney's Rodeo

TO SCHOOL PEOPLE the worst thing about Monday is that it is only the beginning of a whole week's work. For myself as well as the kids I try to pep it up with something new I buy in town on Saturday — workbooks for the little ones, art materials for the big ones. It spoils them; they probably think I'm rich. They look forward; they *expect* a surprise. Okay, today I had a dandy for them — a genuine thriller: a large photograph of our school riding on our float in the rodeo parade last month. It was fun to spring it on them casually.

"Pancho," I said, "Here are two new picture frames. Go get your pliers for the little nails. Take out the fruit pictures and put in these photographs. Hang them over there by the door."

The top photograph, as I handed them to him, was a good eight-by-ten-inch likeness of our friend and patron, Frank M. King, of *Western Livestock Journal*. We had received several letters from him, he had printed excerpts from the *Little Cowpuncher* in his weekly column, and we had met him in person at the rodeo.

"Mr. Frank M. King," said Pancho beaming.

Underneath it, the same size, was a camera shot of Baboquívari School children under the southwestern ramada we built on the wagon that carried us in the parade while we ate a *vaquero lonche*. I was thrilled when I saw the picture displayed in the shop window day before yesterday, and provoked at myself for having waited several weeks to discover it. I hadn't been sure there *was* a picture. The morning of the parade I had seen a city photographer down on West Congress shooting the floats as they passed him. But just as I noticed what he was doing, he exclaimed that some of us had moved and spoiled the exposure. The children, if they heard him, didn't know what he was talking about.

While Pancho went to frame the pictures, I sat down to put my desk in order, pretending not to notice. In a moment I knew the whole room was gathered around him whispering and exclaiming. Then they began shouting to me to come and look. Who had made the picture? Where did I get it? How much did it cost? Look how swell Socorro came out! Teddy, when I went over to clear a place so the little ones could see, kept pointing and saying, "Look, Mrs. Bourne! Here I am!" So, a happy Monday. For a dollar and a half. Every little while pupils found excuses to pass by and take another

Our Float in the Tucson Rodeo Parade

look; at recess and noon the photograph was taken off the wall and examined minutely by groups and individuals. Now we can show it to our visitors when we bring out the big hammered copper tray we won for the best ranch-school entry in the parade.

We won a prize. When I saw the announcement in the paper next morning I thought surely we must have been the only school to enter. At any rate we were from the farthest away; and the only school with a turn-out of total enrollment. However, our appearance was so much below my plans and hopes that winning the prize was embarrassing. It was nice to see the kids glad and excited about it, and I might have felt satisfaction if things had gone right. Nothing was just right except the weather, always the biggest factor in a parade.

Our wagon, a flat hayrack long in use, was hard to fix up, especially with the flimsy material available. We didn't get it the evening before as we had expected, so we had to decorate it the very morning of the parade, in a wild hurry, in the midst of a big crowd of onlookers who were almost all entrants themselves. We were interrupted many times greeting friends and well-wishers; and our boys were so lost in wonder at all the oldtime vehicles, beautiful horses and strange costumes that they forgot our own urgency. The alarming confusion of that hour does not bring me any pleasant memories.

We wanted to represent a bunch of Mexican vaqueros having regular ranch *comida* [midday meal] under a typical *ramada,* the crude shade made of poles and brush to be found beside nearly every dwelling of humble folk in the Southwest. We planned to have a *comal* [iron griddle] over a real fire of coals on a pile of sand, on which the girls were to make tortillas. We were going to eat our lunch *de veras* [in reality] as we rode through the streets. Last year we had worn our "own clothes" as we were truly cow-country natives. But we found the spectators preferred the bright-colored riggings of the private-school pupils. So this year we got dude shirts of many colors, and bottles of red, green, and orange soda-pop to add sparkle to our show.

I tried to plan methodically. The eighth graders headed committees in charge of refreshments and decorations. But it was no use attempting order. When the hour struck we were a bunch of gaping hicks lost in the big city crowded for a fiesta. I vowed that if ever again I had to get two dozen youngsters from over the horizon into a parade, with the town swelled to twice its size by winter visitors and rodeo followers, I'd never let a one out of my sight after passing the city limits. As it was, my little cowpunchers stayed with relatives scattered all over the southern outskirts and western suburbs of Tucson. Some were not able to push their way through the human traffic jams in time and had to climb aboard our float from the sidewalks as it passed up the main street.

The fundamental disorder commenced at the ranch. On the eve of the event I was dismayed at the frenzy of interest involving everybody in the community. Why should I have imagined that Pascual and I were the only ones to go with the little cowpunchers? The fathers and mothers and big brothers and sisters could not possibly miss seeing their own flesh and blood participate in the pageantry of Tucson's great parade. I hadn't the heart to squelch this extravagant enthusiasm, for my people had borrowed money or drawn wages in advance to get their children ready. Of course they wanted to see them in their glory.

We were complimentary guests of Mr. Jack Kinney, the rodeo manager, and wanted to make a good appearance. As a former owner of Poso Nuevo Ranch, he had taken an interest in us. And Pete Waggoner, executive chairman of the parade committee, had helped us. They were furnishing the wagon and team. And Mr. Kinney had taken ten dollars out of his own pocket for a parking space for us at the rodeo grounds that afternoon. We were on our metal.

I still believe the lunch idea was good. In theory it was. All along the way, so packed with people the vehicles could barely squeeze through, there was clapping and exclaiming at the sight of the little cowpunchers busily, joyously, chewing and swallowing. The trouble was to make the chuck last for the hour or more that we were parading. All of it, except the sodas, had to come out of one pocketbook — mine. The Aroses could have donated the beans. Although the Aroses still had beans saved from the last harvest, they couldn't donate frijoles because then they wouldn't have had any way to get enough dimes for the soda fund for all nine of their school kids. So I bought a bucket of beans, and Eleanor De Verl, a town friend, cooked them *chinitos* style *con queso.* They gave off a tantalizing fragrance as I bent over the pot making the "burritos" during the procession through the streets.

Mary and Socorro arose very early and made a big pile of tortillas, wrapped in snowy dish towels, and a pan of *bolitos* [balls of dough] for the ones they were to pat out during the parade. They also fixed the bowl of tomato and green chile salsa.

I made the burritos and passed them out, wrapping the tortillas around the beans and sauce. There would have been enough tortillas to make two for each person aboard. But a bunch of the small fry, led by Víctor (aged nine with a marvelous appetite and capacity), ate one in every two blocks and could easily have doubled their intake rate if they hadn't been warned to eat slowly so the people could see them eating.

Víctor, the insatiable, gave up trying to stand and knelt by the railing, close to my left elbow — intercepting a burrito I was passing out to someone else. He ate with such genuine relish that the crowd applauded in amusement.

"Take little bites, Víctor!" I hissed.

"I am!" he said reproachfully, gulping down a whole burrito.

My impressions of the long ride through the streets are endless circles of thin brown hands extended toward me hopefully around the kettle of beans. I simply could not dish out the burritos fast enough. There were twenty-three empty stomachs riding on that wagon.

"Marcela has had two already," somebody complained.

"No, Mrs. Bourne," she denied indignantly. "I have just one."

Socorro, Mary, Herlinda, and Edward, at the back of the wagon, didn't get any. Ramón didn't ask for one, but I knew he had not had breakfast. The big girls didn't even have a soda until the end of the ride for they were faithfully occupied in making tortillas for the entertainment of the public.

Ramón and I weren't the only ones to appear without breakfast. All the children and their parents had come to town the night before and the friends and relatives they were staying with had crowded homes where the tables for a group had to be set several times each meal. My big boys had to leave before their turn anyway in order to help get the float ready.

The wonder is that we all got dressed and on the wagon at all. Grouped together under the improvised ramada, the little cowpunchers looked very gay as they happily ate and drank. "My-Mother" had made orange, yellow, red, and green rayon shirts for the Aros nine. The four oldest boys capped the climax by bursting out in brand new cowboy hats at four dollars each, leaving Víctor broken-hearted. Days before the festival he declared each morning that he couldn't go because he had nothing to wear. At last one morning he told me, rejoicing, that he had his shirt. Now all he needed was a hat. And shoes. And pants. And a scarf (*mascada*) to wear around his neck. A few days later he announced gladly that he had his pants. But right up to the last he grieved over his wardrobe as any actor about to face an important audition. We borrowed him a hat. Half an hour before he dressed that morning, his mother got some money from José and bought him a silk neckerchief. He never did make the shoes. As he knelt by the rail his raspy earth-encrusted feet stuck out behind, digging me in the thigh as I hovered over the beans and tortillas.

Lolita and Lupe shoved their way across the crowded sidewalk and we hauled them aboard some distance up the street from starting point. Even so Lolita did not have the shirt and jeans, but appeared wearing a blue-striped cotton dress. We stuck somebody's hat on her and made her sit in the midle of the wagon where she wouldn't be seen. She has soft, naturally curling brown hair and the clear, pale skin and starry eyes of an angel, but she was a hidden treasure on the Little Cowpuncher float.

Our biggest trouble was that the parade started before we were ready. Through the driver's misunderstanding we didn't get our wagon until eight o'clock, and the line began forming on various side streets shortly after nine. By 9:45 all the floats but ours were waiting in line. It happened that Pascual's car picked that morning to refuse to start. Mine was the only car available for the several trips to gather up the children. When enough of us arrived at the starting lot we took hammers, saw, and baling wire and began working frantically to build the ramada. Some of our poles turned out to be too short. And in our haste we broke some that we had marked for uprights. And we had underestimated the amount of brush (*batamotes*) for roofing. In the midst of superintending the construction and cutting baling wire with inadequate pliers, I wore out my voice calling the boys back to work. There was too much to see on the lot.

Our troubles were topped off by two last straws. I found that I had brought only one of the signs made to hang on each side of our float, leaving the other at the ranch fifty miles away. Somehow I scrambled through the traffic and stubborn crowds on the main streets and bought cloth and paint and a brush. Our artistic Edward, tormented by haste and nervousness, dashed off another one — fourteen feet long — which we used wet. And at the very end, when our horses were hitched and ready to go, I discovered I had not gone after the cases of soda pop. I had bought and paid for them the afternoon before, but they were to be kept on ice until the last possible moment. Taking Ramón to dash in and get them, for of course there was no place to park, I tore through the packed streets in second gear.

We made it to the bottling works, but couldn't get through the main part of town again. The police had barred it off. I dashed back the opposite direction, ignoring stop signs (cops all being at the parade route), setting Ramón a bad example in breaking traffic regulations, crossed the river on St. Mary's bridge a mile north of the parade starting lot, flew sixty miles an hour through Menlo Park Addition, and came in the back way to the starting point just as the Indian who was detailed to drive our wagon — a one-idea man if ever there was one — was pulling out into line. The kids yelled with joy and managed to halt him long enough for Ramón and me to get the precious soda aboard.

There was nothing to do with my car but leave it where it was. More than two anxious hours later when I had ridden back from the end of the parade behind María Valenzuela on her horse "Medianoche," there sat the car, safely alone in empty spaces.

Triumphantly we had our float, our costumes, our chuck, and our lovely sodas, and the show could go on. The sun was bright and warm, a most precious circumstance for thinly clad paraders. Jouncing along up Congress Street in line, I found we had no bottle opener. Pancho donated his knife which worked well enough until, as the wagon bumped over some streetcar tracks, the knife fell through a crack in the floor and was never seen again. As it slipped through his fingers there was anguish in his face when he looked up at me. His knife! And not a chance in the world to get out and pick it up — years might pass before he would have another.

With no other mishaps, the little cowpunchers gave themselves up to having a wonderful time. The younger ones, eating and drinking with obvious gusto liked the sights along the way so much they seemed to forget their own parts in the parade. They were seeing more people than they had imagined were in the whole world. There were incredible masses of people wedged along the sidewalks, hanging from every window, leaning over the flat roofs of buildings. Occasionally the little ones pointed, shouted from full mouths, and jiggled litter from the ramada into the beans as they waved to friends and relatives along the route. Our public! The older ones, conscious of the honor conferred by our rodeo sponsors, wore their hats and bandanas with swank — keeping perfectly in role.

Treading their brief hour upon the boards as sons and daughters of the true West, they made our staring, gobbling miscellany into a unit. Back at school, while their hearts were still swelled with bubbling excitement, they wrote their stories for *Little Cowpuncher,* telling our subscribers, near and far, what the fiesta meant to them.

ON OUR PARADE WAGON

Socorro, Herlinda, and I made tortillas all along the streets in the parade. We already had the bolas ready. Socorro was the heroine for she could make them bigger. I believe the tortillas was our best triumph for winning the prize. People on the streets called for tortillas as we passed.

We didn't make enough masa (dough) and when our tortillas

tore we made a ball out of them and tried to make another tortilla. But that is not successful. When it was over we had a big bunch of tortillas *sancochadas* (hard but raw) for the fire was not hot enough. The boys fixed a comal (flat iron plate) over coals on the sand. I had fun doing them. Every time I pulled at the masa I tried not to tear it, and I stuck my finger in and made a hole. I sat by the fire to make mine, but Socorro stood all the time, the great tortillas hanging from her arm. She never fell down, with the wagon jerking so hard. But before we stopped Ysidra fell into the kettle of beans.
— Mary Hernández, *8th Grade*

THANK YOU, MR. KINNEY

After the parade about fifteen of us jumped on Mrs. Bourne's car to go to the Rodeo Grounds. The little children with broken hearts could not go in because there was no room for them in the car. With the ticket Mr. Kinney gave us we all went in and got parking place No. 59.

When the show began, whom do you think we saw? Mr. Kinney on his retinto horse. I'm sorry he did not hear us sing at the Santa Rita Hotel the night before, but he wasn't there. And·he did not see us in the long parade for he was riding at the front. I'm glad we got to see his great pretty show. I enjoyed it with great pleasure all the whole day. — Frank Aros, *6th Grade*

MY FUN AT THE RODEO

After the parade all the children of Baboquívari School over ten years old went to the Rodeo looking at the ropers rope the calfs and tying them. But what I liked best was the race horses.

If I were a rodeo cowboy I would rather like to run the race horses than to ride the broncos because I had learned to ride the running horses here at the ranch. Running them at the Rodeo is much easier because there are not holes and ditches and bushes like the ones here. I would not like to ride the broncos because they would throw me down. — Pancho Aros, *5th Grade*

A STORY OF THE BRAHMA BULLS

On Friday afternoon we were on the hay wagon eating tortillas and beans all the way through the parade streets.

When we went in the Rodeo grounds we saw lots of things that we were amused about. The best thing I enjoyed most was the Brahma cattle.

Oh my. They sure knocked off cowboys. Only three stayed on the Brahmas backs. Some even bucked harder than the horses. The horses didn't knock all the cowboys, and the Brahmas knocked all but three.

The Brahmas are the most important cattle in India, and they use them for making farming in that country.

I wouldn't like to be a steer in the Rodeo because they would cripple me and knock me down and maybe break my leg and then what shall I do with a broken leg? — Arturo Aros, *5th Grade*

GANADO FINO

Saturday morning some of us went to the Livestock show to a sale of fine bulls. The most popular bulls were the ragged, big-bone ones born in Arizona at the University. One was sold for one thousand dollars. Our mouths watered when we saw those fine bulls that is how much we would like to have one. They also sold some steers of the Four H that were as fat as pigs.

We could not stay for all the show but we learned very much the two hours we were there listening and looking. And the man who was in charge was amusing all the people with his way of speech. He must have a wonderful throat to talk so fast and so long and so loud all that time. — Edward Hernández, *8th Grade*

What do such experiences as these have to do with schooling? No amount of vicarious learning in the isolated routine of country schooling, or probably any schooling, can equal this firsthand *knowing* about the world. Perhaps as spectators and participants in this "big city" enterprise the children learn respect for the orderliness and efficiency showing on the surface. At their ages they cannot see the seamy side of such events. They are not outraged by the suffering of dumb animals. They know nothing of corrupting influences on the professional contestants. They cannot imagine the underlying high-pressured commercial interests. They see the vividness of pageantry, the grace of practiced skills, the thrill of chance. They grow thus, in contact with the sophisticated world, and they are naturally grateful to those who make it possible.

They had a wonderful time!

We're in the money!

Singing in the Santa Rita

IN THE NEXT ROOM Frank is singing alone this evening. His guitar has a nice, deep tone. He is singing dreamily. I imagine his pleasantly melancholy mood comes from loneliness (he does not take part in riotous play with his half-brothers) and the gentle, nostalgic springtime. His voice is not strong but it is pleasingly husky and sounds musically true. He won't sing in school. The others say it is because of stubbornness and *flojera* [laziness]. I think it's his age. His vocal apparatus is rounding the curve to maturity, and he won't risk it in public. It is a surprise that he is singing in there now when he knows very well that I can hear him. Could it be that my efforts have got somewhere? At any rate he is freely singing in my hearing, and perhaps that is his way of thanking me for the

123

enjoyment we shared on our memorable trip to the Big Town last month.

He is singing "Las Gaviotas" (The Sea Gulls) which is very popular this year along the Mexican border. As he sings the meaningless words to the fascinating tune, it probably reminds him, as it does me, of the night before the rodeo parade and of our triumph as entertainers in the Santa Rita Hotel lobby. This is the song we sang best, the one that made the biggest hit. That night, to my wonder, Frank sang aloud with us, pitching in to make the harmonies right, although at first he was cold with stagefright. Demanding a place to sit in the crowded hotel lobby, he slumped into a tall-backed chair against the wall behind a group of our little ones who stood up facing masses of strangers — well-dressed grownup Americans — and sang for all they were worth.

It was the little cowpunchers' finest hour, and came as a masterstroke of good luck for it was entirely un-planned — a spur-of-the-moment event for all concerned. One reason our audience (a milling group of winter visitors, cattlefolks, rodeo people, and interested towns-people) took our performance with startled gusto was that it came up in an unannounced, offhand way. Sud-denly there we were and the children sang spontaneously as if they were in school singing for their own pleasure. Without fanfare or advertisement, in we walked — a varied group of young Mexicans dressed in Western cos-tumes, singing our hearts out. It was the eve of the big annual Fiesta De Los Vaqueros. The city was full of visi-tors expecting a good time. And we were that something added — an unexpected touch of the authentic ranch-country West.

We had gone to town early in the afternoon, planning to find the wagon set aside for us and decorate it. Hours of anxious waiting passed. No wagon showed up. At dark we separated in search of food, agreeing to return to the grounds after supper. Three young men were on the lot to guard the valuable oldtime vehicles ready for the parade next day. They assured us that our float would eventually arrive and that there would be lights. When we returned, they had news for us. Arrangements had been made with a Papago Indian to bring a load of hay and leave his wagon for Baboquívari School. Because he misunderstood, or prized his wagon too dearly to take chances, he had driven back into the desert — nobody knew where. The young man was positive that it would be there early in the morning and that our materials lying about on the ground would be safe.

I faced the disappointment of my children. We might not have a float after all; if we did it would have to be fixed in such a hurry that it could not make a good showing. There on the big lot lay the long poles Ramón, Edward, and I had gone up the river to get, the two car loads of *batamotes* for the roof, and the sand and wood for our campfire. My little cowpunchers were in town — a rare occasion for most of them — with nothing to do but wait in uncertainty for morning. Impulsively I made suggestions.

"Would you like to go to a show? Or go somewhere and sing? (Now how did I come to pop out with that?) Or go to your quarters and rest?"

Loud and clear came the answer. They wanted to sing.

"You'll have to get into your cowboy costumes."

"Okay."

I had just contrived a crisis: I was an impresario without booking. My mind busily cast about for a ready-made audience. On a hunch I ran across the street to a telephone and called the Santa Rita Hotel manager Nick Hall — the mayor of Old Tucson, a famed movie set — interrupting him with my wild request at his busiest time of the year. He was talking to someone else as he listened with half an ear. Gruffly he uttered three words: "Let 'em sing," and hung up.

I rushed back to my kids with the thrilling announcement that we had permission to sing for the people in the Santa Rita Hotel lobby. Pascual and I loaded the excited bunch for a hurried drive across town to get costumes and as many of the missing little cowpunchers we could find. Somebody said that Víctor was in the picture show. We couldn't sing without Víctor!

"What show is he in?"

"He went to the Plaza."

It was a Spanish-language movie house a few blocks up Congress Street. I parked and went in, telling the young lady at the head of the aisle that I must find a small boy. Sensing an emergency the señorita went along with me turning her flashlight into everybody's eyes, sparking a murmur of protest.

"Never mind," I whispered, "I'll find him."

He and Chelo and a town kid, probably a cousin, were sitting alone in the third row from the screen, Víctor slumped down staring up at the giant figures in the comedy.

"I want you and Chelo," I whispered.

Without a word they got up and followed me outside. Their city companion, curious, came with us. As soon as he saw I was loading them into the crowded car, he protested: "We didn't see all the show."

Taking his hand I ran back to the young usher saying: "I don't want this one." She let him go in again.

Víctor and Chelo were staying too far out of town to go for their costumes. Chelo had to appear in her skimpy gray dress and faded brown coat bursting out at shoulder seams. What matter? Her serious little oval face with straight bangs and remarkable brown eyes shaded by long curving lashes took attention from her clothes. But Víctor. Víctor was a prize. Barefooted, his legs and narrow hips encased in tight patched jeans that had been washed until they were only a milky blue, his chest bulging with the new vest (cut to grow into) My-Mother had made from a man's discarded tan lumberjacket, Víctor was a sight. The proud manner with which he wore the thick homemade vest, with only the thin cotton sleeves of his blue shirt to protect him from the cold as he strode through the brilliantly lighted lobby, marked him as a real personality. And all he had to do was to open his mouth and sing and the audience was his without question.

Little Pili, six years old, was another street singer dressed for the part. His second best jeans had been patched so much in the seat with machine stitching that he looked as if he carried a cushion behind him. Chelo's outgrown candy-striped dress with round collar and puff sleeves served him for a shirt. His slender body was topped by a large well-shaped head. His large melancholy eyes shone through long straight black lashes under a broad brow. He was not self-conscious. He was there to sing, and he knew he could sing.

When we trooped across the sidewalk to the entrance, some of the little ones got cold feet. There were apparently hundreds of fine rich gringos in the glittering lobby. I herded and shoved the children. Some had to be pushed through the revolving doors by force.

Nick Hall gave us a startled glance and waved us toward rear center, then hurried out of sight.

It wasn't a grand entry. In a brown felt hat and last year's short tan coat *with black shoes* instead of my tan boots (I had intended to be decorating a float that evening), I stepped briskly across the tiled floor, my songbirds close around me.

"This *is* Indian Day," I heard an onlooker say.

In the glaring lights our red, yellow, pink, and green shirts showed up sleazy and homemade. We all needed sombreros, chapaderos, chalecos and snappy pants to fulfill our role as *vaqueritos*. Obviously we belonged to the unromantic West of cattle and horses, cactus and canyons, beans and bedrolls. We were not show people.

Frank, the tallest little cowpuncher, seemed trying to hide his guitar with his legs. He slid into the high-backed chair by the wall and waited until I had grouped the others about him and given him a signal. He touched the strings softly and gave me a quick startled look. Our good old guitar which had sounded so well at the ranch twanged inadequately in the vast high-ceilinged hotel lobby. It wouldn't be heard more than a few feet away. But I knew our singers would be heard!

I wish I were a musician. I'd like to know how to teach voice, for it would be a great opportunity to live as I do with a singing family and have their talented youngsters under my wing every day. They are all truly gifted. I have heard it said that all Mexican people are naturally musical, but that isn't true. These children are the first natural singers I have encountered in years of being *maestra* to *"Mejicanitos."* At Redington, in many ways the crack school of my career, most of my Latin-American pupils, gifted in other ways, couldn't carry a tune. Here at Poso Nuevo all the children sing. Every one of them, and most can harmonize. All I can do is to teach them songs and find opportunities for them to be heard.

Some school visitors have wondered because we sing songs in Spanish during school hours. Mexican vaqueros and laborers passing by sometimes stop and grin at hearing for the first time in their lives Spanish words issuing from the little schoolroom over which the Stars and Stripes waves in the breeze. I think of an incident that happened a few years ago while I was teaching in Tucson schools. Owing to language handicap, Mexican children, especially the beginners, were segregated from the Anglos, yet forbidden to use any language but English. Speaking a Spanish word was a misdemeanor. One predominantly Mexican-American school — ten primary rooms — gave an operetta. On the eve of its performance the supervisor discovered that one of the numbers was *Cielito Lindo,* to be sung, while little girls danced, just as it was composed. There was a big to-do in the circle of officialdom. The outcome was that little

Mexican girls, dressed in Mexican costumes, doing Mexican dance steps, were permitted only to hum the tune of a favorite Mexican ballad.

Isolation gives independence in language as well as other matters. Out here we take as a matter of course that two languages are in use and we appreciate the melodious speech that has been spoken in this clear, dry atmosphere for fifteen to twenty generations. It is a language known in modern times to one of three inhabitants of our big state. Poso Nuevo residents welcome a teacher who likes Spanish. The pupils sing better in Spanish, Frank handles his guitar better during Mexican tunes, and the little children have a chance to join in.

It pleases the children to teach me the songs popular along the border, mostly ballads. Sometimes I catch a few words of a new song the boys are singing, and ask about it at school. The words are then written on the board to be copied in notebooks, and we all learn together. One morning I asked Frank about a verse I'd heard him singing, identifying it by the words *"Chiquita . . . chiquita, de puro cristal."*

Edward objected, saying it was nasty. The Aroses hotly denied this. Edward insisted that it wasn't suitable for us to sing at school. To settle the dispute Frank and Arturo explained the words. It was a drinking song.

"Anyway," insisted Edward, "it isn't pretty for us to sing."

Right. But I learned the words. It is catchy to sing late at night while fighting fatigue driving alone on a rough road up a faroff canyon.

That night in the Santa Rita we sang ten songs, repeating some by request. At our first song, a very old one — *Mi Primer Amor* — our audience looked, smiled, and applauded politely. The lobby still buzzed with its own loud affairs. Then we gave them "Boots and Saddles" and the whole vast hall turned to us enthusiastically, crowding around us crescent-wise, laughing and cheering. We had them!

Here were hastily thrown together colored shirts, borrowed hats, Pascual's individualistic haircuts, dark-skinned kids from the lonely desert plains to the south — but singing kids! Spontaneously, Mexican fashion, they sang full blast with simple harmonies curiously effective. Even the smallest knew the words and sang them out. There were wild yells from the cowboys scattered among the audience, and gay shouts of approval from all sides. We were a hit.

A dime fell tinkling on the tiled floor near Marcela's feet. She glanced around at me startled. Later she told me she thought somebody had dropped his money. A quarter came rolling over by Víctor's bare foot. Then a shower of silver and copper covered the floor in front of us. We kept singing. I hadn't expected this, so the children were not warned. The little ones didn't understand, and the bigger ones, with proper dignity, stood and maintained the program. Amid general laughter, the men in front yelled to the kids to pick up the money. Whites of eyes gleamed as glances turned to me. I nodded — and the two front rows ducked as one child to gather the silver manna, darting about like little quails, squatting on the floor to reach under chairs and tables, but never letting go of the song.

We tried to give them "La Rana,"a clever nonsense song suitable for children, but it wouldn't do for grownups in holiday mood. So we sang "La Bola." People laughed, yelled, crowded up, threw their change to us. The clerk, I learned later, began ringing rooms to call the guests downstairs for the show. The lobby overflowed. Men and women were crowded on the mezzanine floor and the stairs. At the end of "La Bola" there was a furious guitar-plunking out in the center of the lobby. Powder River Jack and wife, professional entertainers following rodeos all over the country, and probably guests at the Santa Rita, were singing a cowboy song. They did not get their expected reception. People were used to them, but few had ever heard anything like the little cowpuncher group.

"Give the kids a chance!"

"Don't muscle in on the kids tonight!"

There were loud shouts for them to get out and give the kids the floor, but they wouldn't yield until they had finished their song — quite a long one. We gave them a big "hand" and they graciously withdrew. No doubt they knew that the way we were signing we'd soon split our throats. At the time, however, and for more than half an hour afterwards, we were tops in the amusement line.

Men began calling for "El Rancho Grande." This embarrassed me. It was not a favorite of mine and we had never sung it together.

"They want 'Rancho Grande'," Edward urged.

"Well, let's sing it," declared Ramón.

So we did. It could have been better. But right afterwards we sang "Las Gaviotas," fully redeeming ourselves.

At that high point in our triumph I realized that I was getting more satisfaction out of this performance than anybody concerned. Perhaps the director always does, for the success is his imaginative hope carried over into reality. A dream come true has the added glory of surprise for most dreams do not. As often as I had heard the children sing I had wished that others could share my pleasure. Now we had ventured out of isolation; we were in the thick of things and people were listening to my kids as I had dreamed might happen. It was a fortuitous audience: Easterners, Westerners, highbrows, common folks — all stopped for a moment in genuine enjoyment. The little cowpunchers, possibly excepting Mary and Edward, were taking their success too casually. Children accept miracles. They believe in fairies, angels, Santa Claus, and the wheel of fortune. People liked to hear them sing! Why not? I alone realized the rare chance we had encountered.

A portly, well-dressed official wearing a purple badge came and told me to have one of the little ones pass a hat. I couldn't do that. He did. He shoved his sombrero into Marcela's hands, took her by the shoulders, and, telling us to sing "Las Gaviotas" again, went through the crowd. Marcela looked sweet. Her little jeans and blue shirt fit her thin frame perfectly. She has tiny hands and feet, delicate features, pale olive skin, and medium brown hair cut in a long bob. She wore a rose-colored silk *mascada* (neckerchief) and a black hat from the dime store. Her sponsor ushered her around until she had a double handful of coins; he poured the money from his hat into hers, and backed into the crowd.

Mr. Hopkins came down from the mezzanine floor. He said his wife — "Ma Hopkins" to rodeo contestants — editor of *Hoofs and Horns,* the official rodeo periodical published here in Tucson — told him to go see if the singers were the "Little Cowpunchers" she knew by correspondence. Other friends, some from distant parts of the state, came to speak to me. These amenities had the disadvantage of diverting my attention from the job. The excited children would forget what came next and depend on me for direction. It was necessary for me to come out promptly with the first line of each stanza. During the congratulations I couldn't tend to business and the children sang the same verse twice or the last verse in the middle, confusing themselves if not the listeners.

I was perched with Víctor on the arm of a settee close beside Mary and Ysidra, the leading sopranos. Seated on the bench at my elbow was a lady who became a voice-in-my-ear. She talked and talked. She was a songwriter and offered to send me some songs to teach my youngsters. She wrote her name and address on the back of one of her songs and gave it to me. In the chaos of the evening I never got home with it. While my kids were repeating themselves, she sang close to my ear an original song about musical animals and said I could teach it if I could remember it. With the best will in the world I couldn't.

Soon I began to fear an anti-climax. Our parents, in a natural urge to see their offspring perform, had trailed us down. First they remained on the sidewalk just outside. As excitement increased they passed through the revolving doors, joined the growing crowd, and gradually made their way up to the front. I feared this might make the kids try to show off; or that some of the men who had been celebrating might draw unpleasant attention to us.

Prieto, swaggering from town refreshments, stood opposite me across the cleared space. He was dressed just as he left his horse that afternoon. To keep the unaccustomed glare from his eyes, his encrusted, old hat was pulled down just above the end of his thin prominent nose from which fell away the stiff black hairs of his mustache. His blue jeans had seen a lot of riding. His boots had recently been bogged down in fresh corral dust. He showed no sign of being conscious of his appearance. He was at ease and frankly overjoyed, boasting to those who could understand Spanish about "¡qué maestra tan buena tenemos!" Before this teacher, he said, several of his children did not know Tucson. "Y ahora, ¡mire no más!" While he was bragging that half the singers were his own *chamacos,* Marcela and her sponsor reached the group.

"They're all orphans, boys," said the big-hearted fellow escorting her. "They're all orphans."

Worried about the tribal reinforcements, I gave the signal for our closing song — "Red River Valley" — our best, thanks to Pancho, Ramón, Arturo, and Edward, and I hustled my cowpunchers out of the side door, a strategy to be alone with our gang and our hatful of money.

Around the corner from the front, on the run, came our mothers, aunts, cousins, and big sisters. They stood by, awed — I hoped — by my authoritative manner, as I firmly gathered all the money into my own hat and doled out a few dimes to those present, intending to count the spoils and make the distribution later.

My innocents had been too timid to pick up the money at first, but having got their hands on it they had to be forced to give it up. The older ones had remained in the background doing most of the work. Ysidra had secured only a dime that rolled against her foot and a quarter that landed on top of her head when pitched from the mezzanine floor.

"Víctor has many!" she shrieked.

Violence was necessary to part Víctor from his full pockets. For a few moments his rusty bare feet had trod the invigorating air of riches.

Evading the relatives by telling them we'd meet them at Pascual's daughter's house in a little while, I took my singers to an all-night drug store for a drink. On the way we passed a shooting gallery. Rashly the oldest boys shot away their dimes — big sports! And Víctor loudly exercised his right of protest. At Martin's Drug we took nearly all the long counter seats at the fountain and ordered strawberry ice cream sodas to cool our throats. Edward and Ramón sat with me in a booth to count the money. When we had subtracted for the shooting and the refreshments, we divided the reminder, saving a portion for each little cowpuncher who had been unable to attend. The Badillas had been left out because they were staying with an aunt three miles out of town. The little Emery kids and Ester Bedoy were to arrive in town next morning.

As we hurried through the cold windswept streets to where patient Pascual awaited with his car and mine, out hearts were light. We were united in the pleasant bonds of a shared success. We joked about not getting our wagon decorated, a circumstance that had been completely depressing a few hours earlier. In the warmth of public acclaim, fortified by money in the pocket, we could joke about disappointment and inconvenience. With light heart I realized that at last I could expect full confidence and cooperation in my school projects.

Back at school the first stories written for the February issue of *Little Cowpuncher* were about the singing in the Santa Rita. Edward made an unsolicited illustration, and Socorro conceived the headline.

AN EXCITING REWARD OF $14.85 TO THE LITTLE COWPUNCHERS

The night we went to town to fix the wagon Mrs. Bourne thought out a bright idea to take us to the Santa Rita to sing. Mr. Hall, the manager, gave her permission. None of us had sung in hotels until last Thursday night. We dressed as cowboys and sang our ranch songs. When we got there the little kids were afraid to go in the revolving door. We pushed them in.

Lots of people gathered around when we sang. They started to throw money at us. Lots of coins were falling from different parts while we were singing. After we finished and got together in a drug store for refreshments Ramón and Edward and Mrs. E. B. counted the money and imagine! we got $14.85 just in change — meaning five cents, ten cents, pennies, quarters, two half-dollars and one dollar. With all that money each one had the pleasure to have 75¢ and everybody was happy.   — S. A.

HOW I FELT

I felt excited when we first went in. I didn't think the people would like us. I had a cold and I couldn't sing well. I tried hard to sing loud the best I could. My throat felt dry and ached. When the kids made mistakes I sang loud so that the people wouldn't notice. I had a terrible time making my voice sound clear. Anyway I was proud and glad that we made a hit with all those guests and Tucson people!   — M. H.

MY STORY

I was not nervous neither afraid of the people because I knew all the songs we were singing and our teacher was with us. At first Frank was afraid of the people but we were in front of him and he could not see them very well. He was the only one sitting down because he played the guitar. — Arturo Aros

FROM THE SECOND GRADE

They like it and they threw money to us. I was afraid to pick it up because I thought somebody lost his money. I got 75 cents. And all the ones who sang. And the ones who did not go to sing.
— Marcela Hernández

We went to the Santa Margarita Hotel. To sing to the people. He threw us some money. I was not afrightened. I was happy. I am seven years old. I sing all the songs. — Consuelo Aros

On the ranch there is no money to spend and nothing to spend it on. We eat beans and tortillas and go to bed at dark. It was amusing to ask the children to give accounts of how they spent their gratuities. Some gave their share entirely to their mothers for the family fund. Some saved at least a part. But the majority tossed it away for pleasure.

ARTURO'S EXPENDITURES

- 10¢ for merry-go-round
- 10¢ for popcorn
- 10¢ for bottle soda
- 10¢ for throwing to the bottles
- 40¢ for silk scarf

YSIDRA'S SPREE

- 30¢ scarf
- 5¢ shine for shoes
- 10¢ soda
- 15¢ red socks
- 10¢ ice cream
- 5¢ candy

FRANK'S ACCOUNT

- 5¢ acorns
- 5¢ orange
- 5¢ candy
- 10¢ show
- 5¢ peanuts
- 10¢ taking Pancho to show
- 5¢ for friend of mine
- 15¢ for gum
- 5¢ for another gum

VICTOR'S WILD SPENDING:

- 30¢ for cracker jack and the other for two times riding in the horses (Merry-go-round.)

RAMÓN WROTE:

Spent for the purpose of refreshments and a sandwich for A., and E., and one for me. And I also shot at the turkey's eye three times for 25¢. Altogether my cost 85¢.

A Vacant Desk

AGAINST ALL INCLINATION I have been trying to work
tonight. I *must* work, for work is the panacea for distress.
Tonight I can't stay with it. Twice I have yielded to
interruptions. Without really needing to, I went into the
schoolroom to sharpen all my pencils. And a little while
ago I went out to close the car windows. It isn't likely to
rain. It was just something to do to keep from settling
down under a cloud of gloom. Duty compels me to sit
here at the cleared corner of the little table by the cook-
stove and go over today's school papers. When the children write something original or do an assignment merit-
ing an honor grade they are eager for a verdict. They
can't wait!

"Did I get a hundred in arithmetic yesterday?"

"Do you have my test corrected? I think I missed the third question?"

"I had lots of mistakes in my language story, didn't I?"

Papers should be handed back while interest is hot. Besides, they pile up quickly. The history workbooks must be checked to be ready for the next study period. Tonight I must read a few chapters in *Wells Brothers,* The Andy Adams book sent to us by Mary Kidder Rak, our friend who wrote *Cowman's Wife* — a good book about ranch life that I am reading aloud to the school. I need to read the new book in advance so I can confine reading-aloud periods to about twenty minutes and still give the listeners the best of the book. And this week is especially demanding because it is *Little Cowpuncher* week. There are stories to sift for material; stencils to cut on the typewriter.

The night is hustling by. I loiter at my tasks, my will smothered by disappointment over my little lost Frances. She is gone — snatched away forever. When I took the flashlight and went in to sharpen pencils I stood by her desk staring at it — unwilling to accept the fact that from now on it will be empty and she will be somewhere else. Dear Frances, my blonde little cowpuncher — wherever she lives she will be missed when she moves on.

For the school morale it seemed best this morning to tell the kids that maybe we'll get Frances back. Can a whole school be shattered by one child's being forcibly taken away? This one seems to be. Our group is dispirited, our hearts sore because Frances has been abducted against her will. And so near the end of the term. If only they had let her finish the year here! She never has been able to complete a school term. And she was the star around whom we were building our spring festival for the grand finale of the year. With her light blonde hair, green eyes, and quick lively ways, she was the perfect choice for May Queen.

The special hurt is that everybody knows she did not want to go, and that she is not better off for going. It is clear to all of us that she was happier in this isolated community living with Licha and Charli — her aunt and uncle — than she had ever been in her life. The Aroses say that Charli and Licha are going to court to fight for her. Pascual suggests that I might help them. But no, I realize that the situation is hopeless. Her abductor was her mother. No matter how incompetent or unworthy, a mother has law (and often public opinion) on her side.

Pancho broke the bad news to me this morning when he ran out to open the first gate. "'May Wess' didn't come," he said, leaping on the running board, sniffling in the way he has when he is nervous. The announcement hit me. I knew what it meant. Frances hadn't missed a day all year. Absence could only mean that the disaster threatening her since last December had finally arrived. I drove on through the other two gates without saying a word. Pancho didn't look at me or speak again.

We love Frances, all of us. The big boys tease Arturo about her because he helps her with drawing and spelling. Significantly, he doesn't mind their twits. From the first she has been a general favorite — exciting no malice, no jealousy. Nobody fights with Frances. She gets more valentines than the others. She has more willing partners for dancing. Her aunt and uncle adore her. She has been living with them for more than two years and they pet her, indulge her, are proud of her.

I have never seen her mother, but I have heard much gossip about her. Socorro told me about the way she acted in December when she came to Licha's house to take away the child. "She is what you call a *flapper,*" Socorro confided, and I knew what she meant.

The incident she related (which I verified later) occurred the afternoon following Socorro's saint day — a Saturday not long before Christmas. My-Mother had given a *velorio* [a candlelit evening fiesta] for Socorro here at Poso Nuevo. Frances came with her aunt and uncle from Palo Alto. The prayers, singing, and patient waiting for tamales lasted until midnight. The rest of the night was spent in dancing. Next morning Licha and Charli took My-Mother and the older Aros boys and girls home with them for a turkey dinner. The Hernández family, on their way back from Tucson that Sunday, were invited to stay for the feast.

That afternoon while most of the company were resting (there are about a dozen rooms in the Palo Alto ranch house) in anticipation of the feast, Frances's mother (Licha's younger sister) came out in a taxi with her new "husband" to get her daughter. She had been writing saying that she had married again and she wanted the child to go to live with her. But Frances did not want to go. When she was small she had lived with her mother and some of her mother's "husbands," and she told her aunt that she had suffered very much. When each letter came Licha read it to Frances and asked: "Quica, do you want to live with your mother?"

Frances always answered quickly, "No, No, Tía! I want to live with you."

So Licha wrote saying, "Do not come for Francisca because she does not want to go with you. She wants to stay at Palo Alto where she has a good house and good clothes and good food and a clean warm bed and where she can continue going to Baboquívari School where she is happy."

The afternoon that Victoria (her mother) came, Frances ran and hid inside the big house. Her mother called and called, but she would not come out. At last Licha told the child to go together with her and tell her mother that she was contented and did not want to go away. This enraged Victoria. She grabbed Frances by the arm to force her into the car. The little girl cried out to her aunt for help and Licha took her other arm and held her — the two women shouting and struggling for the terrified child, who, in the hearing of the shocked neighbors kept crying: *"¡No quiero ir! ¡No quiero ir!* (I won't go! I don't want to go!) Auntie, save me! *¡No quiero ir!"*

The men walked over to take part, and Victoria's companion began to scold her for the way she was behaving. He said he had not paid eight dollars for a taxi to bring her out to the ranch to fight, and if the little girl wanted to live with her aunt they should leave her in peace.

He took hold of the distraught woman and pulled her into the car and started the motor and left. But Victoria stuck her head out of the window and screamed threats. Socorro told me that she said, in front of all the people there: *"She shall not live with you.* You will never have her! I will kill her myself before that can happen!"

Pascual did not know that Socorro had told me about it. Soon after the holidays he called me aside and warned me that there might be danger of someone's coming to take Frances from school. He said that as a member of the school board he would assume responsibility for her protection if he were present. But in case he should be working on the road or helping the Aros vaqueros, he urged me on no account to let anybody, no matter who it was, take the little girl away.

"That would be like kidnaping, wouldn't it?" he asked.

I thought it would, and determined to defend Frances to the fullest extent. She and I have had the most pleasant relationship. She likes our school. She likes our singing and dancing. She loves listening to me read. She pays close attention to the story and tells it in Spanish to the little ones on the bus and to her aunt and uncle when she gets home. It would take a court warrant served by an officer, I vowed, to get her from my care.

For several weeks I was uneasy, and kept asking Socorro for developments. As weeks ran into months and no further attempt was made to abduct her, my hopes turned to assurance. I figured Victoria had given up. Now suddenly, only eight weeks before the end of school, it happened.

This morning when I stopped in my parking space under the little tamarisk all the pupils came running to the windows to tell me excitedly that Victoria had kidnaped "May Wess." Nine o'clock came. The bell was rung, the flag saluted, the national anthem played on the victrola. Nobody felt like singing. Nobody wanted to settle down to lessons. They wanted to tell me all about the calamity — as if I could do anything about it!

It happened yesterday, Sunday, at the Santa Cruz Church in Tucson, just after Frances was confirmed. For several weeks I had known that some of the little cowpunchers were preparing for confirmation. Frances, Chelo, Ysidra, Arturo, and Víctor were the candidates from our community. One night Pancho and Ramón, the rascals, with exaggerated inflections and uncontrolled giggling fits, went through the whole ritual, questions and responses, across the partition from me as I sat brushing my hair in silence. Licha bought Frances a pretty white dress and slip, white shoes and socks, and made her a thin soft white veil. Thus arrayed, I imagine Frances had no difficulty in fancying herself an angel. She is a born actress.

After the ceremonies, the little girls ran out of the church ahead of their mothers. Licha had been *madrina* to My-Mother's baby Evangelina who was christened that morning, and was carrying her godchild in her arms, walking slowly down the aisle beside My-Mother. When Frances passed out the door several paces ahead of her aunt, there awaited Victoria. She snatched the startled child by her right arm and left shoulder (Arturo demonstrated for me), dragged her to a car that was waiting at the churchyard gate and whisked away with her. The children heard her screaming as she was being carried away: *"Tillita, Tillita* (Auntie! Auntie!)" But they took her away and hid her where Licha could not find her.

The distracted aunt and uncle went at once to the sheriff's office, then to see a lawyer. But at the inviolable word *mother* they were met with headshakings and shrugs of helplessness.

I don't know who first began calling Frances by her school nickname. When I had been here a few days last year I noticed that the children were calling her something in Spanish (I thought) that sounded like *Mei-Ues.* When I asked what it meant Socorro, surprised that I did not recognize it, repeated the word slowly a few times: "May-Wess, May-Wess."

"Oh!" I cried, catching on, "Mae West."

"Yes," said Socorro. "We call her that because she is different from us."

She is. She's a natural blonde — with a glamorous personality. Her many names testify to her charm and versatility. Christened Francisca, she is called Frances, Quica, 'Jita, and Mae Wess. Bill recognized her gifts before I did. When he came down to introduce me to my new charges and help me register them the first day of school, after they were dismissed for recess he said: "You know which one of your pupils I like best? The little blonde."

"Not me," I answered. "Over seven years old and in the first grade."

"Well, I don't know," Bill insisted. "She looks bright to me. I'll bet on her."

His hunch was good. She was retarded because she

had never been sent to school regularly. There were two first grades when I came here — one entering for the first time, and one held over from the year before. As a beginner Frances was in the lower class, but she at once determined to get into the upper group where Marcela was. It was inspiring to see her determination to learn to read English. One afternoon while the others were climbing into the bus she ran back to say:

"My *tío* (uncle) talk English. I take my book to my house?"

With permission she hugged her book with both arms and dashed out to demand her regular place in the sputtering, gun-popping old car.

Soon she wanted to take home a bunch of flash cards we use for teaching sight words. I hesitated, saying they might get spoiled in transit. She quickly explained in Spanish that she would wrap them in paper and keep them perfectly clean. She took thirteen cards with words on both sides; next morning she knew every one. It wasn't long until she was reciting in Marcela's class.

But after the holidays her progress got another of the setbacks that had plagued her. Her aunt had a baby, a tiny little boy with no grip on life. He lingered on, in poor health, all spring. There would be two or three weeks when Frances missed school because they were in town having the baby treated by a doctor. When the baby died her aunt did not return immediately to the ranch. Frances's schooling ended for the term as she stayed in town to help and cheer her grieving aunt.

But I needn't have spent so much time and thought puzzling over her report card and filling it with finely written explanations for her retention. When school began again in the fall she promoted herself to the second grade, determined to keep up with Marcela, Lolita, and Lupe. She writes well, is excellent in number work, and has learned English rapidly. Although she has missed some necessary first steps in reading, her interest and industry carry her over many handicaps. If only I could have had her these last few weeks! I can only hope that the versatile little girl will be equal to whatever comes to her.

Her immediate forebear on the paternal side does not seem to be a matter of record. (She bears her mother's surname.) But whoever the father was he surely was Anglo. She has the coloring, the wide-apart eyes, and tall slender figure of the Northern peoples. And she has their grit, their storied daring and vivid imagination. Probably my worries are unfounded. "Mae Wess" will get along.

For the time being, I imagine, her mother and her associates will do whatever they can to win her favor —which won't be too hard. She is fond of pleasure and flattery. I hesitate to admit that she has been impressed by the fact that her aunt has bought more clothes and toys for her than her mother did. The eternal female. Or, perhaps, the eternal child!

Whatever happens to her, the loss is ours — mine, the school's, her playmates' and fellow pupils'. In so many ways she was the piquant dash in our combination of little cowpunchers. Everyone accepted her popularity. Perhaps because she had been living as an only child in a household of adults, she looked upon school as an exciting social opportunity and never tired of directing and inciting amusements for her classmates. This has been a boon to me as I have to turn the primary grades outdoors, unless the weather is severe, at two-thirty each afternoon. From then until four o'clock they are on their own. Squabbles and petty battles are bound to occur. Ester, a delicate, thin-limbed little girl, is so sensitive that the least offense throws her into tears. Chelo (Consuelo) has the Aros fighting spirit. Teddy, sweet little doll, is used to being petted. Marcela, with the soft voice and flashing eyes, is a scrapper. But nobody has ever quarreled with "Mae Wess." A natural leader, she invents games, has a good memory for all she has seen and heard, is always mistress-of-ceremonies, and makes her playmates share her fun.

Last fall she started a fad of christening parties for dolls. Disappointed to find that the other little girls did not name their dolls, she organized a party and stimulated Eloísa, one of Chelo's big sisters, into making christening robes and to help make cocoa and cinnamon cookies. The festive afternoon the whole school seethed with scarcely suppressed excitement. The unusual stir and all the whispered *comadres* and *compadres* made me know that something was up. They were wild to get through with reading, writing, and spelling lessons, and begged that the older pupils be allowed to hear their lessons. Dismissed early, the girls, who had worn best dresses that day, put their arms around each other and skipped down to the Aros *sala* where Edward had built and decorated an altar for them. From *Little Cow-puncher*:

THE CHRISTENING PARTY AT POSO NUEVO

Wednesday afternoon, when the little boys and girls went out of school they had a party to christen the dolls of Marcela and Teddy. Eloisa made little white dresses for the dolls and my mother made some *viscochuelos* and they had chocolate to drink. They invited the big ones and our teacher to the cute party.

One of the dolls was name "Shirley," and one was "Helen." Frances was the priest. Lupe and Chelo were the godfathers of Marcela's doll, and Pili and Chelo stood up for Teddy's doll. I cannot explain the ceremony as I did not see it. I had to thresh beans. Now the little children are calling each other "Comadre" and "Compadre" because they are godparents together.   — R .A.

This theatrical performance had consequences. A few weeks later Licha bought Frances a new doll so that she could have her own christening party during Thanksgiving vacation. This kind of inventive art is new to the children of vaqueros. Most of the young Mexican-Americans I have tutored have clever hands because all their lives they practice patting out intractable dabs of dough into thin round tortillas — a skill to command respect. Also the girls learn early to use a needle expertly. And the boys' supple fingers make fine ropes of intricately braided rawhide strips, or tightly braided strands of stout hairs from horse tails.

My six-year-old Chelo is a skilled seamstress. For Christmas she made me a pretty red silk pincushion with lace ruffles and my name, "Eulalia," embellished with flowers, embroidered neatly in outline stitches. Her handwriting is smoothly flowing, definitely controlled. Marcela and Teddy draw well, write well, and make attractive pottery of the native clay we sometimes play with for "Art." Frances does not have that peculiar quality of hand-eye coordination. Her gifts seem to be the Anglo-Saxon rather than the Latin type. She would rather read books, learn riddles and folk tales, write stories, and invent dramatic games than make pots or embroider dish towels. It was my pleasure — and privilege — to be the first to tell her the classic English masterpieces in fairy stories, folk tales, and nursery rhymes. She has sat before me in a kindergarten chair too small for her, good-naturedly whacking any of her classmates who grew restless and threatened to interrupt the tale, raptly enjoying every story period. When a story was finished — and I gave each one the best within me — Frances sighed, coming back to earth from the Land of Magic, and thanked me. Then she asked in Spanish if it were true. And in the next breath begged for another one. If the story were sad, she demanded a happy one. If it were short she positively insisted on an encore.

"Mrs. Bourne!" she exclaimed. *"Please,* another!"

How often I have heard her say that in her bright, wheedling voice.

Short of time, I have had to limit the storytelling to Friday afternoons. She counted the days and never let me forget. She knew all the folk stories, rhymes, and riddles in Spanish that were to be heard from her schoolmates, uncle, and aunt She liked to tell stories, too, and to write them. When the older pupils began handing in stories for *Little Cowpuncher,* she handed in stories too. And if her literary contributions did not come out in the paper she interviewed the editor! As it is hard to write the simplest story without running into spelling blockades, her compositions were usually dictated to Arturo, Mary, or anybody who had time to spare. She stood by her secretary and dictated aloud. Noisy? Oh, yes. But there are things better than silence.

Once she was dictating a Spanish tale, "Juan Sin Miedo," to Edward. It went on and on until, having filled four pages of scratch paper, he cried: "No. I'm not going to write any more for you. I quit. I'm going to do my arithmetic!"

She stamped her foot and cried: "Mrs. Bourne!"

"What's the matter, Frances?"

"Edward!"

"Edward, why don't you want to help her?"

"But this story goes from here to Tucson and back again. It has no end!"

Mary gently offered to finish it for her. And after all it was too long to put in our paper. She was very disappointed.

There will be no story next Friday. I can't do it.

Why should it mean so much for a teacher to lose one of her pupils? Why can't I say: "Now there is one less to struggle with," and make sensible use of the extra minutes? Wouldn't that be the professional attitude? But my little Frances was taken by force. We all feel the sorrow. There was no fun, no enthusiasm in school today.

When you give your heart to children you can expect it to be broken. You always lose them in one way or another. When I had a schoolroom in the city "system" I used to raise a howl when my pre-first-graders were promoted and I couldn't pass on with them to continue teaching them to read. At peak enrollments the powers sometimes promoted me at the same time as my precious pupils; but gave them to another teacher and handed me a group started by someone else. This was done arbitrarily. I was paid to teach *the course of study*.

So I quit the cruel city and came to the country where I can teach *children* — *my* children, year after year.

My sister says I suffer a misplaced maternal instinct. What do you do about it? Is affection for the young under your care a fault? Perhaps love is always selfish. It is no less sincere. In losing this little girl the structure of the school, the patiently built-up morale, has been genuinely disrupted. This unit of human relationships, created by daily application, imagination and much work, has suffered what seems like irreparable loss. Lessons will go on. Interesting and pleasant things will happen. But we'll never be the same without our "May Wess." No day will pass that we do not miss her, and worry about her welfare and happiness.

What spontaneity she had! Curious as a bluejay, she was the first to see my ring after the holidays. She had come up front to her reading class, but she spoke up immediately:

"Mrs. Bourne! You get marry?"

"Yes."

Pin-dropping silence all over the room.

"You had cho-co-la-te? And cakes?"

The second grade and I were close together up in the little alcove between my desk and the supply closet, their small chairs crowded close to my big one. I glanced down at the eager faces, shining with interest, shook my head, and raised my book for the lesson. But Frances had an inspiration. Poised and sincere, she exclaimed:

"Mrs. Bourne, when you have baby, bring to the school. When he cry, I — " she moved her arms to show how to quiet a fretful infant. Then she said in her own language that she had really enjoyed tending her aunt's little baby. It was her triumph that the adolescent rabble seated beyond my desk didn't burst out snickering.

Stacked here on the back of my utility table are piles of material the pupils have been handing in for the March *Little Cowpuncher*. Today they wrote about what happened to Frances. Here is Frank's:

WHAT SHALL WE DO?

We miss MayWes very, very much. We miss her when we practice the dance we are going to have in May. She was the star here at Poso Nuevo. Of the little children now there are six boys and only five little girls for partners for the Maypole. We don't know what we shall do without her. She was going to be the Queen of the May. She is a good little girl and likes to hear stories and to sing and dance. She is a happy little girl. She is not very fat and not very thin and weighs 63 pounds. They say they are going to talk in Court as soon as her uncle gets his check. We hope she will come back again. She had been here all the days since school was open this year. She had not missed a day.   — F. A.

Edward K.

On the Trail of Culture

IF ORDER is its first law, heaven can never be in a country one-room school. One person's time just isn't enough. The thirty-first of March is now on its way out and I have only begun to cut the stencils for the March issue of *Little Cowpuncher*. Shortage of time (yes, and space) is incongruous in this environment. There are localities in America in which the terrific rush that drives me is probably a commonplace. Here on this vast Arizona semidesert at this lonely cattle water, among slow-moving animals and people to whom leisure is as instinctive as respiration, I am a curiosity.

When I first came Ramón and Pancho sometimes asked me if I would like a horse to ride after four o'clock. My percentage in finding an hour or two for outdoor fun discouraged them. They have given up trying to entertain me in any way except by singing to me beyond the partition. My-Mother and the girls used to come to my room evenings to visit, making themselves quite at home, as if I were but a guest in their house, fingering the things on my tables, asking many questions. Evidently my distress, as I perched on the edge of a table, itching to get at my papers, was clearly transmitted. They don't come any more.

When my typewriter, the first ever to click in the wide silence surrounding Poso Nuevo, began its initial staccato in these quarters, there were bug-eyed spectators crouching outside the screens on my window and door, for it was hot weather and I was the only one on the ranch choosing to spend the after-supper hours indoors. Now the typewriter bangs away unnoticed after the boys in the next room have laid aside their guitar and are tired of their horseplay. They don't object (I'd know it if they did!) no matter how long past midnight it continues.

The neighbors are tolerant, asking only non-interference in their own affairs. They are not rushed. They were never rushed in their lives. Their time is not cut to bits by clocks and ground out to them grudgingly. They work in easy tempo. If the washing, gardening, cleaning, rope-braiding, embroidering, or any other task doesn't get done before dark, there is *mañana*. They don't want anything that will cost their birthright of sitting in the sun when the weather is cold, or in the shade when it is hot.

Living close to nature, they are not subjected to the disintegrating influences of shop windows and high-powered advertisements. Beans and flour are reasonably cheap. In the country areas of the Southwest clothes are chiefly covering. And one can keep warm and dry without a great deal of trouble most of the year. These people don't have much, but in the main they live in contentment and revel in the fantasy of hope. Apparently, to them, whether you have goods and money is merely a matter of accident.

At any rate young and old of the country people here accept their life-long poverty with resignation. They can't understand people who storm the firmaments by sheer human activity. They watch me curiously, as they would a caged squirrel running on his treadmill. If I retire during daylight hours, close the door, and draw the oilcloth curtain across the small window, they pad up and down, front and back, as if to figure out the meaning of this unusual occurrence. At times, fighting illness, fatigue, and depression, I am near the point of blessed sleep — even if the sun hasn't yet set — when one of the kids, usually accompanied by two or three younger ones, comes tapping at my door. She brings wild flowers, almost stemless, clutched in a hot moist hand. Or perhaps a handful of small sticks for kindling. Or that is the propitious moment a middlesized girl comes asking for aspirin, rubbing alcohol, shoe cleaner, baking powder, sugar, a cup of lard, a can of tomatoes, or a bottle of lamp oil. When I close shop and lie down I suppose they wonder if I've blown up at last.

They may be right in expecting that. There isn't room on this table for all the papers, books, devices, and gimcracks I want it to hold. There isn't room in this twelve-by-twelve space for all the eating, sleeping, bathing, laundering, storing, living, and working I try to crowd into it. In fact, human life is considered short because there isn't room in it for a person's aims, not to speak of hopes and dreams.

It *is* ridiculous to be so cramped for space here in this vast corner of North America. The truth is that the limits that crowd and hinder me close in from many sides. Here is my immediate problem: there isn't room in eight pages of *Little Cowpuncher* for all the stories and drawings that my children have originated and turned in for printing. I must fret over selecting materials and cutting them to required size, knowing that this will hurt some feelings and discourage some ambitions.

The little "magazine" is not intended, as anybody can see, to afford journalistic training. Even providing language exercises is secondary. The high aim is literature — an attempt to hold the mirror up to life as we live it here, a record of what happens to us — something we can smile over nostalgically in years to come. Of course I want its influence to play a vital part educationally — that is, to bring some of the big world (through letters, subscriptions, visits) over the mountains into this makeshift schoolroom. To do this its scope must be varied enough to interest many different kinds of people. We want children to like it. And grownups. We want to amuse Easterners who wonder about our ways, and Westerners who know our ways well and have perhaps served their day as little cowpunchers. We want to be read by families and neighbors in this community, many of lowly status in learning; and by friends famous as educators, editors, authors.

This is the *Library Books Issue*. It is our spring roundup of individual reading lists, and a presentation of certain volumes chosen by pupils for spontaneous book reviews or reports. To save cutting too drastically, I'll have to use another dollar's worth of paper, making a twelve-page issue. Well, the subject is *books,* the very foundation of schools and learning. Most of one page will be used to list the grades, the individuals and the number of books each has read this year. That is, supplementary books selected from the 211 volumes brought out from the Pima County School Library to this date. Grade One (four pupils) has 46 primary books to credit — Chelo topping the list with 20 books read. There are 83 books listed for Grade Two (5 pupils, including our lost Frances.) Víctor is the entire third grade. He has read 19 library books. In the fifth grade, Arturo and Pancho have read 22 books each, and Inez Jane, here only half the year, has read 19. In the three upper grades, Mary wins honors with 76 volumes; Socorro and Herlinda are close runners up.

So my pupils have been incited, persuaded, nagged, and forced into reading; some of them (sweet triumph!) really like to read. No psychologist is needed to tell a mother or teacher that reading is the hardest thing there is to learn. To read skillfully, purposefully, thoughtfully, critically, is still an outstanding accomplishment. Nor is it easy to convince children that reading is the most important subject offered in school curriculums. If they enjoy reading they may have a guilty feeling that they are neglecting more important lessons. Country children are inclined to prefer arithmetic and spelling, subjects definitely prescribed in textbooks so that they can be attacked in a cut-and-dried manner.

Happily there are always a few natural readers like Chelo. She has a good memory, a desire to please, and a gift for comprehending the mystery of sounds and symbols. Mary must have been like that in her early classes. When I got her last year (seventh grader) all I had to do was provide her with books and say "Bravo!" Víctor and Arturo "savvy" and if the interest is kept alive each will go through a volume profitably. Many of the others, some willing enough to try, have been drags on this trail to learning's green pastures — prodded along each day with bribes and penalties.

One of the spurs is that under this teacher no child in school above the first grade will be promoted unless his record shows that he has read at least 18 supplementary books, preferably from the county library. To offset this do-it-or-else regulation, there are three substantial annual prizes from teacher: first and second prizes for the most books read during the term, and a special prize for the one having the most reading credits based on the difficulty of books read in relation to his grade. This arrangement has drawbacks. How can I know that a child has read an entire book? I make an effort to give a reasonable, if hasty, oral examination of each book brought up to me for posting in my ledger, but this is a time-consuming process. Usually I judge by my knowledge of the pupil and the length of time he has had the book. Fudging creeps in, but it is not significant. To one familiar with the practices of university classmates of good repute, it is not shocking when a Mexican child cheats on some of the more verbose chapters of English literature. And three cheers for authors who write books that children really like to read!

Now and then an incentive is offered for the reading of some particular book. Last spring we concentrated on Mrs. Montgomery's masterpiece, as this excerpt from *Little Cowpuncher* manifests:

E. B.'S GUESTS AT THE PICTURE SHOW

Monday, April the 8, we went to Tucson after school to see "Anne of Green Gables" at the Plaza Theater. Mrs. Bourne told us that when we finished reading the book she would take the ones who had read it. Socorro, Ramón, Edward, Frank, and I read it. It was a thrilling show. Anne, spelled it with an "e," was a little orphan girl. And an old man and old maid, they lived at Prince Edward's Island in Canada, took her out of the orphanage to live in a house of green gables. She had a great imagination, and put names to everything she saw. We liked the show and all had a good time. — Mary Hernández

What of the money spent for gasoline, tickets, sandwiches, and sodas? What of driving a second long stretch (the return fifty late at night) after Monday's pre-dawn arising? *No le hace.* It was worth it. If I remember correctly Socrates supplied refreshments and diversions to his scholars. A reading teacher has no off hours. A country teacher is on twenty-four-hour duty. When a long day closes and I lie yearning for sleep, problems still buzz in my head. That backward child. What can I do to help him learn to read?

Precious Saturday time for personal activities, I spend instead in the stuffy county library pawing over misused books that have been handled, many of them, for years by young hands bearing germs of scabies, impetigo, granulated eyelids, and trench mouth. These weighty boxes of books have to be loaded, and unloaded, and reloaded on my journeys back to Pepper Sauce Canyon and on down to Poso Nuevo.

Last year, before I won my battle for book reading, the library project was disheartening. After I had struggled to pick stories to fit into twenty-odd different capacities and tastes, and set the heavy box on a front desk and called up the children by grades to get a book, I had to stand and see the volumes dug out, glanced through for pictures, and tossed back; or carried off and forgotten so that Friday afternoon had to be interrupted by frantic searches for the "libraries." Except for Mary, at that time the only way these children wanted to read was to drone aloud in my ears a few paragraphs a day.

There came an afternoon when in desperate attack I made every kid in the room spread a library book out on his desk and duly turn the pages while I stalked up and down the aisles armed with a long hardwood ruler. Impulsively I snatched *Robin Hood* out of a boy's hands, flipped the pages to the meeting with Little John, and began reading aloud as I walked, skipping incomprehensible passages, translating English into Spanish, making full use of whatever dramatic power I was born with. They listened! They applauded! That was the turning point. Every afternoon from then to the end of the book I read a few chapters aloud, rejoicing in the interest displayed in the young faces turned my way. Before the year ended we went through eleven books in that way.

At first I perched on a front desk, keeping an eye watchfully on my audience. Later I could move back behind my desk to my big chair, still maintaining interest and order. "Books," said Isabel Paterson "afford a valuable extension of living." For the little cowpunchers the extension began in Sherwood Forest.

This year I have read aloud a variety of books. Some old favorites such as *Little Lord Fauntleroy* and *King of the Golden River;* and some non-fiction: for instance, Mary Kidder Rak's *Cowman's Wife*. There could have been a longer list if I hadn't chosen, at Socorro's request, that great old romance *Lorna Doone*. It took many weeks to read it together, but we loved it. At thought of that book I am reminded of that cold wet December Friday afternoon that I sat, my chilled feet wrapped in a sweater, in the car in the arroyo at Fresnal turning, reading to Mary and Edward (who were hitching a ride to town) of how John Ridd rescued Lorna during Great Britain's greatest, most destructive blizzard. The all-day rain had melted the snow on the Baboquívaris, and we were stuck in the muddy roaring flood in the dip.

It was my fault. To the right, where I should have been, not two feet from the tires' passway, there was about a 4 foot deep dropoff. The swift, dark water shot over a low cement curbing and poured down into the lower stream bed with such force and clamor that I was scared, and veered left, skidded in the sticky red mud, and plunged into the dip where the flood had cut a twenty-inch jumpoff into the road. We screamed, the car settled, stalled, couldn't pull out. The water gurgled over the running boards. Taking off my boots (Edward is susceptible to pneumonia if he gets wet and cold) I reconnoitered. There was nothing to do but wait for a car to come along and tow us ashore. The nearest house was ten miles away. Darkness was less than two hours off. And it still rained.

We wrapped up in coats and blankets and I read *Lorna Doone* aloud for an hour. No car showed up. I had kept an eye on a stone on the opposite shore and saw that the water was gradually receding. It was raining on us, but not in the mountains where the arroyo headed.

The light faded. The cold increased. Absently, as I closed the book after a long chapter, I sighed and murmured: "Oh, God." Remembering the kids, I added plaintively: "help us out of this river!"

Then I stepped on the starter, just in case, and lo, out we went.

"Just as you were praying," said Mary happily.

We laughed, and laughed again, not so merrily, two minutes later when I stopped to put on my boots and along came a man in a truck and kindly asked if we needed any help. Since then we call that place "Lorna Doone Dip."

Of course in writing book reports and keeping reading records, the children do not include the books we read aloud. Among their stories I must condense to use are these:

NOTES ON BOOKS FROM THE PIMA COUNTY LIBRARY
I.

I have read to now 27 books this year. I know they are few but the reason is that I haven't enough time to read. My father runs the schoolbus 70 miles around trip each day, and we have to go all the way with him. We get home very late. After I get home I have to do my everyday chores in carrying water from the canyon up about one hundred feet deep and awfully steep. I also cut wood and carry it and do other things. We eat our supper by the light of lamps and have to go to bed early to get up at five o'clock to start to school next morning. If you read while going on the bus as my sister does you get dizzy and hurt your eyes. In school I am busy all the day. That is why I have not read more books.

I have enjoyed books by Madeline Brandeis like *Little Tony of Italy*, *Little Anne of Canada*, *Little Tom of England*, *Little Dutch Tulip Girl*, *Bah, the Little Indian Weaver*. They are easy to read and teach about different ways of living of many races of people. I also caught a few words in foreign languages from them.

But the book that I read that I liked best was *Wild Life of The Southwest* by Oren Arnold. It teaches the ways of living of all the animals of the Southwest. It tells in what part of the country certain kinds of native animals are densely populated. It teaches how to treat wild animals. It tells what are their real names and what the names mean. The *armadillo* from Texas — it means a coat of armor. The roadrunner is called *paisano* which means *a native* in Spanish. It tells the adventures of some cowboys hunting lions and gives the name of the famous government hunter Frank Colcord who has killed 500 lions. It also tells which animals are to be killed and which not. The buzzard should be protected. The lion killed. The book has beautiful pictures. I copied some of them in water colors to hang on the wall at home. I wish I could own the book.

— Edward Hernández

II.

I have read 42 books since I started school this year. The last book I read was *Stories Pictures Tell — Book Seven* by Carpenter. It tells about famous artists that made beautiful pictures of little Dutch girls and others. Long, long ago these famous artists liked to draw and paint. Some of them were very poor and drew people in the streets and old people and ragged children. Some of them made pictures of rich people and kings and princesses and little princes. These artists when they were little they liked to draw very much. When they grew up they became famous and made lovely pictures that lasted until now. — Herlinda B.

III.

I have read 21 library books this year. Some of them are *The Wee Scotch Piper* by Madeline Brandeis. *George Washington* by James Baldwin. *Cedric the Saxon* by Strange. *Moufflon* by Luise de la Ramee and *The Tailor of Gloucester* which goes like this — "Out stepped a little live lady mouse and made a courtesy to the tailor. Then she hopped down off the dresser and under the wainscot. The tailor sat down again by the fire warming his poor cold hands and mumbling to himself." — Pancho Aros

IV.
"COWMAN'S WIFE"

One of the books Mrs. Bourne read to us and I have read it to myself is *Cowman's Wife* by Mary Kidder Rak — a true Arizona author.

She is an educated woman who married a cowman and went to live in a ranch where she had many exciting adventures. She was not only busy in the house making bread and butter and cooking and entertaining. She learned how to ride horses and work cattle.

She even went to look at the traps. And she was always hoping that nothing would be caught in them. Once near Christmas time she found a dear little fox terrier dog and saved it from the trap and took it home for a Christmas present.

For pleasure she went to a dance in a school house, and it was a little sad because she had to go home before tasting any of the nice cakes though she brought one herself to the party.

— Mary Hernández

V.

I have read 28 books. *Three Little Kittens. Little Red Riding Hood. Humply Dumply. Little Dog Cracker. Magic Boat.* And *Many Book One* and *Book Two.* I have read much books but I don't remember. — Marcela, *Second Grade*

VI.
WELLS BROTHERS

Wells Brothers by Andy Adams is a story of two orphan boys who had a little homestead on the plains of Texas in the times of the big herds they used to drive over land for thousand of miles.

These two boys were very poor and were just going out to look for jobs when something happened. They made a trail hospital because they had to take care of a wounded man. That was their start in the cattle business because their patient and the boss helped the boys to get some cattle and range for them so they could have a ranch.

They were brave honest boys and would not give up until they did what they started to do. They held their cattle in terrible blizzards with no fences or mountains to help stop the herds. The book gets better as it gets longer. I liked it very much. — Ramón Aros

VII.
RIKKI-TIKKI-TAVI

From the *Jungle Book* by Rudyard Kipling. Rikki-Tikki-Tavi was a mongoose that licked all kinds of snakes. Two cobras snakes were always bothering him. Their names were Nag and Nagaina and they wanted to eat little birds and to kill the white people.

Nag was always wanting to kill Rikki-Tikki-Tavi too but he was too smart. At last the little mongoose killed Nag. And Nagaina was very sad because she was a widow. Rikki-Takki-Tavi said You are not going to be a widow any longer. So he killed her. — Arturo Aros

VIII.

The *Snow Baby* was one of the books I liked best this year. It is written by Josephine D. Peary. It is a true story with real photographs of a little girl who was born far north among the Eskimos. She was a very bright and friendly little girl. — Víctor Aros

What has been the effect of the book-reading I have imposed on my pupils for almost two years? What has been my aim in insisting that every one read books in addition to text books? I can't claim it as a method to give efficiency in the Arizona schools' course of study, but it helps. Reading always helps.

Our superintendent gave standard achievement tests to all the children in our county schools for six years. She found that non-English-speaking children were taking two years for the first grade, then doing as well as any others in the tests up to and including the fourth grade. Beginning with the fifth grade they were falling behind. She suggested that this drop might be overcome by stimulating the children to read, hoping that library books might balance the lack of home advantages.

My best readers — Mary and Edward and Chelo and Víctor — make the best test scores. But to carry out a purposeful program for each grade and pupil, we would have to have passing tests as a goal. And where would the time come from?

I have another aim which may be described fairly well by calling it culture. The dictionary defines it as "The training of the mental or moral powers, or the result of such training as shown in intellectual, aesthetic, and spiritual development." I believe reading can excite thought, imagination, and appreciation, and refine personalities. Such a goal cannot be reached in a few months; but I think even the surface-scratching possible in less than two years is worthwhile. I can see the changes in attitudes that literature has brought toward school activities, toward each other, toward animals (Oh, the need for that!) and toward the world beyond the children's immediate knowledge and environment.

Just one little story, Ouida's *Moufflon,* has changed for the better the lives of the dogs and cats in our district. To my knowledge, no little puppies or kittens have been carried off into the desert and abandoned within the last year. I have not seen outrages such as happened to Leo my first week here. Leo was a cat who wasn't wanted. The teacher preceding me had left him. The kids brought him to me and said he was the teacher's cat — mine. But I had two little dogs in my room, and two canaries in the schoolroom. I declined the cat. Late one afternoon I heard terrified cries of a tormented cat above a commotion in the back yard. I tried to ignore the situation, for my own status in the locale was none too secure, and I hesitated to start a contention right off the bat. But it was impossible to ignore the screams and choking moans accompanied by shrill, wild laughter from young barbarians. I forced myself to look out of my window. The biggest boy had lassoed Leo and tied some tin cans to his tail and was wearing him out by jerking, choking, and dragging. When the cat got to his feet, the boy yanked the rope and ran a few steps causing the victim to choke and drag in the dust, yowling and moaning.

An enraged woman flew out of my door and around the house.

"What are you doing to that cat?"

"Just scaring him." The boy's insolent eyes were on a level with mine.

"Why do you do such a brutal thing to a helpless animal?"

"So he will go away. My-Mother does not want him."

"HE IS MY CAT! Give him to me!"

Among other unpleasant episodes before *Moufflon* came to Poso Nuevo were ill-matched rooster fights at which the whole family, big and little, followed the bleeding gladiators around the yard yelling: *Mátalo, Mátalo,* and unprintable additions. And there was baiting, tormenting, and torturing of coyotes caught in traps and dragged up alive for indulgencies in brutality which were supposed to condition the dogs to killing varmints. I ran out one morning in pajamas, face grease-smeared, hair tousled, and demanded a *golpe de gracia* for one of these victims.

One evening a few days ago Pancho, flanked by the little kids, brought a live woodpecker to my window just at dusk. The little boys had found her on her nest while out looking for wood, and had captured her. Pancho rescued her and brought her to show her to me. When I asked what he intended to do with her he answered: "Let her free."

When she whirred off straight to the thicket where her nest was, we laughed. At present a flycatcher, unmolested, is also sitting on a nest of tiny eggs in a shed by the arroyo back of the house.

I remember when I first began to like Pancho. One morning at recess my little dog Cherry had a sticker in her *mano* and was hunkered down licking at it. Pancho, running out to the ballfield, saw her distress, stopped and picked her up, took out his knife and removed the thorn.

I don't know anything better than literature to promote civilized attitudes toward underdog life. If I did, I'd try it.

Eastern writers and city writers everywhere are unanimous in praise of range life and "characters" produced by outdoor environment. The general impression given is that the cowboy is about the finest person who ever walked the earth (if he ever did any walking!). Millions of pounds of pulpwood are used in exploiting his reputation. Even slick publications devote space to the lone, free individual who spurs and lashes his horse across the roughs, through spiney brush and cactus, over dangerous bluffs and gullies to practice roping, throwing, and hogtying cattle that as often as not do not belong to him. I have seen a horse white with the cruel spines of chollas which could not penetrate the rider's stiff leather chaps.

"Wait!" I cried. "Let's pull the chollas out of your horse!"

No. He says let him learn to dodge.

This ruthless young man is presented as a hero living an envious life in wholesome, uncomplicated relatively unpopulated scenery. Writers who have actually lived and worked with cowmen and cowboys see another side. Ted Bronson and Owen Wister give the good and bad of plainsmen and mountaineers. They lived with them. But they did not stay with them.

Why should a schoolteacher take on the job of trying to dim the cowboy illusion? Why try to weaken the chain of tradition that binds son to father so that the cowboy mores go on for generations? Why try to round the rough edges off the reckless "roving barbarians?"

The answer: there are better patterns to follow. The jaunty range riders are often not what they seem. Their bodies are seldom sound beyond their youth, and, as a rule, get little hygienic care. Their daily life and responses are primitive. Their future, speaking specifically of the scores who have come within my ken, is old-age destitution. As I read of the glories of cowboys and rodeo performers I wish the West-smitten authors would follow these individualistic persons to their homes and observe their personal habits, their speech and way of joking, their tyranny of their wives, their children, their hired help, their domestic animals and beasts of burden. If *en vino veritas* holds true, then this man is a savage — whatever his ancestry. He has no inhibitions. He is as free of inhibitions as the stratosphere is of gnats. He has a bandit's boldness and unscrupulousness. He has stubborn tenacity that has withstood generations of human development toward higher ideals. He is monarch of all he surveys. And I truly hope that his sons don't take after him.

Teachers must give their children an appreciation of the beauty and value of the environment which our forebears seemed to be doing their best to destroy. Where is the tree that some outdoorsman doesn't go after with his axe — for fence posts, maybe; or just because it is there? In campaigns to conserve forests, soil, wild life, and historical monuments, Westerners have not been famed for cooperation. Considering the problem, I am grateful for the words of Stan Adler, noted for his quizzical wit in the pages of *Brewery Gulch Gazette* and *Hoofs and Horns*:

I tangle with a heap of papers in the course of newspaper plugging, but *Little Cowpuncher* always gives me a wallop on account of a spirit which drives the paper along and which might be termed a sense of civilization. I was impressed with last year's stories of the horse who herded the kids to school and with the youngster who spotted the herd of deer but didn't want to mention the fact for fear that somebody would trek out and blast them with a rifle; and with the clinical treatment dished out to the indisposed goldfish.

Civilized intelligence is an unusual attribute in this world and its predominance in the outfit of the Baboquívari School is something for the book. There will be times, kiddies, when you will be ridiculed and ribbed by savage and stupid humanity for this attitude. But keep the spirit on the prod — because *you are right and they are wrong.*

"Lassoing A Bronco"

Edward Hernandez

Reading Leads to Writing

ANOTHER MONTH IS PASSING. It is April. Tonight, looking over material to illustrate the page of rhymes we've done for our March issue, I am pleased to find a sketch Edward made of a man roping a bronco. I don't know when he did it, or why; but it fits. The little cowpunchers could rope a bronco easier than they could catch and tie down in conventional form the imaginative ideas that range through their heads. It was fun to see them struggling to write verses. Working out seat lessons for the little ones, now and then I peeked over the row of books on my cluttered desk to watch the combatants in the literary field. A face screwed up in dark concentration would suddenly break into light as an idea dropped from the blue. These little rhymes, trivial as they are, represent

174

COWBOY'S LAMENT

On the hills and plains of Arizona
Where the earth is wide as the sky,
All the cowboys get stuck with chollas
And wish they had wings to fly.

— S.A.

EL JINETE

A horse was bucking and cracked my head.
The other [next] day I was lying in bed,
And I was mad with the thoroughbred.

— Arturo

LIFE ON THE RANGE

It's tough for a young cowpuncher
Riding in wet cloudy weather.
Thick and strong shines his saddle leather.
As he lopes his lasso switches
And swats him on the britches.

— Mary

WHERE I FALL

A bronco, a bronco,
As hard as a bronze.
He threw his soft rider
Across ditches and ponds.

— Herlinda

THE CORRAL'S NEW TENANT

We have a soft red calf.
We feed him thin blue milk.
And what if he didn't have that to drink?
His hair wouldn't look like silk.

— F. A.

A NAUGHTY HORSE

I got on a horse.
He went to throw me off.
I said if you do I'll —
Then he made me cough.

— Bill

serious, mental effort. In some cases, after we did samples together on the board, books and magazines were consulted for inspiration and technique. At the final scratch many of the last lines were brought up to the maestra for a critical yank.

As was to be expected, some of the pupils balked. Pancho can be prodded just so far. Last year he didn't want to try.

"I can't," he said flatly. (That means *I won't try.*)

As a way around this roadblock, speaking casually, I told him to write a few sentences telling what he had seen out in the pasture, and what he thought about it, because I wanted to see if he knew where to use periods and capitals. Nervously sniffling, he picked up his pencil to show me what he knew about punctuation — and I liked what he wrote.

When I was doing the spade work today on the rhymes lesson, he sat deeply concentrating on a library book. I took the hint. Poetry, even in thinnest brew, cannot be forced through stony filters. Víctor and Luis gave up also. And Ysidra. But young Bill Emery made the grade.

There is gallantry in this little fellow. After he came to us I met one of his former teachers. She said that he had been moved and buffeted around until he was behind in his grade but she didn't have the heart to fail him. She said she used to feel like holding him on her lap while teaching geography (it was a departmental school) to his fellow-pupils. He is nine, small and frail, but spunky. His white skin and pale eyes are striking in this crop of brunets — more so than Inez Jane's or Jack's. They tan but he doesn't.

The little Emerys descended on us last January, leaving a city school with special teachers, equipment, and social services to live at an abandoned mining camp off in the Sierritas — with no apparent ties in the community to which they have come. Their mother is dead. Their father is a disabled veteran — which is all the information I have about him. The children say he stays in town, then they clam up. They get up before day, walk a mile to the bus stop, and ride nearly three hours a day over rough roads to attend our school, and they seem happy to do so.

At first the newcomers weren't welcomed with pleasure. I imagine that many women who have many children (until they adjust to the confusing prospects) greet the advent of the next ones with desperation. When Pascual announced that some new "childrens" from a "mine" above his homestead were going to come to our school I had to bite my tongue. I wanted to cry *Oh, no! I've got more than I can take care of already!*

I managed a smile and a nod, and hoped he was having an exercise of imagination common in this section of limited communications where rumors thrive.

"Mrs. Bourne, the Clarks are coming back to Las Carpas next month. Lambert and Freddie will come to this school."

"How do you know?"

"A man in town told My-Mother."

"You know something, Mrs. Bourne? Dolores is coming back and they are going to live at Espinosa again. Gilberto and María Luísa will come again to this school."

"How do you know?"

"Alfredo's mother told my father."

"Another family is coming to Palo Alto and three more children will come to this chool."

"Who said so?"

"Some cowboys told my father, I think."

Few of these skies fall upon us. But the little *gringos* actually appeared. The ethnic problem didn't worry me much, although of course it is there. My Redington School taught me that in a country school Latins and Anglos mix successfully with advantages to both. For several years I preferred to have Mexican pupils exclusively. They seemed more in need of my services, and the Anglos were likely to have parents satisfied with the status quo and opposed to innovations. But America is a melting pot. We have to work with what shows up.

On the bus the new kids became acquainted with the Hernández and Badilla children. When the bell rang they tried to sneak in without creating a stir. But Lalo, quite at ease and wanting to be clever and at the same time friendly, came forward to introduce them.

"This is Hoover," he told me, pushing forth bashful round-faced Jack, "because he looks like Hoover. And Bill here is Roosevelt because he doesn't look like Hoover."

Bill and Jack grinned, and I laughed at Edward.

Then he pointed to Inez, corrupting her name to "Highness."

All of us — even I — accepted the newcomers warmly. It was obvious they were used to hardships. Wary of questions, murmuring "I don't know," it was plain they had been cautioned about giving family information. I took them at face value as they wanted to be taken, resolving to shield them as much as I could from rude jokes and teasing. They were different, so they would be picked on, the boys especially.

The myth that primitive people are inherently polite was probably begun by travelers going about the earth seeing only surface behavior. No person is born polite. Courtesy is acquired by long exposure to precept and example. People in lowly circumstances are too engrossed in sustaining life to take on refinements. Of course our youngsters here have learned certain traditional expressions sanctioned by their elders to murmur to strangers. They are not customarily polite to each other and to others who fall within their power. Living in the house with a large group of young country folk like this, you wince at the names they call each other, at the way brothers and sisters snarl and shove for food and comforts, and the abuse they are used to heaping on their helpless animals.

Surprisingly, in view of some of the hardships of their lives, these mothers are wont to indulge their children. The six youngest Aroses have nothing to do but eat, sleep, go to school, and amuse themselves. The younger Hernándezes and Badillas have no tasks to assume when they reach home. Socorro and Mary, sixteen and fifteen, let their fingernails grow to absurd lengths which, Edward observes, proves they do not have much work to do. They beg for new shoes and dresses as if these things were procured by persuaison.

On the other hand there is Inez Emery, eleven and delicate, taking care of her younger brothers, cooking and washing for them. She is so destitute for clothes that

My-Mother (Socorro told me when she rode to town with me Friday) hopes to buy some cloth and make Inez some slips and dresses when she gets her check from Prieto's boss. And My-Mother has eighteen to feed and clothe.

One day recently I went into the schoolroom at noon and found Inez sitting at her desk, head cradled in her arms.

"My stomach hurts so bad," she whimpered.

When she showed me how tight her jeans were, I felt guilty. I wear jeans, my girls wear jeans, so she wears jeans. It seems she has only one pair which she washes each week-end and they have grown too tight for her, squeezing her in like a wasp. They are not cow country jeans. They have a wide belt with three buttons to one side of the placket.

"Unfasten the belt," I suggested.

"I did the other day," she complained, "and the boys made fun of me."

I reached down and undid the buttons, assuring her that I'd "git" the first smartie who made a crack. So. Inez Jane must have new jeans whether school keeps or not. She deserves to be rewarded. And to be loved. She never gets so deep in work or play that she doesn't keep an eye out for her family. She leaves her map-drawing to see that slow-poke Jack gets his writing lesson. She nags Bill about his arithmetic, trusting to luck for her own, and holds up the bus to see that he gets credit for the library book he has read. She and Bill read at home by lamplight. She makes Jack read aloud to her if he can keep awake after an eleven-hour day. She sets the alarm, she tells me, at four o'clock, to get breakfast and lunches for them. The big boys banteringly asked Bill if she were a good cook.

"Not very," he said. "She can't make cakes and pies."

On our print days Bill works faithfully, taking the ink-wet sheets from the mimeograph and laying them out on the desk tops to dry — stopping now and then to look at a drawing or short story.

Inez is really thrilled by our *Little Cowpuncher* and its concomitant activities. She likes all our extra-curricular doings, particularly dancing — which we have taught her. It is comforting to feel the loyal spirit in which she attempts any assignment, although writing is not easy for her. (Is it for anyone?)

This was her Valentine story for our *Romance* number.

COWBOY JACK AND BETTY
There was a handsome young cowboy riding into town.
His name I do not know.
But soon after they knew each other she began to call him Jack.
When he saw her he fell in love with Betty for she was pretty.
They went horseback riding that evening and had a good time. But Betty's father wanted her to marry a rich man and she wanted
    Jack only.
Their romance lasted a long time. But in a month they were married and they lived happy.— Inez Jane, *5th Grade*

Trying to fit our writing to the calendar, some of our "authors," on Valentine's Day, took a shot at romantic fiction. Volunteers were called for, and they were given time and a free rein. These school-crafted love stories were written by ranch children who have listened to *Lorna Doone, Mrs. Wiggs of the Cabbage Patch, Ramona,* and various other romances, as well as viewing at least a limited number of movies.

Mary's shows the influence of the cinema. The dash and assurance with which she tackled the task came right out of Hollywood. Socorro hasn't seen many movies. Her story is more traditional. Both stories amused our subscribers. I shall treasure them and remember how good my girls were to make the effort. It was work.

ROMANCE OF A LONE WOLF COWBOY

Once at an Arizona roundup there were lots of cowboys and among them there were lots of jokers. There was a nice, quiet boy there named Frank López. He was always apart from the rest. The boss seemed to like him so he gave him a job to work at his ranch.

The day the roundup was all over the vaqueros grew wild for they were going to town to spend their money. At town everybody had a girl friend so they all had a good time. They ate and drank and danced and sang. Except Frank. He stood alone. All the girls stared at him for he was a handsome cowboy. Then the boys made a plan to play a joke on him whom they nicknamed Lone Wolf. When he got ready to go they had the joke all ready to play on him.

One of the girls at the party — Dorothy — had a friend, a pretty sweet bashful girl just come from Texas. Adaline was her name. Dorothy agreed to the boys' plan so she went home early and asked Adaline to come to her house to stay with her. When they were about half the way Adaline felt something wrapped over her and she heard a gruff voice say: Don't make a sound or I'll plug you. And finally she felt herself lifted on a saddled horse.

Well, the boys were telling Lone Wolf not to go so soon, to wait for them. But finally they let him go. And he was riding home thinking of the party. He didn't like the girls there because they were real crazy and lovable with all.

Suddenly he heard a cry for help in the dark. He stopped and listened. Soon he heard it again, coming from a little ditch. He went right away for he heard it was a woman's voice. He lit a match and saw a pretty girl binded to a tree. They stared at each other. She blushed and said: Won't you please unbind me?

So Lone Wolf smiled at her a very romantic smile and went to untie her. She was very cold so he built a fire and wrapped her up in his coat. He asked her questions and she told him that she was from Texas, that her mother died and the rustlers were stealing her father's cattle so they sold their ranch and cattle and came here, for her father had a ranch in Arizona also. He told her what was the name of the ranch. She said it was the "A Slash B" Ranch. Now it happened that was the ranch where he had the job. So they became friends.

While they were talking they heard the trample of horse hoofs and he drew her behind him and waited. Then a familiar voice shouted: He's not a Lone Wolf any more.

Then a whole lot of cowboys and girls got down and started teasing them. We better get the ceremony over with, said one. They had a judge there but he was dressed like a cowboy too so they did not know he was real. Lone Wolf cried: You can't play jokes like this on a strange sweet girl. And farther more it is serious because she was kidnaped.

Oh, said the boys, we did it to play a joke on you. Then Frank said to Adaline: I'm sure sorry for all this. Don't blame me.

Well, she said, now that you were the prince charming who rescued me don't you want to get the rest of it over with?

What?, said Frank, do you mean you don't care about this joke? She said: Not if you don't.

So they married them and after that the boy who had been called Lone Wolf said: I wish this was really true and not only a joke.

Then Dorothy stuck her head out of the bushes and said it was true — that it was Judge Clark who had married them.

So they were happy, and they went home to celebrate and break the news. Adaline's father liked Frank so he gave him the ranch and they are still living there.

— By Mary Hernández, *8th Grade*

ROMANCE OF THREE WESTERN GIRLS

Once there was a family in where there were three girls — Esperanza, Margarita, and Alicia the smallest who for a nickname was called Beauty. Their father didn't let them dance or go anywhere aione.

It happened that there was a roundup and nobody but the boss knew there were three girls near the camp. But there were three brothers there looking for wives. One day while they were at the roundup the sisters were out walking. When they became tired they sat down to rest a little. While there they heard horses prancing along the road.

At this noise they wanted to run away but imagine what they saw — three handsome boys on horseback. These girls had never talked about love to any boys so when they got acquainted they talked and they talked until it was getting dark. Each girl had fallen in love with a cowboy.

The boys who were tempted to ask about getting married wanted to walk all the road home with them but the girls refused them. Their father was mad at them and asked them questions.

Then Beauty got disgusted and said "Please, papa, we have met three boys and we are to be husbands and wives some day." Her father said "Hum, hum," and became horribly frightened.

The next day the boys looking very handsome in their best costumes came to see their ladies. The youngest brought a letter to Beauty's father in which he wanted the consent to be married with her. The father was very angry and in a rage ran for his suitcase to get his gun. He said he did not want his daughters married to cowboys. While he was gone each girl mounted a horse with the boys and ran away with them where they lived.

When they arrived there was great excitement. On February 20, 1870 the three boys and girls got married at a wedding that lasted three days. Afterwards they all lived together happily. When their children were about eight or nine years old they went for a visit to their grandfather and grandmother and begged them to be contented and to come and see them. When the old man saw what the children were saying he became sad and wanted to see his daughters even if they had married against his wish. So he went with the children and the grandmother went too.

And Oh my, they were glad — all of them. They gave them a room to live with them and there they all lived happily until they died. — Socorro Aros, *8th Grade*

THE YOUNG COWBOY OF LA OSA RANCH
[True Story. Really Happened]

There is a cowboy now working for Mr. Manning who before he got married with his wife he liked another girl very much. He was working for La Osa Ranch when this happened. This girl lived at a ranch far from there.

One day all of the cowboys went to a roundup and he — instead of going to the roundup he went to visit his *novia.* When he came to the camp at last his father said, Where were you? Why didn't you come in time for supper?

Well, he said, you know my horse is not very strong and he got tired.

That was a *mentira.* And his father didn't believe him.

Three days past and he was anxious to see his sweetheart again. So when all the cowboys started on the circle he followed them a little and then what do you think? The young cowboy went to see his girl again. This time he stayed three days.

When he came to camp his father said, What happened?

So C. E. said, My horse got tired again.

Well, said his father, don't saddle that horse again. Don't saddle any horse. The only way to keep you in camp is to keep you on foot. — Written by Ramón Aros, *8th Grade*

THE TWO COWBOYS AND THE SWEETHEART
[Not True]

Two cowboys lived together in a little log hut. One had a sweetheart and he loved her very much. The other one was jealous because she was his sister. The boys were named John and Robert.

One day they were camping [range riding] in the forest and they began to see a little spot far away. Robert said, Let's go there.

All right, said John the brother, Let's gallop.

So they galloped very hard. But they didn't find anything so they came home very tired and hungry. They took off their saddles and came to make dinner and there was a big surprise — a cake on the table. The girl had come and made a big cake for her sweetheart and her brother.

While the two cowboys were eating the girl was just laughing and laughing at Robert because she liked him. And Robert couldn't eat because he was very amazed.

Yours sincerely, Arturo Aros, *5th Grade*

A HAPPY STORY
It was Juanita's birthday.
She was dressed very pretty.
She made a fiesta.
Her sweetheart was going to the party
    but he didn't come.
She waited and waited.
Then she got a horse and went to look
    for him and found him in
    the arroyo with a leg broke.
She help him and he get well and they
    get married.
They had a big wedding.

— Marcela Hernández, *Second Grade*

A SWEETHEART STORY
One day there were two sweethearts.
The man was a cowboy and every day he
    came to see the girl.
The man is Jose and the girl is Maria.
They like so much that when Jose do not come
    to see her she cry.
One day he came for Maria and they don't
    let her go.
Then she ran away and they marry and
    have a big party and live
    on a ranch.
They are happy.

— Frances Salazar, *Second Grade*

COWBOY JOE

There was a cowboy and his name was Joe. Every day he went out to herd the cattle. When he came back his wife would have a big pie or a cake.
One day she cooked a big turkey for dinner.
That day he took me riding with him. It was fun.
But when we came back his dog named Wolf had got in and he ate all the turkey.

— Bill Emery, *Fourth Grade*

These primary stories were greatly influenced by the compositions of my Redington pupils — the original "little cowpunchers" — in our tiny school in a remote corner of the San Pedro River Valley. There, working happily together (with the support and encouragement of the mothers in the district) with our lessons, our library books, our tests, our pottery, our excursions, our dancing, and our *Little Cowpuncher,* we created an organization so alive that its influence will still be shining when all of us who participated have become but shadows of memory.

In perfect spring weather those wonder-working children at Redington went out — each one alone under the April skies — and brought me back specimens of original poetry. (Yes, *poetry.*) I tried the idea on the Baboquívari eighth graders with these results:

MESQUITE TREE

Under the shady green mesquite
I feel the breezes of the great
            swinging earth.
They whisper in my ear, and seem
            to say "Spring is here."
I sit in the cool shadows
And try to think of spring —
Spring with its beautiful weather,
And beautiful flowers and trees
Moving in the light wind
            like fairy wings.   — S. A.

OCOTILLOS IN BLOOM

The ocotillos on the hillside
        Are tall dark maidens on a stage
Dancing with April breezes.
        As they sway and dance in rhythm
The red plumes lightly held in
                their fingers
Spring and dive like the play
        Of flying cardinals.   — E. H.

SWEET BIRDS

I like to see the birds in the mesquite tree,
Swinging from branch to branch,
        Singing softly to cheer the earth.
All the little children go out
        To see the birds springing,
Flying like soft dark leaves.   — M. H.

THE DRINKING HERDS

I sit under this mesquite tree
        To watch the cattle coming in for their
                morning drinks.
I like to see them in April
When they are getting slick
        And good and heavy.   — R. A.

One day at noon Mary, Socorro, Edward, Ramón, and I took a book of language exercises and spent most of the hour hammering out a little poem. Socorro timorously suggested the first line. We struggled over the second and third, and had to go to the dictionary for "ominous." When the piece was finished, Edward drew a picture for it.

SAHUAROS

(A poem written by the Eighth-Grade Language Class)

The sahuaros in the valley
Grow dim when the sun goes down,
And seem to stretch in the shadows,
And wait in ominous silence,
        Like giants in the dark.

Storm on the desert — Edward Hernandez

For the Fun of It

IT IS STRANGE to be here at Poso Nuevo this evening. Sunday nights are few that find me away from the homestead.

Also it is strange to have cold feet propped on an oven-warmed brick in April. Southern Arizona should be right on the doorstep of summer, tempering our skins for the blazing heat to come. My city friends have been wearing fashionable cottons for a month.

It is the rain that makes it so cold, the big rain that drove me down Pepper Sauce Canyon today ahead of the flood. No complaints. Rain is a blessing any time. Let the dark floods rage. Let the car get stuck in mud or quicksand. Just let it rain!

It has been a promising spring for cows. Not a good

spring, but promising. The showers that have fallen regularly for several weeks promise the cattle something to eat if they can keep alive on cactus and browse until it warms enough for something to grow. It has been too cold for feed, although it has a start. The hopeful cows seem to sense the connection between rain and grass. They follow the showers up and down the rocky ridges and canyons from river to mountains and back, apparently expecting a good stand of *quelites* — before the puddles dry and arroyos quit running. This constant traveling makes the animals look like survivors of a famine.

Poor old "Nannie" came plodding up the steep rocky trail this morning in the light sprinkle that scouted ahead of the main downpour. I was in the hay-pantry (too small to be called a barn) shoving the precious remaining bales around so they wouldn't get leaked on. Hearing a distinctly maternal "moo," I stuck my head out and there, where she had occasionally picked up a few bites of hay, came the sad-faced, humpbacked old cow with (surprise!) a wobbly new calf in tow!

The pitiful old cow should have gone to market with the bunch last summer. At the last minute I opened the gate and let her out. My excuse was that I wanted her six-months-old heifer "Lily Violet" to have a fair chance. Truthfully I felt a special tie to the cow because my young friend Vi, and I, with no man around to help, had roped her and thrown her down and milked her out when she had a swollen udder. Furthermore, there is a human-like quality about her. She seems to attract trouble. Here she comes with a new calf when last year's pasturage is gone and this year's still only fresh air and walk-about. I named the little calf "Target." He has a round red spot in his forehead.

A livestock ranch in a dry country, no matter the size, is no place for a soft heart. Range animals can't hide their miseries. If you are out among them you see them tormented by hunger in hard times, and by flies, worms, ticks, pinkeye, and other afflictions such as lump jaw, wooden tongue, and — most dreaded of all — cancer eye. The corrals usually hold some unfortunates to be treated, mostly by amateurs and ignoramuses. Anybody who owns livestock practices medicine.

Tonight little Target, who has known only the warmth and security of the womb, is unsheltered in the cold, wet rain.

What music it makes steadily drumming on the tin roof. It is the most joyous sound to desert people. The ancient hunters and herdsmen and dry farmers who lived in the Indian ruins on the flat down by the arroyo where the children go now to pick up bits of broken pottery must have heard its cadences with the same assuring satisfaction; although what they had instead of a tin roof I don't know.

But even with the advantage of rain, I have been deprived of the peaceful afternoon I had planed to spend transplanting margaritas in my little ocotillo-fenced garden at the homestead, as remote from the sounds and excitement of our industrial world as a lamasery in Tibet. And I've missed a contented evening by the open fire in the little canyon shack listening to the old German tunes on Aunt A's little music box she bought in Paris a life-

time ago; and playing double canfield with J. as if we
we had all the time in the world and didn't need to hit
the floor at three-thirty a.m., he to ride horseback twelve
miles to join a "works" (roundup) and I to speed a
hundred miles to school.

The rain which has cut me out of my home life
immediately benefits my little cowpunchers. Tomorrow
they'll have a teacher whose nerves have been steadied
by four extra hours of sleep instead of being worn raw
by fighting road hazards against the clock.

This morning I flung things into the car and fled
down the sandy box-sided Pepper Sauce Canyon gorge
ahead of the inevitable flood from the melting snow that
still clings high in the Catalina Mountains. In a country
of makeshift roads you start off with time to spare, especially in weather. When they finish oiling the Ajo road as
far as Robles, exactly fifty of my hundred miles will be
on pavement. At each end of my journey will remain
twenty-five miles meant for dry days only. Rain fouls the
slick clay hills and sand and rocks fill the dips. I've had
the car stuck to the chassis, the rear end buried in mud,
and had to wait for help. I've sat for an hour in cold
dampness, burdened with worry for my dogs, my birds,
my personal luggage, and provisions, waiting for a roaring flood to be on its way to the wide gulping desert, that
I might pass.

One homeward trip I got stuck in sand in Pepper
Sauce Canyon a half-mile below the cabin. I had to take
off my shoes and, by flashlight, carrying the little dogs
and my purse, wade the rest of the way through ankle-
deep water underlaid with small sharp-edged rocks and

gravel. Certainly rain wrecks the roads. But who wants roads if the alternative is the life-giving rain? And it could be worse. It could be snow.

The worst trip ever was during the record snow last year. I had gone home Friday night as usual and the next morning ranch business sent us back to town. It was after dark and pouring rain when we left the city. The rain turned into snow as soon as we left Oracle Junction and started climbing to Oracle. Blinded by heavy snow on the windshield, skidding and spinning, we fought our way through. At Oracle we had to be helped to the crest of the divide. Four men shoved while I took a running start and gunned the motor. The rest of the way was mostly downhill and the car tiptoed along, weaving drunkenly in soft snow. Sunday morning the sun shone blindingly on eighteen inches of wet whiteness. My little dog Cherry, desert-raised, refused to set a foot outside. I tossed her out. She went in over her head. But without making an extra track she leaped back inside.

I started southward about nine o'clock with J. to escort me to Oracle and borrow a horse for the return. We were three hours making the twelve uphill miles. He with a shovel and I with a stout old broom cleared the ruts for the rope-wrapped tires until we arrived at the Flag Ranch where we borrowed chains. It was two o'clock that night before I landed at Poso Nuevo, the car double its normal weight with several coats, inside and out, of Arizona mud.

Compared with that seventeen-hour trek, the jaunt down today in the exhilaration of a spring rain was a lark — including the dangerous passage of four miles of road-under-construction, and the plunge through the raging Cañada del Oro which would have swallowed me, car, baggage, and all, if I hadn't raced ahead of the full flood. In town I detoured to the southern outskirts to pick up Frank where I had left him with Doña Apolonia Friday night. He had gone to see the county school doctor about his sore throat.

Frank is a pleasant traveling companion. He doesn't fell obliged to make small talk as Mary and Socorro do; or feel free to burst into Edward's continuous chatter — often containing detailed accounts of movies he has seen, related in a voice uncomfortably raised. Yet Frank's silences are not embarrassing. He radiates a friendly feeling of comradeship. He does, though, make himself comfortable whether anybody else is or not. If several of the kids are going anywhere in my car, he takes the front seat until asked to give it to the girls. His mother gives him privileges. He is her first son.

Ordinarily I am glad to travel alone the fifty miles from town to school. Always in a hurry, driving alone gives me a chance to organize plans and duties. If it is daylight I can absorb rest from the scenic grandeur of the mountains that rim the horizons, and enjoy the quiet beauty of the desert growth — palo verdes, Spanish daggers, and mesquites, doubly loved for their familiarity. Their spring blossoms and foliage give me a personal, and intimate delight.

At such times also, I am free from childish banter and giggling and ceaseless questions, and don't have to bear the inspection of critical eyes and ears. But it is seldom that I don't have riders. On payday Fridays some of the Hernández kids usually go with me. Their father has to deliver the other children and pick up his wife and mother at his homestead before he can start on his bi-weekly trip for gasoline and supplies. The young ones want to get to town in time to dress up and see a show.

And it is a rare Friday that some of the Aroses don't decide to go with me. One of the small children is sent tapping at my door to announce, right at the hour of departure, that My-Mother says So-and-so can go with me to town, for this or that reason — and the matter is settled. A few times I have said I did not have room; but I've never made it stick. My car is their convenience. They don't mean to impose. The car is ready to go and they don't mind squeezing in somewhere, no matter how crowded. On return trips they have many packages.

Monday mornings time must be spent picking them up. Their hostess, Doña Apolonia, lives on the south side where dirt streets are dustiest and bumpiest. I have a guilty conscience about that poor woman. She must hate the sight of me — every weekend bringing to her two rooms from one to six guests. They bring her fresh corn and squashes in season and the children told me My-Mother buys some food for her household.

But often, as with Frank this weekend, the kids hop out at her door with no resources whatever. I gave Frank a dime and told him to go to Lee Hop's store across the street and buy her a candy bar as a greeting gift. She is a middle-aged widow who works at cleaning and ironing when midwifery is slow.

Perhaps the arrangements with Doña Apolonia are more satisfactory than appearances indicate. The girls told me that My-Mother paid her twenty-five dollars last fall when Evangelina was born. News that another little Aros had seen the light of day was brought out by messenger (a relative) one morning. When the car drew up in the yard Socorro jumped from her desk and ran out for news. At noon everyone knew that Don Prieto was making hurried preparations for his paternal visit. There was a great commotion of shrieking and squawking — chickens and children all over the place. Ysidra yelled to me: "They are taking a hen to My-Mother."

Don Prieto had to be back at the ranch at saddling time early next morning. The whole family gathered in the kitchen while he drank his coffee and told them about the little new baby. Her hands were so plump, he said, there were deep creases in her wrists. Her hair was long and black and very soft. She had big round eyes that stared at him when he picked her up. The children were happy and excited when they told me these details after the school bell had dragged them away from the father's thrilling account of his fifteenth child.

He seems to think even more of Socorro than his own daughters. But Frank doesn't share this stepfather affection. "My father is better now," he told me as we plowed through the slushy road. "He talks to me."

Several weeks ago I had an errand to do at Las Delicias and asked Pancho and Frank to go along as gate-openers. Pancho was not given permission, but Frank didn't bother to ask, he said, because his father did not talk to him.

"You mean he doesn't speak to you?"

That's what he meant.

"But why?"

"I don't know. Since about two months he does not talk with me. That is why I have been going to stay with Pascual all the nights. And I help Pascual work on the road."

Now he is happy because he is accepted back in his home.

As we turned eastward on the narrow Poso Nuevo road, we saw a dim light gleam through the rain in the direction of the hill we call El Cerro Negro. I said it was perhaps a wood-gatherer on the Old Black Hawk Mine road. But Frank wasn't sure that it wasn't the phantom believed to do his ghosting around that place, proving by inexplicable lights that some money is buried there. Many of our far-circling mountains are credited with these mysterious "buried treasure" lights. The fact that many have seen them and no one has found any treasure does not deter the natives from hoping. Nearly all of the fathers in our community have hunted for ghost-haunted lost fortunes.

Maybe it wasn't "cricket" for me to have the children write about these local legends. But printing the tales has brought them out into the open — a procedure that cools off irrational beliefs and practices. Pascual, who has some fortune-hunting in his past, was chagrined. He told me that our faraway readers (our *Little Cowpunchers* go across the continent and to Europe, South Africa and Australia) would think Mexicans were ignorant and superstitious. I wonder if he thought of that during the times he hunted caches of ancient silver?

Of course I want the little cowpunchers in my care

to be free from superstitions. But in this issue of our
paper, as indeed, in all of them, I had no axe to grind.
Our stories were done purely for fun — fun for the writers
and the readers, especially the readers to whom our way
of life is truly novel.

GHOSTS ON SIERRA DEL ABANICO

One night I saw the ghost lights on the Sierra del Abanico.
They say a Papago went to see if he could find the gold, but he
could not find it. And my father sometimes goes to see if he can
get it.

Sometimes on the mountain Sierra del Abanico it burns, but
when men go to find the gold the ghosts blow out the light.

STORY OF A DEAD MAN AT POSO NUEVO

Once upon a time this ranch belonged to Mr. Kinney. And when
his cowboys were on a roundup here in the night they heard a noise
like a man with boots walking.

Charli Escalante and one of his friends were sleeping beside
the tanks. They saw the man coming out of the pumphouse close by
and they awoke all the other cowboys to watch their saddles. Everyone in camp got up. But when they went to see — they didn't find
the man at all.

My sisters and Chato and I heard the noise one time since we
have been living here. We heard boot steps. We went to see and
we found nothing. Chato took the pistol but we could not find anything. The girls went inside the house and were scared to death.

GRAY HORSE WITHOUT HEAD

Once we went to Batamote Ranch and it was too dark to come
home. Graciela, a girl who lived there, told us that sometimes a wild
horse used to pass by the window. The horse was gray without
any head.

It was about nine o'clock when we went to bed. We were all
of us girls talking and laughing in a bed by the window when
we heard a noise on the roof like someone throwing rocks. That
happened just on Fridays — noises like that. And that night when
they stopped the rocks the horse passed by! We girls were scared
to death. We jumped out of bed and went to the next room to be
with the others. We could not sleep that night for one minute.

Akin to such stories as these are the folk tales we

gathered for the April Fool issue. These are stories that Mexican people tell their children just as English-speaking people tell their little ones "The Old Woman And The Pig" and "Little Red Riding Hood." I doubt if any of these have been collected for publication. The translations made by my young writers are entirely original and written spontaneously. Here they are, errors and all.

TILÍ-TALÓN
[A folk story translated from Spanish by Mary Hernández]

Once there was an old woman and a little boy. The old woman said: "My son, go buy ten cents of menudo so that we can eat it for breakfast."

The little boy went a little way till he met some boys playing marbles. They invited him to play. He said, "No, I must go to buy menudo."

The little boys argued with him so much that he got down on his knees and played with them. After awhile he remembered about the errand and stood up to look for his dime. It was not there. He looked everywhere and the boys helped him but they couldn't find it. So he said: "Now what shall I do? It was the only dime we had to buy breakfast."

Soon one of the boys said: "I know a man who died and was buried yesterday and his wife put a pot of menudo on his grave because that is what he liked. Let us go get it." So they did.

When the little boy got home his mother said: "My! you stayed long, my son. Now I'll warm up the menudo so that you can eat."

When it was warm the boy said, "I don't want any. I am not hungry."

When it was noon she said, "Come to eat menudo, my little son."

But he refused again. And for supper he refused again.

Soon it was dark and they went to bed. He had a separate bed in the attic upstairs. In the middle of the night he heard a voice saying:

"Tilí-Talón, Little Boy, I am near your house . . . Tilí-Talón, Little Boy, I am in your yard . . . Tilí-Talón, Little Boy, I am in your house . . . Tilí-Talón, Little Boy, I am sharping my knife . . . Tilí-Talón, Little Boy, YOU ARE DEAD."

The little boy screamed and his mother ran up to see what was the matter, but he was dead. They buried him and that was the end of him.

THE TWO LITTLE GIRLS

Once there were two girls. One was a bad girl but she was very pretty. The other one was very good, but she was ugly. They both had little goats.

One day the bad girl said to her father, "Let us kill the goat of my sister." And they killed it. He gave the tripes of the goat to the good girl and told her to take them to the brook and wash them. She took them and while she was washing them she fell asleep. When she awoke the tripes were gone. She said, "Oh, my father is going to get mad with me!"

A little man passed by and the girl said, "Dear old man, haven't you seen my little goat tripes that I lost?"

The little man said he hadn't see them. Then a woman came by and the little girl said the same thing. The woman said she hadn't seen them but she said "over there is a little house and a little woman who knew where to find lost things."

The little girl ran to ask the woman who said, "Yes, I know where they are. Go to that little house in the woods and sweep the floor and put wood in the stove and rock the baby."

The little girl did all that she was told.

Then a voice said "Go to the door and look up." When the girl looked up many little golden stars fell on her face and all of a sudden she was prettier than her sister and there was a little box and in it were the tripes. She took the little box and went home.

When her father saw that she was beautiful he wanted to cut all the stars off so that the other sister could still be more pretty than she. But then more stars fell on her body and the other sister became very ugly.

She said, "Father, let me kill the goat and do the same thing."

And she did. But when she went to the little door and looked up her face was all with worms. Her father tried to get them off, but he could not. Soon she died and no one came to see her. But her sister, the good one, lived happy all the time after.

The above story was translated by Rosa Álvarez, fourth grade, who came from town to our school for awhile when she was visiting relatives out here. As a postscript to the editor she wrote: "Go to the show and then come and tell a story more pretty than that."

More translations:

THE DONKEY AND THE COYOTE

Once upon a time a little old woman and man lived in a little house and they had a donkey who served them. One day they told the donkey to go bring them some cheese and bread.

The little donkey went on his way till he came to the store. "I want some bread and cheese," said the donkey and the man put them to his neck [hung them around his neck.] When he was going home he met a coyote who said, "Please take me through this big river. It has lots of water."

While they were passing the river the coyote was eating all the time. The donkey felt something and he said: "Don't be eating my food." The coyote was very smart. He said, "I am only scaring the flies."

    — Translated from Spanish by yours sincerely Arturo Aros

A BADGER AND A COYOTE

Once a coyote living in a cave by the river got lonesome and went to ask a badger if he had a little money to play him a race. The badger said "Yes with one condition. You run above the ground and I will run below the ground just under you."

Now the badger's cave had two doors. He told his wife to place herself in the back door and when the coyote came to tell him "You see I have won the race."

Then they started. The coyote ran as fast as he could but the wife of the badger was at the door first.

So the coyote lost the race. But anyway the badger did not play fair. — Translated for *Little Cowpuncher* by Ramón Aros

Writing may require some talent to begin with, but its growth is probably like that of a hemlock tree. At any rate the common variety of personal expression in print has a universal appeal even for children. As long as we publish *Little Cowpuncher* the kids will all want to see their stories in it. The primary pupils don't have to be given assignments. They see the older ones writing and they want to write stories, too. After printing some second-grade stories about our picnic at Gill's Lake, a friend who teaches college students asked if the little ones really wrote their own stories.

They do. Of course they can't spell most of the words they want to use, and they are constantly asking how to say in English the words they have in mind. If

I have time I help them when they come up with requests such as: "How to put *picnic?*" Or "Please write me *water.*" Many times the little ones know where to find the word they're after, remembering the stories and even the pages in their reading and spelling textbooks where they have seen it. I enjoy seeing them make their own *Little Cow-punchers* when they are playing school in the shade of the house just outside the door. They fold little pages from discarded newsprint and cover them with pictures and stories that are entirely spontaneous. Even then they come in to get their readers and spellers for dictionaries.

Most of the time when they write for *Little Cow-puncher,* they ask some of the big children to write the hard words for them. Often someone in an intermediate grade, glad enough to break the monotony of his own desultory studying, takes a stand at the blackboard near the primary section and spells on demand.

The compositions are always original, although the little rascals get hints from the words their classmates are asking to have spelled, and feel free to copy ideas. In country schools, first-grade children learn to write as they learn to read. They must have something to do on their own during long periods when their teacher is busy with upper grades. Besides, they *want* to learn to write. Pencils are fascinating.

As for their stories, some incident happens and a child asks if he (more usually *she*) can write a story about it for *Little Cowpuncher*. That is the way the pieces about superstitions were written by the little girls in the second grade who heard the older pupils discussing the subject.

We had a reading lesson about wrens and I was try-ing to describe them.

"They are not afraid of people. Sometimes they come into houses."

"Ah, then somebody die," said Frances.

She told me and the class that the day before her grandmother died a hen came into the house, jumped on the bed, and sang: "cock-a-doodle-do." With appropriate gestures she told that the hen lost her head at once. All the same her grandmother died.

Then Chelo and Marcela wanted to know if they could write stories about birds coming into houses. With permission they happily snatched up scratch paper and skipped to their desks.

THE CROWING HEN

We have a hen that sings like a rooster.
The people say that when a hen sing somebody is going to die.
We have a hen that sing and my mother wants to kill her.
But my father doesn't want to kill her Little Cowpuncher.

— Marcela H.

TWO BAD SIGNS

1. When a black butterfly went inside the house
        somebody died.
2. When the flag is half ways it means that a Governor died.

— Dolores, *Second Grade*

SEEING SHADOWS

I am Frances Salazar.
On New Year Day if they see a shadow [that is, if one
        sees his own] that do not have any neck
                they are going to die.
This year I did not look to my shadow because I
        don't want to know if I am going to die this year.
That is all Little Cowpuncher.

— F. S., *Second Grade*

Play-Pretties

DAY AFTER DAY scheduled tasks spin out time and strength to weave a curtain of seemingly secure order against the world outside. Life becomes a routine of getting the job done. Some call it a rut, but it is more. It's a plodding try for a better tomorrow. However, orderly systems are against nature. So they blow up. Suddenly something unplanned occurs and I am jerked out of my appointed rounds. Tonight I had company. Guests for dinner! Monday is a bad day for social activities. It begins at three-thirty a.m. It is fouled up with Friday's uncorrected papers and no prepared lessons or busywork for the little ones, and thus double duty to get ready for Tuesday's rush. But tonight was just for pleasure, and routine to the four winds.

Bill and Sally came down from Las Delicias to see the pottery we have been making. We sang a few songs for Sally, and Bill took over our art class with a lecture on good taste. When the bus left, the visitors were mine alone. It was so good to have them that I ignored the chaotic state of my den. It takes more than an hour a day to make an uncluttered home out of one small room. The open shelves Bill put in for me last summer are crowded with phonograph records, school supplies, files of *Little Cowpunchers,* two dozen books, piles of school catalogues, old registers, and elementary-grade tests. It would be a chore to inventory the odds and ends of water colors, ink and tempera bottles, correction fluid tubes, clay pots, letters, kodak pictures, cosmetics, toilet articles, sewing equipment (for mending only), colored chalk, note paper and envelopes that cover my big table.

My nerves will frazzle when I try to find all the materials I took off the small table and stuck out of sight to clear the way for the dinner party. Hurriedly I jammed articles into suitcases, table drawers already bulging, and packing boxes on the floor. While doing so I ruefully remembered the smart New England neatness these walls enclosed when my predecessor lived here. Nothing on the big table but a bowl of flowers and a magazine. Nothing on the small table but a carefully folded bright table-cover. Rugs on a floor not obscured by boxes of school-lunch provisions. No little dogs curled up on the bed. No birds scattering seeds over the little drainboard. H. didn't have hundreds of papers, manuscripts, letters, pictures, watercolor daubs, art materials, and this and that of medical supplies strewn about everywhere. No clay pots

"It is natural for me to see more in these crude clay pots than anyone else."

were tempering in her wood stove. No old magazines for cut-outs, posters, and models were piled under the tables. And goodness only knows what she did with the paper flowers and plants in tin pails given to her by her pupils.

While we sat crowded at my little table, Sally — happily possessed of a home having spacious rooms and many closets and cupboards — put her mind to my problem. But thought alone cannot add cubic measure. Building supply cupboards, even if there were adequate space, cannot be considered. No money. By careful management Bill makes the school-district funds come out even with the school expenditures. The irony of one living in a *tuza's* nest asking an artist to give a talk on good taste! But Bill is a godsend to these children and I want them to have full advantage of him. As for me, I pitch in and try. These excerpts from *Little Cowpuncher* give evidence of the effort:

THE ART PICTURES

Saturday at four o'clock we met Mrs. Bourne at the Library Park in town and went to the Temple of Music and Art to see the pictures by the artists of Tucson hanging there on exhibit. There were some of the most beautiful pictures and also some very skillful work done in water colors. In the next room were some lovely landscapes of missions made by using ink in different ways. We were fortunate to have a chance to see those works of art and I'll always remember it. — Edward Hernández

OUR PROGRESS IN ART

For a few weeks we have been drawing faces, practicing on hair, noses, eyes, and shading parts to show where the light hits. We have been drawing faces from our own pupils and have some of them on the walls. If anyone would like to see them you have our permission to criticize them. We are not very good and not too bad.

Before this we were practicing on landscapes in water colors. We are supposed to do a little bit of everything. We make landscapes, pottery, drawing heads and features, experimenting with warm and cool colors, and printing our *Little Cowpuncher.* We have a teacher who gives her spare time for such things. And sometimes Bill Ronstadt our school board clerk who is a real artist comes to criticize our work and give us ideas. We appreciate all this great help. — Socorro Aros

ON ART APPRECIATION

In showing us the difference between a poor picture and a true picture Bill said that a really good picture doesn't have to have every bit of details and all different colors. Just something that gives you room for your imagination for a long time.

For instance some calendars have pretty pictures but you get tired of looking at them. He showed us some prints so beautiful that they give stimulation for your imaginations and pleasure forever. — Mary

Our trial-and-error art studies have had, I am sure, forceful influences. What the children have learned about form and color will stay with them. Several besides Edward are now willing to try self-revealing compositions. As for Edward, that talented boy instead of copying and following instructions is now confident enough to work out his own ideas. An example is the original line drawing for the frontispiece of our March issue. He had been coming down with a cold that day, running a slight temperature. His father and I worried. He has had pneumonia twice, both times in March, and he has come to have a dread of that month.

When school opened I saw his distress and suggested that he had better go to my room and lie down. No. He wanted to see what was on the program for the day. It wasn't art, but my sympathy made me say: "When you feel able to draw maybe you could do the front page for *Little Cowpuncher.*"

"I feel like drawing now," he said, perking up.

He sat chewing on his pencil for awhile thinking up something appropriate for our Library Books number. In a few minutes I became absorbed in primary reading classes and forgot him. When he sent Víctor up with his drawing I cried out in delight. He had drawn a bookcase full of books, labelling the top shelf "Nature Books," his favorites; the middle shelf "Cowboy Stories," Ramón's choice; and the third shelf held a row of encyclopedias. He and Ramón sat with volumes in their hands at a little table, discussing their reading. Dear Edward! A joy to a teacher all too used to hearing "I can't" and "What shall I make?"

But back to the dinner party. As I have indicated, Monday is always a short-on-sleep day. Yet it has one advantage: groceries are more plentiful and fresher. I had a chunk of boiled ham I had intended to lunch on for several days. And two small cans of yams made a dish.

Incidentally Monday is special for the school-lunch kids because it is hamburger day! We have no ice so it is the only day they get fresh meat.

The lunch program, sponsored by a state branch of a federal relief organization, is a pesky nuisance. Of course I don't have to do it. It is a voluntary thing — up to the teacher. I am bullied by a horror of hunger so that I must take on whatever underfed creatures come within sight and sound of me. In the fall, the Pima County Schools instituted an optional program, endowed by relief money known as the "Governor's Fund," so that teachers could serve hot cocoa to underweight youngsters. A sixth-grade girl wrote a thank-you note for our December issue:

THANK YOU FOR THE COCOA

Last month the Government of Arizona began to give the Baboquívari School children some cocoa, and lots of them have gained. Here are some of the names:

1. Arturo Aros has gained 5 lbs.
2. Pancho Aros has gained 7 lbs.
3. Herlinda Badilla has gained 4 lbs.
4. Ramón Aros has gained 3 lbs.

We thank the Government very much. — Herlinda Badilla

But in February there was an upheaval in relief administrations. They discontinued the Governor's Fund and substituted an optional hot lunch program which was several weeks getting set and was snarled up with red tape. Even now, some time later, the lunches are bought from the teacher's private funds. So far, no reimbursement. Reason enough for some of the schools to discontinue the program. I snatch at straws. It is sad to think of hungry children all over the world, and especially those in food-rich America. But sufficient unto one boldly clucking hen are the chicks she can get under her wing.

Pascual sometimes complains about the monotonous task of making the cocoa; but he can sit in the rocker and keep warm, look over my books, and perhaps feel superior from his intimate knowledge of my disgraceful housekeeping.

At 11:45 a.m. I dismiss the little ones, warn the big ones that rioters will get no orange, and take over the sandwich making. We have no dishes or cooking utensils (save my big kettle for the cocoa) so it is sandwiches, hot cocoa, cookies, and oranges.

There are fourteen on the lunch list, the others being of normal weight; but I have fudged a little and each of the pupils on roll gets an orange and a cup of cocoa (bringing his own cup). Sandwiches vary. Mondays, hamburger (the favorite!); Tuesdays, peanut butter;

Wednesdays, eggs; Thursdays, jelly; Friday, canned tuna. In spite of many explanations and much weight inspection, the children — except the eighth graders — still look upon the sandwiches as dainties acquired by favoritism or good luck. To understand this, consider a permanent diet of frijoles and tortillas. Teddy is plump, but her six-year-old heart would break if she didn't get cocoa with her thin sister Marcela. Inez Jane, (thirteen pounds underweight by our chart) and Bill are on the lunch list, but not Jack who still has the soft curves of infancy. He stands quietly under the tamarisk in front of my door while the sandwich tray is being passed. Nothing is said. But there just happens to be one left over for him.

The Aros kids have the rather engaging Mexican custom of sharing with their parents. When you give something to the little ones their coattails pop around the corner and down the line to My-Mother. They seldom share with brothers and sisters, but invariably divide treats with parents.

H. said she gave an apple a day to have her wood brought in. I find candy more convenient. I get small pieces, wrapped, so that a handful will go round. The presence of visitors this evening didn't interrupt our daily wood routine. Chelo came first.

"You want some wood?" she asked softly.

When she brought her armload her payment was a pink candy Easter egg and she made tracks down to My-Mother with her "surprise." Pili came running to bring his quota. A moment later Meli, three and a half years old, began piping outside my window: "M's Bone, I-wan-some-good?" When she puffed in with three tiny sticks, for fun I asked her if she wanted a banana, an apple, or candy.

"Candies."

"How many do you want?"

"Two."

With a pink egg clutched in one grubby little hand and a yellow one in the other she pattered out, letting the screen door slam.

Bill turned to Sally and said: "Sister spends nine dollars and eighty-nine cents a month that way."

After dinner he settled himself in the rocking chair and Sally and I reclined somewhat on the studio couch he designed and built for the teacher's room last summer. It is a good bed, with nice rows of bookshelves for its headboard. One night a little spider crawled out of the books into my ear; but she vacated when I turned the flashlight in on her.

The window curtain drawn, we were now out of sight of the curious children but they played near enough to be noticed in case anyone happened to look out and care to see some fancy roping or hopscotching. The boys in the next room were unusually quiet. No singing. Bill's voice is too good at penetrating partitions to be missed. The story in *Little Cowpuncher* reported how the children joined the party:

THE NIGHT GAME

Monday night Mr. and Mrs. William Ronstadt had supper with Mrs. Bourne and at night they played a game. Mrs. E. B. came out and said, Don't you have some marbles to play a game? Yes, said Pancho I have some. Christmas all the boys got marbles but now Pancho has all the marbles. He won them and keeps them in a little sack.

When Pancho brought the bag of marbles Mrs. Bourne said Come in childrens and see us play.

The game is a board and it has twelve holes. Some count for 100 and some count for 10 or 5 or other numbers. And so and so. They put the marbles on the board and try to make them go into the holes with big numbers. When Bill's turn came we all said *Achíscala* and the marbles went out of the track. When Sally's turn came we said *Cién, Cién* and it came and fell in the hole of one hundred. When Mrs. Bourne's turn came Arturo and I were praying on our knees for her to win the game from Bill. But Bill won it.
— Ysidra Aros

Bill likes to teach. He likes anything related to art. Or life. This school is his personal interest — not merely a civic duty. Perhaps he, too, cannot see where these children are heading; but he takes satisfaction in seeing their progress as individuals. We both want to teach them, and he teaches a fascinating subject. Probably the happiest study in the world is learning to create something beautiful and good. Sherwood Anderson has written immortal prose on the relationship of men and the materials they work with. Our country is slowly finding money, time, and thought to devote to the encouragement of its young who are especially talented. What of those who are not? They also like to use their heads and hands in the enjoyment of creation. I wish these children (many of whom will never go beyond this elementary classroom) could have practical vocational training. Not that I want them to find an easy way to make a living. I hope they every one will have to work hard. I worry about what little work they do — excepting Edward, Luis, Ramón, and Pancho, for I know that in a sense work is their salvation.

By keeping my little cowpunchers busy with their hands (art), and feet (dancing), and voices (singing), there is a chance they may be inveigled into using their heads. If the things we do are showy it is because we like them and we hope to interest people outside our isolation, bringing us closer to their world.

We would achieve more competence if we concentrated on only one extracurricula activity, for instance, writing — a field in which practice probably yields better harvests than in any other. But how about dancing, play-acting, baseball, water-colors, and pottery-making? We cannot be specialists for this is an elementary school — introductory experience for pupils of different talents and tastes.

Our writing has a definite goal: to bring the world out to us. Bill gets the credit for the drawing and painting. But pottery, as we make it, is my own particular "baby." Like *Little Cowpuncher,* it began at Redington School, far off on the San Pedro River. It grew out of three factors: the clay my little car was so often stuck in; an article in *Normal Instructor;* and the need of Christmas gifts for parents. Also there was a happy coincidence. Our school at Redington was situated on a little mesa that had been the site in 1697 of a Sobáipuri Indian settlement visited by the Spaniards. Among the visitors was the soldier-historian Captain Cristóbal Bernal. The surface of the mesa abounds with broken bits of ancient pottery. The kids would go out at recess and bring me handfuls of these shards impressed by their strange beauty. It seemed to mean something for all of us. We experimented with some of the clay.

Our products were exhibited at the Pima County Fair, the Office of the County Superintendent of Schools, and the Tucson Chamber of Commerce. We sold a considerable number at ten and fifteen cents each and used the money for materials for *Little Cowpuncher*. A newsreel scout came out and took our pictures while we were making pottery and sold the "documentary" to a national newsreel company. But when I lost contact with the Redington kids I thought I never wanted to get my fiingers in "mud pies" again.

When Constance Smith, my superintendent, sent me to Baboquívari School she said: "There's some good clay in the Poso Nuevo country."

"Nothing doing!" I declared, my heart aching for the cherished and skillful little hands that had delighted me at Redington.

I had been here a few weeks when Mrs. Smith came to visit and to bring us a picture show. She slyly brought along samples of our Redington pottery and dropped broad hints to the children. One day Edward pinned me down.

"Oh, it's lots of work. Takes lots of time," I answered. "And besides we don't have any clay near the school."

The next day he brought some. He had tried to fashion three little unbaked figures from unstrained red clay he had found along the road. I gave him a carton and told him to bring some to school. That was all we needed to get us into it up to our necks.

Surely there must be a primitive urge in the human race toward clay manipulation. It is of course the oldest known form of art. Anthropologists consider it the most ancient of human industries, preceding agriculture and domestication of animals. Some scholars even give it credit for fostering the first inventions and mechanical developments. It would hardly be possible to overestimate the interest in humanity in this mother of arts. I like to think of the loving appreciation and proud care originally given to the fine specimens of ceramics in our museums.

Mexican-Americans that I know seem to feel self-conscious and furtive about their native culture and arts. They have not maintained a pride in teaching traditional crafts to their children as they did before our public school systems absorbed them. Apparently, some of the Indians, Indians of the Southwest, aloof and clannish, have kept their arts. At any rate I am glad when a child brings in a suggestion about clay-mixing, smoothing, and firing that was given to him by a grandmother or some old *tío*.

These children find our "pots" fascinating. They are easy to decorate. They make fine displays of form and color when grouped together. They satisfy the child's impulse to pick up his "play-pretties" and carry them around. I myself like to handle them. Tonight I unpacked a box I had ready to take to town. Bill and Sally and I got down on the rug and spread them out in the space in the center and handed them around in admiration. Socorro's lovely little bowls, a nest fitting into each other perfectly, all round and smooth and delicately colored, took Bill's eye.

"I'd give a left leg for this," he said enthusiastically. But I couldn't part with them. I'm losing Socorro this year. I gave him Luis's bowl with the bright, stylized fruit design, and I confess it hurt to see him take it away with him.

It is natural for me to see more in these crude clay pots than anybody else. As I look I see the restless chapped brown hands that formed them, the absorbed faces of the children as they painted them — faces shining with the happy vitality of expressive activity.

The experiment has helped develop ingenuity and resourcefulness in the girls and boys. (But oh, the time it takes!) They smear the desks with mud, waste soap, and paper towels, sneak into the carefully mixed clay I have earmarked for a special purpose. But not mischievously. The smallest kids, busy as little beavers, spend extra time and energy making toy figures and doll dishes to play with. In a way it is constructive. It keeps them from spitball throwing and tripping up classmates.

Mrs. Ewing, from Illinois, who came out from town to see our pictures and pottery and hear us sing compared our school activity to that of Montessori. No, the only extraordinary thing we are doing is to try to teach children instead of teaching a course of study.

When there is no clay the small children who have so much surplus time use an alarming quantity of crayons and water colors. There is a constant stream of colored daubs being brought to my desk. They seem to think I have an endless need for lean horses and purple cows. The Aroses all sense that I am thrilled by beauty. They call me out of my room to see a fiery sunset in a jagged mass of pastel colors; or a full moon bulging up out of the dark peaks of the Santa Rita Mountains. They swamp me with wild flowers and pretty rocks. Chelo, Pili, and Meli spend hours down in the arroyo picking up special pebbles and curiosities for me.

Pancho capped the climax, bringing in a full-grown land turtle, on horseback. I heard him telling the little kids in Spanish that he was going to give something to the maestra, so I was ready to radiate pleasure when he called at my door. But when I saw the unhappy gift my face must have betrayed my dismay.

"She eats grass," he hastily assured me. "You can take her to your ranch to put in your garden."

And poor "Tillie the Toiler" scooped a path around the tight ocotillo pickets in my garden fence until Uncle Jim left the gate open and she escaped.

Perhaps this intense enterprise of life enjoyment was brought upon me to some extent by a suggestion in Edward Eggleston's *Hoosier Schoolmaster*: "The artist of originality will work courageously with the material he finds in his environment."

Trophies

I MUST TYPE Socorro's letter to the governor so that I can mail it as I go through town on the way home tomorrow. I'd like to send it in her own neat handwriting, but it is so bulky it might discourage a busy executive. I am anxious for him to read it because she volunteered to write it and it gives her "true thoughts."

We had great pleasure and real enthusiasm in receiving your interesting letter which our teacher read to us. It was some excitement to all the little cowpunchers. We never expected a letter from a real governor, because we imagined you were too associated in great business being the State Governor to have leisure time.

We have the honor to invite you for our May Festival if you can come without inconvenience. We will give a big performance. There will be three parts to it, and we'll dance different dances for each part. We are planning to organize a good show for the 8th of May, and it will be very attractive. We are practically working with great enthusiasm, and I hope you can come.

BENJAMIN B. MOEUR
GOVERNOR

H. H. HOTCHKISS
SECRETARY

Executive Office
State House
Phoenix, Arizona

April 7,

Dear Boys and Girls:

I was very pleased to have
the March issue of your school publication the "Little Cowpuncher", and
wish to compliment you upon its ingenuity.

This is a very interesting
little paper and I am glad to know
of your activities.

Very sincerely yours,

Governor

Baboquivari School,
Poso Nuevo Ranch - Sasabe Star Route,
Tucson, Arizona

BBM-H

You seemed to enjoy our *Little Cowpuncher* and we'll be sending you another one soon. We won't be able to print one every month of the year because our school term is ending. And four pupils are graduating: Mary, Edward, Ramón, and I. You won't have more stories written by us next year.

We are greatly pleased with you for making your duty nicely and developing our State, and for furnishing things to the schools, helping us in our education. All the children are gaining with the hot cocoa and oranges and sandwiches you furnished to help the underweight children who need to be built in normal weights.

I shall put writing aside now. All this year we have been writing and answering letters to faraway friends. We even write to a little school in Alaska. Please accept our invitation.

Yours truly, Socorro Aros, *Eighth Grade*

Since the art of recording sound symbols on a surface was invented, letters have been preserved and treasured. They are perhaps the most intimate, revealing, and authentic evidence of human minds that can be kept in permanent form. We are proud of our letters. In our March issue we printed some of the answers the little cowpunchers wrote to a few of the eminently busy friends we are indebted to for encouragement and material help with our little paper.

Dear Mr. Frank M. King:

We all thank Mr. Frank M. King an editor of the *Western Livestock Journal* and author of a book called *Wranglin' the Past,* for giving us a present of the beautiful book *Western Poems* by a real cowpuncher Bruce Kiskaddon. We enjoyed them very much. They are real poems of cowboy life with horses and cattle, and they have pictures of cows, horses, colts, bulls, calves, and steers. All animals are drawn very well by Miss Katherine Field.

We also thank you Mr. King, and your wife and friends, for coming and hunting us in the Rodeo before the parade. We were very glad to know you. We thank you for this honor.

— Frank Aros, *Sixth Grade*

Dear Mrs. Mary Kidder Rak and Mr. Charlie:

We are now sending thanks to Mrs. Mary Kidder Rak and Mr.

Charlie her husband for the four interesting, exciting, and charming books:

> *Jungle Book,* by Rudyard Kipling
> *Second Jungle Book,* by Rudyard Kipling
> *Wells Brothers,* by Andy Adams
> *A Loyal Little Red-Coat,* by Ruth Ogden

The package of books by mail was a surprise to us and a great pleasure. All seemed to like them. They are a nice gift and help us in our education.

Mrs. Bourne has a book she bought by the name of *Cowman's Wife* — written by you. And she has read it to us because it tells truly of the life of our state, cattle raising, and the way ranch people live and make their lives interesting. We surely enjoyed a paragraph where once your car got stuck and Mr. Rak began to throw out the load and threw out the new glasses from the Kress. And one thing he carried with great care was a package of horse shoes.

Mrs. Rak, please receive your sincere thanks from the cowpunchers and our teacher. — Socorro Aros

Dear Betty Jane Hansen:

We are sorry we did not write to you before. One thing is that we haven't got any time. We do so many things we never get enough done in one day.

We want to tell you now that those pictures you sent us in the little book you made we think they were very nice drawings. Your book helped us in our vocabulary such as "caricature" and "ballet" dancing girls. Your pictures help us because we are having lessons in art sometimes and we always are trying to draw. We are happy you like *Little Cowpuncher* and please send us more pictures.

— Frank Aros

Dear Mrs. "Picture Lady" (Mrs. J. W. U., Watseka, Ill.):

We are thanking you for the pictures you sent us from the Chicago Sunday papers. We like them very much and the teacher liked them too. Some of us have put them on our walls at our houses. — Herlinda Badilla

We write so many letters that only a few of them can crowd into our little paper. They are not models of English composition, but all are written in sincerity.

Dearest Friend, Mrs. Mary Kidder Rak:

We intended to answer your last letter sooner, but we had bad luck the same as you. We felt sorrow for Mr. Rak's sickness. Most of us including Mrs. Bourne have had the flu. She couldn't even talk a word.

We are having a Dance Drama the 8th of May and hope we have success. We all wish you and Mr. Rak could come. Mrs. Smith, the superintendent of schools, is coming to give us a speech, because four of us are graduating this year. Two girls and two boys. Next year we won't be able to hear from you. We hate to quit school and never write stories for the *Little Cowpuncher* again. But we are glad we all passed the eighth-grade examinations thanks to God.

Exceeding thanks for being interested in *Little Cowpuncher,*
Cordially yours, Socorro Aros

Dear Mrs. Mary Kidder Rak:

I wish you could come and visit our school some day. Thank you for the books. The *Wells Brothers* is a very good book because it shows that the two boys are brave to protect their cattle in the storm. We have received from our friends this year many books, pictures, funnypapers, *Hoofs & Horns* magazine, *Brewery Gulch Gazette* from Mr. Stan Adler, a picture book, and a Mexican song book. And many one dollars to help us in our paper. I wish you good luck with your cattle and your book.

Pancho Aros, *Fifth Grade*

Pancho not only admires courage, he makes it a plank in his daily platform. Monday afternoon occurred his latest. The work horses being hitched to the wagon in the courtyard got scared and bolted when the dogs rushed out barking at Chato riding in across the arroyo. I had been lying down. When I heard the commotion I jumped up and ran to the door. Pancho had beat the runaways to the west pasture gate which often stands open, and waved his arms under the horses's noses, turning them aside. Still lunging, they made a dash into the back yard through the narrow passage between the end of the schoolroom and the pasture fence. Pancho dived to the ground and caught the drive-lines. They dragged him, stiff as a board, about thirty feet in a stream of dust but he held on and stopped them.

"Are you hurt?" I shouted, running to him.

"No," he answered brusquely. His face was white from the fine dust, making his black eyes look piercing. His family had stood watching in frozen attention and made no comment when he brought the horses back to the wagon. Ysidra, who had been standing in the door holding the baby, yelled to him in Spanish, "The dogs frightened them."

Ramón was not present. He was off helping his father. He is made of the same stuff, but is less sensitive and more sociable. He likes to be bold and dashing and to have an audience. In his letter to Mrs. Rak he said:

We have been very successful with our *Little Cowpuncher*. We are getting to be known all around the world. And we are going to have a big May Festival the eighth of May with the ERA orchestra to play at intermissions for our outdoor dance drama. We would be very glad to meet you there if you can come.

By a nice coincidence we received letters from my former pupils at Redington and from these children's former teacher in the same mail. We printed excerpts from them in the April issue.

Every *Little Cowpuncher* that arrives is declared by the children here to be better than the last one. You have no idea what an incentive your children's writings and their library book work are to the other children of the county. At least they are to mine.
— H. C. *Sahuarita School*

I always enjoy reading your *Little Cowpuncher* because I like the news and stories you write, and I wish I was there to write in it.
— Manuel Valdez

I like *Little Cowpuncher*. It is good. I would write to all the kids but I don't know all their names. — Donna Bingham

I wish I could join in the *Little Cowpuncher* with you. I wasn't jealous. I was very glad that you took it up and I certainly like it.
— Carlota Valdez

I enjoy reading your *Little Cowpuncher* which I think is very thrilling indeed. You have good imaginations to write such lovely stories and news for it. Of course you know that we used to print it when Mrs. Bourne was teaching us. I remember when we voted on a name for the little papers. Gareth Bingham was the one who thought to call it *Little Cowpuncher* ... I loved to write stories, especially those original ones. But now I think I have forgotten how.
— Clara Valdez

It is a pleasure that the little paper has become a bond between the two groups of children who have been closest to me. Both schools are small, isolated, patronized entirely by ranchers, serve only a few families. The letters the Baboquívari children wrote to the first little cowpunchers were not printed in the paper, but I have kept them in my files.

Dear Manuel,

I live out in a ranch near the border of Mexico.'We are twenty-three now in our school. Most of us live very far and have to get up early to come on the bus. As for me I live right near the schoolroom. I don't have to worry.

Here the roundup is coming very soon. That is what I like. I go Saturdays and Sundays to help the cowboys. It is fun to run after the calves and steers and cows. Oh boy!

Do you ever ride bronco horses? If you haven't I am going to give you an advice so that you will know how when you ride one. You press your laps very hard against the saddle and loose your legs from the knees. And don't take your eye off the horse's head. If you do you go down. That is the way I have been taught. I would like to know you. — Ramón Aros

Dear Carlota Valdez:

We received your lovely letters Wednesday morning and they were so nice. We liked your pictures too. I wish you could know all of us and come and write stories in our *Little Cowpuncher.* You are good readers and good children we know because Mrs. Bourne told us.

I have read thirty-five books from the library. The teacher brings books, but we don't have time to read them all. We have to do other things. The teacher told us you were good readers. I wish you pass a happy Easter. — Herlinda Badilla

Dear Otilia Valdez

I am in the second grade. I have read 27 books. Mrs. Bourne likes to have good readers and she brings lots of books. She is a very nice teacher. I like her very much and I wish she can be my teacher till I finish school. I will cry when school close. I think I would like you if I saw you.   — Marcela Hernández

Miss Clara Valdez, Dear Friend:

It was such a pleasure to receive such an interesting letter from you that I felt near you. I am so glad that you like our *Little Cowpuncher* which I think is really interesting. I wish all of you kids could be with us here; I'm sure the paper would be more interesting. E. B. tells us about you kids and how nice you all are and how she misses you. We all think that we won't have another teacher like her. I surely hate to leave her this year.

She is reading aloud to us now about five books at the same time — sometimes one and then the other. I have read 26 books only I am ashameful to say. When Mrs. B. taught here last year she was really the one who got me interested in reading.

My father drives the school bus. We make over seventy miles round trip and it isn't any fun bcause you really get tired. We have two places where my father dumps a big load to wait until he goes for some other kids. The places where we stop and wait we have them named such as "Station Number One" and "Number Two." My father is hauling now fifteen kids and we surely look like sardines in a can. We get home very late and that is why I haven't many books read.

The ranch where our school is at is quite large to compare with our little homestead. I am sending a little sketch of the Poso Nuevo Ranch. Our school is really named after the big mountains near, the Baboquívaris.

Do you dance there? We do here. We have a dance every Wednesday morning — that is half an hour. We learn folk dances and sometimes we can dance what we like. We are going to have a big dance drama which will be the eighth of May. I wish to invite you to come because I heard you are excellent dancers.

We got some letters from Alaska yesterday which were very interesting. I think you have heard of E. B.'s friend, Mrs. Marguerite Tiffany Naas. She is teaching the little Alaskans. They write cute letters. Answer, please. Yours truly, Edward Hernández

The first letters we got from the young Alaskans (their fathers are Scandinavian; their mothers are natives) excited us perhaps more than any tribute we ever received. We used excerpts from them in our January issue of *Little Cowpuncher*.

LETTERS FROM THE FAR NORTH

From Arthur Johnson:

I am in the eighth grade, weighing 120 pounds, 5 ft. 2½ inches tall and I am 15 years old. I have three brothers and one sister. We have five dogs using them most for hauling wood. Dogs are not used as much as they were before airplanes came into use. In time I think they won't be used at all.

Our school is a one room log cabin lined on the inside with beaver board. It has windows on the south side because of the prevailing north wind. . . . The fox season opened on the 16th of November. I have three traps set now and expect to set six more. A man caught one fox already. The skin is worth from ten to fifteen dollars. There are not many foxes around but there are lots of ptarmigan.

I will keep a weather chart from the first of December till we receive your answer to these letters. I will use only the five school days. Would you keep one for us for about a month?

From Edna Swanson:

We don't live in snow houses like your geography says. I never in my life saw anybody live in a snow house, and they don't. We dress about the same as you do except in winter we use mucklucks and parkas with our clothes. The food we eat is about the same as you eat, except we don't get fresh vegetables and fruit all the year round, but canned food we do get. For our meat, instead of chicken, beef, and mutton, we use reindeer and ptarmigan. In summer of course we add fish and different wild fowl.

We get mail twice a month. In winter the mail comes from Seattle to Juneau by boat, from Juneau to Nome by airplane, and from Nome to here by dogteam. From here to northern places by airplane. It takes a month for mail to get here from the United States.

There is daylight all night and day in summer with twenty-two hours of sunlight. In winter about one to two hours of sunlight and about four to five hours of daylight. The country is covered with snow from October to May and the rest of the time it is not. In winter the average temperature is 40 degrees below zero. And in summer 70 to 80 degrees above. In summer the people plant turnips, lettuce, and radishes, and a few plant carrots and spinach too.

Wallace Johnson, seventh grade (who signs himself "Unknown Friend"):

The natives dry the fish for the dogs. When they kill a whale they take the blubber and store it away. They sell the fish and blubber to the traders.

My father mines for gold. In winter he chops wood for sale.

Tom Beltz, seventh grade:

It is storming today but it is not very cold. It is about twelve degrees above zero. Sometimes it gets to sixty degrees below zero here.

I am setting traps for foxes. I work for wages in the summer and spend it all in the winter time just fulish.

Trygve Jorgenson, sixth grade:

I just took my skis to a man and told him to fix them. He said he would so I will be skiing after school.

We use gasoline lamps in the morning at school and at home up till about eleven o'clock before lunch. (Early in November.)

George Johnson (the other sixth grader):

Our school is 22 feet by 22 feet and is 12 feet high. We have to have lights in the morning. We had them till noon today because it is cloudy and snowing. We have three blackboards and a piano. It is heated by a heater and it burns wood. A new floor was put in our school this year. I hope you will answer and tell about you.

Martha Jorgenson, fifth grade:

It is snowing all day. Snow is little drops. They are white and make drifts all over. The ground is all white in winter. When spring comes we have the most fun. In summer we swim and go wading. We also pick berries. The names of the berries are salmon berries, blue berries, black berries, cran berries, and currants.

We have Northern Lights. They are of all kinds of colors.

We ride on sleds and dogs pull them. We go fast. Instead of automobiles. We go skating on the lake and creek. We also go sliding on a hill. Its name is Headache Hill.

Betty Johnson, Martha's classmate:

I am in the fifth grade and I am ten years old. I am 68 pounds. I am four feet and one eighth inches tall. I have light brown eyes and light brown hair. I am tall and slender.... There are seven people in our family. I have four brothers and no sisters.

There are fourteen children in our school. Our teacher's name is Mrs. Marguerite Naas. Our ganator's name is Miss Elba Swanson. Tom Beltz carrys water for our teacher.

Snow is little flakes and sometimes the flakes are bigger than other times. I would send you some because the teacher says you don't have snow in the desert near Mexico, but it would melt. We use it for water sometimes because when winter comes it freezes all the water into ice. We use the ice and snow to make water.

From the third grade:

We had 5 dogs but we sold them to Tomy Utbuk. I had good rides with a dogteme. In school we made books. Mine was the best.
— Holger Jorgenson

We are playing tag today on the tractor sleds. Buddy and Bobby fell of the sled and hert their nieces. Our teacher is Mrs. Naas. She has a bolldog. The bolldog's name is Chiquita.
— David Johnson

In our school are nine boys and five girls. Sometimes some of the children go outside of the schoolhouse and make a snow man.
— Emile Olsen

It is very cold up here now. But in spring it is warm and we play. What does the tempetcher get down there? — Bobby H.

Both the second grade wrote letters:
We are glad to rite you.
We have no flag the rope is broken.
but she is a good teacher. — B. H. *Six Years Old*

In winter it snows.
sumtimes we eat dry fish and seal oil
But we do not very much.
Northern lights are red and blue and yellow.
ther are other collers But.
I do not no them. — L. J.

The little cowpunchers wrote prompt and enthusiastic letters to these faraway friends. And in April the Alaskans wrote again, and sent us Wallace's weather chart. He wrote to Pancho who had answered his first letter.

Dear Pancho,

Well it is spring now for nearly all the creeks are running. The geese and ducks are going to be here in a few weeks. Then we will go out on the Peace River and the Koyuk flats to hunt them.

I went to Landing with a fellow who was freighting stuff from there. We took up 500 pounds with eleven dogs. At one of the bridges the water was over them, and we crossed anyway. The water went over the bed of the sleigh but the flour and sugar never got wet because we put the canned milk in the bottom.

To the Landing it is seven miles and we made it in about fifty minutes. It took one hour to come up. We got here at three o'clock and caught Trazan [a nickname for a short fellow] outdoors.

Your friend, Wallace G. Johnson

Dear Socorro:

I was glad to receive your letter and will try to answer your questions. You asked if I would like to live in Arizona. I certainly would like to take the trip. But I think it would be too hot for me.

Yes, we have flowers in summertime. Some of the flowers are poppies, roses, violets, for-get-me-nots, bluebells, buttercups, water-lilies, and many others.

The Eskimos do have a language of their own. Here is an Eskimo sentence: Na-vak-sac koo-nick-dak coos-kuk. Meaning, Maiden is kissing the cat. The Eskimos have not a written language. I understand most of it, but I can't talk it — only a few words.

We have instruments to play on. I have a guitar but I don't know how to play. I intend to learn this summer if I can. Dan, Hamm, and Ebba play two guitars and a mandolin at dances.

We do not have farms to raise vegetables, but we have little gardens. Nobody raises chickens here, but in Nome I saw some.

The kind of fish we eat are salmon, white fish, greylings, trout, tomcod, and she-fish. Some of the fish is salted or either dried and lasts all winter.

I have never been outside Alaska. Please send me a picture of yourself and I will send you one of myself when I get my pictures developed. *Bu-ra-in,* meaning Goodbye. — Edna Swanson

Through the interesting letters we receive the little cowpunchers, living almost as isolated and primitively limited lives as their ancestors, are getting acquainted with the great moving modern world. Johnny, our sailor-boy pal whom Mary wrote of as being "away up there in the ocean" brought us in intimate touch with the sea and the navy.

The great floating fortress, U.S.S. Pennsylvania, proud flagship of the U.S. fleet, and home of Admiral J. M. Reeves, sails this week to parts unknown to fire the second of the year's battle practice. It is fired on the world's longest range, the blue Pacific. The firing consists of shooting at a target which cannot be seen by the crews who fire the fourteen inch guns. All the aiming is done by the eyes of the fleet, the ship's fast airplanes. Now let us interview one of the men behind the guns, one of the men who fire at the invisible targets. We overhear him talking to one of his shipmates.

"It is about time for Long Range, Paul. I always get sick after we fire one of those blasted salvos. The first isn't so bad, but those last five surely get me. It's that wait between shots that hurts. There I am with my fingers on the firing key, eyes on the repeater, waiting for the buzzer, nerves like a taut line, and then those guns go off. No bang to those guns — just a roar which keeps getting louder all the time. No wonder we all get sick. Powder, smoke, concussion, and nerves on edge. But I wouldn't miss it for anything. There is something in firing those big guns that makes you forget everything but to keep them loaded and going off!"

Paul, who has yet to fire his first time, asks questions. "Say, Joe, how do you shoot at something you can't see? Those targets are 27 miles away."

"Well, Paul, it is this way. The spotting officer gets the range, and the deflection, which he sends to the ship by radio. The ship picks it up and plots it out on a big board, then sends it on down to my repeater. The face of the repeater looks something like a clock. The red hands move as the plotting room directs, and all I have to do is pop the white hand up to match with the red one. When the two hands match, then the gun is aimed at the target."

"One thing more, Joe. How much powder do we use in firing?"

"Say, kid, you should know that. Each gun takes four ninety-pound sacks. There are three guns to a turret, four turrets on the ship. Figure it out yourself. And each turret fires six salvos. But here is your answer: twenty-five thousand nine hundred and twenty pounds of powder. Now let's see how much steel that throws 27 miles. Each shell weighs fourteen hundred pounds; that makes one hundred thousand eight hundred pounds of steel. Wow! That is certainly throwing a lot of steel a long ways!" — J. F. H.

Fan letters not only give encouragement, they refresh the spirit which has strained hard in endeavor.

I am very proud to know that we have such good student editors in our state. I like the *Little Cowpuncher* because it is so very original. It says everything as if someone were telling what was happening at the moment. I also think it is quite amusing with humor that fits well in the stories.

You have put us to shame because we live in a city and do not edit a school newspaper, while you who live in the country do. I hope you will keep on in the years to come as well as you are doing now. I wish you success in your wonderful little paper and above all success in life.

Yours sincerely, Edna Aguirre, 7A, *Roskruge Junior High School,* Tucson

Mrs. E. ――― and I read every issue of the *Little Cowpuncher* with great interest. We think you are a very enterprising school to publish a newspaper and make it so entertaining with your parties, games, trips to town, and everyday happenings. I have become familiar with the literary style of your contributors and find it unusual and refreshing. I much prefer it to some of the cosmopolitan newspaper types of writing; for at least we know it is sincere. The illustrations are most intriguing. I congratulate the pupils and teacher of Baboquívari School for having the imagination to make everyday life and tasks full of interest.

With best wishes, I. K. E., *Decatur, Illinois*

Sometimes when it is not convenient for each child to write to friends who send us presents, we print notes of thanks in our paper:

A GIFT FROM ILLINOIS

When school started after Christmas, on the sixth of January Bill came from Tucson and brought one box of oranges — a gift sent by a lady who lives two thousand miles from here. Mrs. Charles A. Ewing sent them because she liked the *Little Cowpuncher.* We appreciated them very much and they have lasted us nearly two weeks. —Luis Badilla, *Sixth Grade*

A PRESENT FROM IOWA

Miss Olga who lives in Iowa where the tall corn grows has sent us a present of two dollars. Mrs. Bourne bought us some work books to help us in our education. They are of history and reading. We thank this lady very much. — P. A., *Fifth Grade*

THANKS TO MRS. RHODES

We owe a debt of thanks to Mrs. Rosa Rhodes of Redington for her generous interest in *Little Cowpuncher.* All the little cow-punchers of Baboquívari appreciate her very much for helping us with our paper. She bought the newsprint for this issue. And we thank her for sending us the little book of Mexican songs. We were glad to get it and some of the girls began to copy some words out of it.

We wish we could go to see Mrs. Rhodes and sing for her before our school closes. Thank you very much.   — Ramón Aros

MRS. J. M. HILL GIVES LITTLE COWPUNCHERS LOVELY GIFT

Thursday we never expected a visit from Mrs. Hill. But she and a daughter of the Picture Lady, and a brother of Johnny, and even Johnny himself whom we thought was away off in the ocean, came in the night and brought us a fascinating gift which we appreciate very much.

We would like in return of the beautiful fish to give Mrs. Hill something interesting that she would enjoy, but what can we give her? Our only gift to her will have to be our *Little Cowpuncher.*

The next day at school all the children were full of joy and very grateful to Mrs. Hill for bringing these strange beautiful fish. There are eight of them and we have given them names. The weather fish we named them Torpedo Twins, One and Two. The gold ones are named the Gold Dust Twins, Tip and Top. The black one that is a Chinese Moor is Tin-Lung, and the one with him is Silver Mate. The pink one is Strawberry, and the small one in her bowl is called Pee-Wee. They brought them and some snails in four glass jars. And they also brought us some very curious shells from the Picture Lady. Thank you, folks, we all thank you very much.   — S. A.

Little Cowpuncher has been much obliged to the editors of the *Tucson Daily Citizen,* the *Arizona Daily Star,* the *Western Livestock Journal, Hoofs & Horns, Brewery Gulch Gazette,* and *Arizona Stockman* for their words of encouragement. Quoting:

I am thankful to the little school children of the Pozo Nuevo Ranch down there on the border of Old Mexico in Arizona south of Tucson for the nice write-up they gave me recently in their school paper *Little Cowpuncher.* The children in this school are all good little Americans born of Mexican parents, and they are taking their school duties seriously. They respond easily to English education and are making rapid strides. Members of all grades in the school from the second to the eighth write for *Little Cowpuncher* and show great talent in writing and their art work published in each issue is hard to beat. — *Western Livestock Journal*

The *Little Cowpuncher,* published by the Baboquívari School, under the direction of Mrs. Eulalia Bourne, herself a fullfledged cow woman, is attracting the attention of many people. The convictions and imagery of the children are reproduced untouched and it would take a cold heart indeed not to enjoy the journalistic efforts of these little Mexican-Americans. — *Arizona Stockman*

I do wish that all of you readers could see a copy of this paper *(Little Cowpuncher)*. It is an eight-page mimeographed tabloid size sheet. The writing is done entirely by the children who are Mexicans; Mrs. Bourne, the teacher, types the stencils and the children run off the copies on the mimeographing machine. Most of their pages are illustrated with drawings by the children. They write about everyday happenings and familiar scenes, and their ability to express themselves is remarkable. — Ethel A. Hopkins, *Hoofs & Horns*

SCHOOL NEWSPAPER ATTRACTS PRAISE

Strikingly original is the school newspaper *Little Cowpuncher,* which comes out once a month at Baboquívari School. All of the articles and items appearing in the mimeographed sheet are signed by their writers from the second grade to the eighth grade.... A short promotional article, signed by Ramón Aros, appeared in a recent issue, as follows: "This little paper is written once a month by the Baboquívari pupils. We call it *Little Cowpuncher* because we all live on ranches, including our teacher and we are all born of cowboys. If you subscribe to it we will try to make a larger copy. We are Mexican boys and girls and that's why the English is not perfect." — *Tucson Daily Citizen*

... *The Little Cowpuncher,* a mimeographed school paper of the Baboquívari School, Pozo Nuevo Ranch, reached many friends yesterday throughout Arizona and the west, for the little cowpunchers are growing famous.... And as their fame grows, so grow the students of this isolated school which graduates four students from the eighth grade at commencement exercises "which will be talked about for weeks and weeks to come" the eighth of May.

— *The Arizona Daily Star*

Instead of stultifying her students with questions on what happened to Amo when the Amozans got hold of it or whether MacBeth or his missus put King Duncan on the spot, Mrs. Bourne keeps them right on the prod on the highlights of modernity and is developing a bunch of youngsters who will be of more use to society than a carload of professors of the old school of pedantry ... The most decorative flowers sometimes grow wild on the prairie and likewise intelligent education may bloom far from the swank of the metropoli.
— by Stan
Brewery Gulch Gazette

VARI SCHOOL

Edward Hernandez Four Say Farewell

Four Ride Away

THE PRIM LITTLE French clock held captive in the wild
forest of my shelves has just chimed the hour of two a.m.
and all Poso Nuevo creatures are sound asleep except
me. I drank coffee at midnight before we left the dance
at Sahuarita.

Mary and Edward stopped in town with relatives.
I might have stayed with my friend Lolita and been half
way home on my weekend trip if I had not had to drive
back here with Socorro and Ramón. They have slipped
in to crowd their bedfellows and are surely asleep already.
When we saw the light as we drove up I wondered if
My-Mother had waited up for us. Then I remembered
the night lamp that burns before her shrine.

The place belongs to the livestock now — as it was

meant to do. When I went out with the flashlight to get some chips for the morning's fire a bunch of horses broke out of the corral where they had come for a drink and galloped away. They like to come in at night when the human peril is lowest. It is like the shutdown of a big mill when the family here stops its clattering *barullo* and retires for a long deep slumber. I am probably the only inhabitant of the Altar Valley who is not asleep.

The forty miles of it we tore through after midnight — and the six or seven hundred sections of surrounding land so open to view by day that we feel their vastness even on nights too dark to see — form great areas of scenery apparently suspended in shadowy mystery. In our wide sparsely settled corner of earth, harboring no factories, mines, or crowded thoroughfares, there is little activity visible at any time; but by day our brilliant sun and restless winds give the illusion of vigor and liveliness. When the sun is gone and the wind swishes softly, the quietness that haunts lonely places is depressive. The stillness, not so much of degree as of quantity, has a saddening effect however grand and peaceful it seems.

Yet I laugh if someone asks if I get lonely. I don't have time for rest, to say nothing of the additional contacts and activities of the non-lonely. Perhaps, however, there is deep down inside a suppressed emotion or yearning that accounts for the endless chain of multiple-action I indulge in. Is it a fellow feeling for these underprivileged children that prompts me to take the trouble and expense of escorting the four graduating pupils with me here and there over the country to give them social experiences no one can have in these remote environments?

This much I know — I can't educate kids by keeping them shut up in a tidy supervised room reading about the annexation of Texas and the ancient Chinese methods of agriculture. To live with them in something like pleasant progression I must go out with them, share dangers and good times with them, give them contacts that will wake them up to their possibilities. If pupils are bored they will be sullen, impudent. Monotonous routine does not arouse the spirit. If school is quartered into fifteen minutes of arithmetic, fifteen minutes of history, fifteen minutes of spelling — and grammar, reading, and penmanship, on and on (Go day; Come day; Lord send Sunday) the reaction at each dismissal time is: *I'm glad I got out of that!*

Human needs surely must interrupt systematic schedules. Yet such interruptions take their toll. Instead of this late hour and hundred fifty mile drive at night, I might have shooed the kids off at four o'clock and tackled the disorder of my room. This is *Little Cowpuncher* week, so it hasn't received the usual lick and promise. I can only hope that whoever enters here will realize that this is the den of a busy woman. It is my workshop, furnished with odds and ends of somebody's discards. Generally I can find my way around, and I'm happy because the mice can't get in, my feet can be kept warm, and the bed is a comfortable place to read. Too bad about the cleaning. But the loss of sleep is serious.

Instead of chaperoning the young to a neighborhood dance I should have been resting against the ordeal of Saturday-in-town. Of all the disagreeable, disintegrating, soul-destroying tasks, the worst is doing Saturday errands in the city. So far this year, twenty-seven out of thirty Saturdays have been detailed to this misery. I must shop for the homestead and the three men working there at present; for the school; for the school lunch program; for myself, and for the neighbors. Everybody in the county apparently chooses Saturday for the same purpose. The salespeople are rushed and cross. Banks, post-offices, lumber yards, hardware stores, office supply houses, wholesale groceries, and welfare departments (where I get the cocoa stuff and, occasionally, shoes for barefoot youngsters) all close at noon *en punto,* if open at all.

There are, of course, other errands and appointments besides shopping. During this long ordeal I stamp about on unyielding stone and pavement, punishing my feet (too often) with wooden heels, with no chance to relax and freshen up, so that I am always in distress over my appearance. It is impossible to look nice when you've dressed before daylight, humped for two hours over the steering wheel on a cold morning drive, and go tearing around all day with no opportunity to do more than dab on powder and lipstick. As I rush down Congress Street, arms bulging with clumsy ill-wrapped packages from the five-and-ten, my hair wandering from under my seldom-cleaned hat, I meet city friends — smart, collected, groomed for inspection — never frowsled by haste.

It is seldom possible to get away from the city before dark. Even then I often have to stop at the feed store on Oracle Road for a few sacks of grain and chicken scratch. Sometimes I tie two bales of hay on the rear bumper to take to Buddy, my cherished horse who, alas, now knows other riders better than he does me. Then, car

"I can't educate kids by keeping them shut up in a tidy, supervised room.

tilted nose-up from the load, the fumes of kerosene or lamp gas polluting the air inside, I take off on the rough fifty miles to Pepper Sauce Canyon. When I eventually get up the sand wash, there is still unloading to do or supervise. Cowboys sleep when cattle sleep. As a rule they think very little of shopping and doing errands. They just won't do it. It's being cruel to ask one, however intimately related, to crawl out of his soogans at ten or eleven o'clock at night, if the weather forces him to pull on his boots, to make a dozen trips carting in the debris a woman loads up with.

"Leave the things in the car. I'll unload in the morning."

But there are bundles and boxes on top of my per-

must go out with them . . . give them contacts. . . ."

sonal luggage. A poor imitation of a cowboy, I can't flop at the drop of a hat. I have to dig out the laundry, my toothbrush, skin lotions, hairbrush, and slippers before I hit the hay.

And with all that looming over the eastern horizon, I take the eighth grade to a dance at Sahuarita — far over the Sierrita Mountains. Well, the dance happened to be on Friday. Helen had invited my graduates, and I felt they should keep in touch with her. Besides, she and Rex came to our Halloween festival and are coming to our dance drama two weeks from now. We reciprocate!

It's good for my bashful four to go out under my care. It stimulates them in a way just going with their parents does not. We have gone to picture shows, art exhibits, and Gen Brown's dance recital — besides the picnics and rodeo parades. I wish I could take them to the old Mission of San Xavier, the museum at the University, the observatory for a peek at the moon and stars, and the summit of the Catalina Mountains where they could see pine trees and mountaintop views for the first time.

Tonight I was proud of my four. They behaved well and looked nice. As we left town at eight-thirty for the twenty miles southward to Sahuarita. I gave them some gum and told them to chew their heads off until we arrived and not to touch any more until we started home. In this respect alone they were outstanding among the hordes of jaw whackers.

Socorro wore a white sport skirt, yellow sweater, and neat flat-heeled white sandals. Mary wore her little linen suit with the pink blouse. Edward, who loves to be formal, wore light trousers and his dark blue coat. Ramón doesn't have a coat, but his clothes were clean and his beautiful hair neatly arranged. Both boys looked alert with none of that deadpan rural stare.

Our boys were cramped at first because we had not brought any money. I had two dollars but I needed it to buy gasoline. Used to the Mexican way of entertaining, I had forgotten that at *bailes americanos* where there is expensive music and many different cliques who stay in their own select groups, the male dancers buy bits of ribbon to pin on their jackets or ties to show they are eligible to use the dance floor. Last December Mary wrote an item for *Little Cowpuncher* on this topic:

PARTIES, MEXICAN AND AMERICAN STYLES

There is a difference in Mexican and American parties. When the Mexicans make parties they are always the ones to pay for all the expenses to entertain their guests. All can go and enjoy the fiesta as the one giving the party pays for the orchestra, the dinner or supper of Mexican food, and whatever there is to drink. The hosts pay these things.

And Americans when they are going to make a party and invite people, they ask them to pay a dollar each for the music and then to buy the pies and coffee or whatever is to eat and drink. So the Americans have the least expensive parties. But my choice would be the Mexican host. — M. H.

On the same page appeared a write-up of a party Socorro had attended the night before:

EL VELORIO DE ANOCHE

Last night at the Hernández Ranch far up in the Sierritas we had a velorio which means praying to a great saint. Those are promises which we make to our own saints. We Mexicans do. It is a night when nobody sleeps and it is the same as a party.

We had *enchiladas* and *vinos* for all night we prayed to *Nuestra Señora de Guadalupe* and from twelve o'clock until two-thirty we danced. And now the next morning we are all sleepy working on our favorite project our own *Little Cowpuncher.* — S. A.

Helen did not notice our embarrassment. She had her hands full being chairman of a dance committee at a party numbering over a hundred people of almost every social status. And at last Pascual, and Henry, his son-in-law, arrived with their group and cheerfully bought ribbons for my two young cowpunchers who forthwith stepped out to help make the dance a success. Edward dutifully danced with his hostesses, Helen and Mrs. E. Ramón, noticing the segregation practiced in this community, held back. Both asked me to dance, but I saved my strength to dance with Frances.

Yes, our little *Mae Wess* was there. She wore the

white dress and shoes that Licha had bought for her confirmation. We knew that she had entered school at Sahuarita, and hoped we might see her at the dance. I had kept up with her by inquiring at the office of the county probation officer, and by now and then running into Helen in town on Saturdays. Helen said that as soon as she entered school, she, the principal, Miss Keller, the primary teacher, and all the children in her room loved her at once. When I met Miss Keller I apologized for her poor reading, explaining that she had missed so much the year before.

"Oh," the teacher surprised me by saying: "she is the best reader in her class!"

"Is she in the second grade?" I asked anxiously.

"Yes."

Tonight, her face flushed with pleasure, she ran and threw her arms around me.

"Is that your mother, Frances?"

"Yes."

"I want to meet her."

She took her mother's arm and pulled her over to me. There stared at me over Quica's bright head a thick pudgy woman with a dark expressionless face. Nothing at all of Frances in her. Her small eyes were blank — neither hostile nor friendly. Her thick black hair hung long on her heavy shoulers. Her purplish lips opened wide as she chewed her gum. I spoke to her in Spanish.

"You are the mother of my little Francisca?"

"Uh-huh," busily chewing.

"I am her teacher. We loved her very much at Baboquívari. She is a good little girl."

"Uh-huh."

"May she come to sit with us?"

"Uh-huh."

Frances wanted to dance. It was the first chance she had found since she left us. My big kids were dancing with the Sahuarita young people of their own age. So Frances danced with me, who had taught her to dance. She glided, floated, and improvised in ecstasy. I held her lightly, firmly, letting her show off before her mother and her new school admirers.

"Frances, are you happy here?"

"Yes, ma'am. But I like the Baboquívari School, too."

Plainly she was enjoying the limelight, and the grand, new sweep of popularity that had engulfed her in this larger community. It was this taint of vanity that had caused Charli to hesitate about trying to get the law to give her back to us. When she had been gone three weeks he went over and asked her point-blank whom she wanted to live with. Her answer was ambiguous.

"Quiero vivir con mi 'amá, y con mi tía, también," the little minx had said, wanting, not unnaturally, the affection and devotion of both sides. After that Charli stopped suit.

When Pascual came bringing Marcela, I was happy watching my two little second-grade girls dance together. They were on the floor all the time, head to head, little feet flying, graceful and lively as humming birds. They danced so well they were not in anybody's way on the crowded dance floor.

I sighed at not being able to have our little blonde

bailerina for our May program. (Only two weeks off!) We are working frantically to make it the biggest blow-out we've ever had in our district. Lolita is to be the May Queen. She is a lovely sweet child, but a meek, soft-voiced angel with none of the fiery sparkle of *May Wess*. Graceful, pretty, she is as aloof as the sky. Marcela, dark and slender, is pretty and a good dancer, but self-conscious. Chelo is stiff with reserve. Teddy is more free like Frances, but she is still a rolypoly baby. Socorro and Mary are the stars of the show and neither can be featured above the other. The three middle-sized girls — Herlinda, Ysidra, and Inez make the biggest problem dramatically. They have lost the charm of infancy and have not acquired the poise of maidenhood.

It is surprising that Inez, the latest comer, excels. It has been tough work for her. One handicap has been that nobody wants to help her but me. I give her regular class drill on Wednesday mornings for half an hour, but that isn't enough. The good dancers, of whatever size, are those who practice and practice, with or without supervision, not only at class time but at recess, noon hour, and at home. Inez doesn't have a chance at this help. The Aros boys won't voluntarily dance with her, afraid of being teased by their fellows. Edward will dance with her if she specifically asks him — but he is very popular. One morning during practice Pancho was detailed to schottische with her. She missed some steps. He was furious — not so much at her as at the smirks on the faces of his brothers. He left her and stalked off the floor muttering. I know she will learn to dance because her spirit is

245

determined to conquer her flesh. I am glad I've had a chance to show her how to dance.

We have been weeks generating skill and enthusiasm for this show. We want it to be something to remember; something fitting to crown the school work of these four young people who have now finished the eighth grade. We have attempted to put this thought into this issue of *Little Cowpuncher,* their special number.

ADDRESS TO OUR GRADUATES TO BE GIVEN BY MRS. SMITH

Four of the pupils of "Little Cowpuncher School" are going to finish from the eighth grade on the 8th of May. Mrs. Constance F. Smith, our school superintendent from Tucson, Pima County, will give an address which means a talk. It is a great honor to our little school and we appreciate it very much. — Ramón Aros

EIGHTH GRADE TEST RESULTS

The other day Mrs. Bourne brought the news that we — all the eighth graders — had passed the Standard Achievement Tests given by the county office. The tests were a long time being corrected. But I am especially glad that I passed. I was doing the seventh and eighth grade work together. It was understood that if I could pass the eighth grade tests I could graduate this year because we already passed the Constitution tests. The average I made in all the subjects taken together was eighth grade, sixth month, which is probably the national average as we took the tests in the sixth month of the school year. I am glad I passed with Mary, Socorro, and Ramón. — Edward Hernández

LONG TIME AGO

A May Festival of Dance
By Bavoquívari School
Friday, May 8th at 8:00 P.M.
Visitors Invited — Gratis

At last about two weeks ago, we got started to get organized for our big day. We have our story that holds our dances together.

It is about some Southern troupers who are going from Louisiana to California, and are passing through our land here in the Altar Valley about fifty or sixty years ago when the Apaches were bad.

They have been passing quietly through Arizona because they were afraid of an Indian attack. But at last they think they are safe for they have met an Indian who seems friendly and tells them there is no danger from his people.

But he is deceiving them. That night when they are happy practicing their songs and dances that they are going to give on the theaters of California where they are going, the Indian gives a sign and a tribe attacks them. Before they are driven away they steal one of the loveliest maidens (who is afterwards the May Queen in the Third Act).

In the Indian camp Mari-Rose manages to win the favor of the old Chief who is sick with melancholy and his people cannot cheer him with anything. But Mari-Rose is a dancer and she teaches some folk dances to the little children captives and the old Chief is so pleased he allows her the favor to be sent back to her people. They are happy to have her back with them and so pleased with the spring in California when they arrive that they celebrate a great May festival which ends by the winding of a big Maypole.

Some of the characters which we thought up names for are Chief Horseface, Big Deer, Juan John, Chicken Hawk; and Sammy, Pa Hugh, Dixie, and so on. We want to have pretty costumes and to know our dances like professionals so that it will be the best program we have given in this school. It will be outside. We are going to build a stage of green boughs, and have lights from cars. We want everybody who can to come, and we will entertain all the best we can and hope to let them see something they will always want to remember of our little Baboquívari School.

— Mary Hernández

For the next two weeks we'll use practically all the school day, including play periods, for dancing and rehearsing. We have worked in the words to be memorized during language and reading periods. Now we must draw the whole dance together into a unit. Only practice can do that. There is a terrific strain on the director in a program like this where the performers' bread and future are not definitely dependent on their acting. For the sake of our nerves we must halt at intervals and turn to regular lessons. This will be spasmodic, informal — four or five classes going at once. It may look like madness, but there is method in it. I give each eighth-grader a class while I take the little ones. Thus the primary children are disciplined in drills and kept advancing while the graduating pupils review basic skills such as long division, "tricky zero," inversion of divisors, dates and outlines in middle-grade history, and hundreds of spelling words. This also gives them responsibility for their school and for their younger brothers and sisters. (And they get an idea of what a teacher endures.)

Ramón can't have Ysidra in his class. They are both straight Aros explosives. Pancho, too. He was at the board with her to show her some arithmetic fundamentals. All at once he bellowed loudly and she bellowed right back. "Mrs. Bourne!" he shouted. "She is telling me bad words!"

When she shouted a denial and denunciation, he blurted out her remark — an obscene insult common among the people here. "And I'm going to hit her!" he cried.

"Go ahead. I don't like to hit her, and she surely deserves it."

So he won't try to help her any more.

One day Edward went to the board with her and Víctor to show them long division. He labored, getting louder and louder. At last he startled the whole room by crying out in despair: *"My God you're dumb!"*

It takes a long run of terms for the common-school

instruction of many of our isolated, language-handicapped pupils. Not for any lack of brains or ability, but mostly on account of their stubborn attitude of putting the entire load on the teacher. (Even the saintly Padre Eusebio Kino was accused by colleagues of using passionate violence on some of the natives in his charge for educational and religious instruction.)

But if a child can't make a grade in one year, he can do it in two, or perhaps three. Time is not at a premium to sun-loving rancheritos. Suppose they wore themselves and their teacher out and finished the eighth grade at the age of fourteen. Then what? They're too young to enter the field of labor. Few can go to secondary schools. Mary and Edward hope to go through high school. Their economic security may not endure for the four-year stretch, but at least they'll start next fall. And the fact that they'll enter ninth grade in a city junior high school in September has been a whip over us.

Sometimes when country pupils go to city classes they are put back — and not always just one grade. On the other hand many country teachers seem to regard it as an act of cruelty to retain a child, especially if he is physically out of proportion to his mental growth. This may be the fault of parents whose pride is jeopardized. In a one-room school, if a child is not *passed* he has been insulted and his family held up to shame. It took nerve last year to retain nine of the twenty-six pupils here, but this year we all enjoy the benefits.

I am sure that my eighth graders have a pretty good smattering of elementary school subject-matter. They have been faithful in attendance, personal manners and sanitation, all our extra-curricular activities, and have managed to pass creditable achievement tests. I can't imagine my school without them — sons and daughters to me now. It is good that in the rush of closing the term and directing a fitting blaze of glory for their exit I am too busy to realize that when this is over I won't have them any more.

It was our plan for each to write a little autobiography for this, their special *Little Cowpuncher*. But there were slips. Ramón thought he had lived so long that a story short enough to go into our paper would not do justice to his whole life. Mary worked several days on her story at home and at school. It must have had two thousand words. But I'm afraid it was destroyed. I know she showed it to me; but in the rush we're in, neither of us can remember whether she left it on my desk or took it back to hers. And when you've written your story, you're through with it. Only a Lawrence of Arabia would have the superhuman energy to write his own life twice.

Socorro's and Edward's are revealing:

MYSELF

I am a girl who still has a mother and a step-father. When I was about two years old my father died. I have step-brothers on account of my step-father who had a family when he married my mother. She has two of her own, my brother Franqui and I. My father and mother have seven of their own now, so that makes sixteen children that are living. And I am one of them.

I have lived in Arizona all my life. I am sixteen years old and I still go to school. I am in the eighth grade. My dear teacher is Eulalia Bourne from Oracle, Arizona.

I am a Mexican. I have brown eyes and brown hair. I weigh one hundred twenty-nine pounds and am sixty-four inches tall. To my best estimate I am not a very good girl, and not very bad. I like to help my teacher in all that I can. I never in my life wanted to discourage my teachers. Of all I ever had I love Mrs. Bourne better than the others. I am not saying this because she is my teacher now, but it is my true thought.

I am able to do all the things my grown people command me to do. Sometimes I get a little stubborn with my mother when I don't like to wash dishes or do several things. What I like when I get out of school is to read and eat something while I am reading. I like to go walking in good weather. I like dances, shows, and I like to be dressed in good clothes. In school I am poor in my subjects. Sometimes I do well, but sometimes I am ashamed of the low grades I get. The subjects I like best are physiology, spelling, English literature, and geography.

I live a happy life with my mother and step-father. One thing I don't like is that we are so many and we all have to have the same. Some times I think I wish I were the only daughter of my mother. And I wish she didn't have so many babies. That's my true thought. I hate to take care of babies. I wish I could go places and wouldn't have to worry about small children all the time.

I haven't been in any other counties but Pima and Santa Cruz. And I haven't been to any other state. I have lived all my life on ranches.   — Socorro Aros

MYSELF IN LIFE

As I start to tell my life I will say that my name is Edward Delahánte Hernández. I am sixteen years old, five feet five inches tall, and weigh one hundred twenty pounds. I am both in the seventh and eighth grades and the teacher knows why.

In school the lessons I like best are arithmetic, art, geography, literature and history. Art is where I am strong. If it was for me to decide I would draw all day long from sun up to sun down. But of course I convince myself that just drawing won't get me anywhere.

I am a book lover. I would like to have a library of my own and so let my friends read my books. I hope that some day I will see my book shelves full of interesting books to read and study while in spare time. The books I like best are of things that will help me in my knowledge, such as nature books, adventure books, lives of great men, and books of the Wild West of both animals and men.

I don't like to brag of myself, but they say that I do well in art. I have painted several pictures for different friends. I may yet get to be a good artist, who can tell? It is my ambition.

Now about behavior. I'm not an angel because every human

being has faults, no matter if rich or poor, or even king or queen. My good virtues are that I don't like to use bad language or mix with bad companions. That is what pleases my parents about me. I like to make good friends and entertain them in some way. My bad virtues are that I loose my temper sometimes when I find my sisters getting my things. And I spend too much money in going to movies every chance I get. Also I don't really mind my parents when I think they are wrong.

To return to my appearance, I am not fat nor thin. I have dark eyes, straight black hair, and my skin is sort of tan. I am a Mexican, but born in America so I am an American citizen.

I have four hobbies besides art and books. I can drive a car. I have been doing it since I was eight years old. I can play the piano (by ear). I know how to handle a gun. And I know how to ride a horse.

As I was telling you, I love to know about nature. I like to plant trees, and gardens of flowers and vegetables and watch them grow. I like to have a little pond with fish in it, and many dogs and cats.

If I'm of any value to the world that I cannot say. Only people who read my life can judge. My parents say that they will depend on me to take care of them when thew grow weaker and I am stronger. That is natural. That is why they brought us to this world.

I am writing a few lines as truly as I can. Perhaps the rest of my life as I grow older will be more interesting.

— Edward Hernández

The biography idea was not a hundred per cent successful. But another thought served practically the same purpose of getting boys and girls to open their hearts in sincerity.

Assignment: Write an imaginative story of what happens to you after you graduate from the eighth grade.

MY LOOK INTO THE FUTURE

After Ramón Aros graduated from the eighth grade in the Baboquívari School, he went out of his family's crowded room to look for a job. When he was out trying to get a job he remembered all of his playmates and teacher and felt very sad, but that was all the chance he had to be with them.

Long before he had finished his school his father wanted to make him quit school. But he wanted a little study before he did as his father wanted. His father wanted him to quit school because he needed him very much for he always knew that with him he could help him get a job and earn more money for the support of the family. And his father could have more rest for he is getting old very fast.

From there on he has had very good times because he has worked and earned money enough to spend. But he will never have money enough to go all around the world because he is in a big, big family and his parents need his help. All Ramón could do was to work as hard as he could all of his life. — R. A.

WHAT HAPPENED TO MARY

Mary felt glad to have finished her school ready to go on to high school, but there was a lump in her throat when she left her old school and dear teacher. She had a summer vacation in Los Angeles to enjoy herself and have good times before she was ready to start to school again in a Tucson Junior High School.

She was determined to study hard and get a good education to become a teacher, so she went on through high school with perfect grades.

During this time her father made a success with in their homestead. He had lots of cattle and a beautiful home. Mary spent all her part of the big hacienda, but she went to the University and to the Teachers' College in Flagstaff. She got her teaching diploma in dancing and art.

After that summer she got a job in Boston and made good money. When she had enough she went around the world and met lots of interesting people. When she was in Paris she met a very handsome Englishman who wanted to marry her. He had lots of money, but she was not ready to marry anybody yet. While she was still in Paris she received a telegram from a director in Hollywood who wanted her to take the leading part in a musical hit picture. And she accepted.

Her name came out in the papers nearly every day, and all the people wanted to see her in person. Afterwards the papers announced that she had married her leading man. She lived in Hollywood in a fine house with twenty servants, among them a chauffeur and a hairdresser. Now she has gone to New York to sing and dance in the Metropolitan. — M. H.

A FORWARD GLANCE

Edward graduated in May, saying farewell with a heavy heart to his teacher, school, and schoolmates. When he left the eighth grade he determined to get a job for three months of vacation. So he got one with a store. With this money he bought everything he needed to start the ninth grade in the fall.

There in town he suffered very much with the teachers and the pupils. One bad look from the teacher and he used to remember the kind looks of dear E. B. Every festival day that came he used to remember the lovely parties and dance dramas she used to give. Sometimes in his dreams thinking of his chums and teacher having fun, he wished he had never graduated. Once he dreamed that he had E. B. in every grade he passed until he finished high school.

One day he and his mother planned to give a party just for his old schoolmates and his dear old teacher. So they were all very happy while the party lasted, then they had to depart again.

Soon he graduated from high school, getting his diploma from the Art Department, and was able to get a swell job. He bought a new car and had money enough to give to his teacher and former schoolmates at the ranch. So he lived happily ever afterwards.

— E. H.

SOCORRO'S DAY DREAM

After Socorro graduated in May she kept on going to school. She went to high school, through the University, and through college, and now she is teaching in New York. It is her first year of being a teacher and she is having a grand time having parties similar to the shows E. B., her darling and lovable teacher, had. She is also making her pupils write stories for a *Little Cowpuncher.* She is getting $2000 every month and she is sending her mother and father half of it. For her own advantage she is putting $50 in the bank, and of the rest she buys groceries and nice clothing and other expenses. She has her own home. On Saturdays she goes to dances, to picture shows, to picnics with her friends. On Sundays she teaches dancing to American girls. She has become very good at drawing, and still remembers the art lessons William E. Ronstadt used to give her when she was just a kid at Baboquívari School.

— S. A.

While Socorro was composing her "day dream," I was seated on a desk top facing the blackboard in the northwest corner of the room giving dictation to the second and third grades. Glancing over my shoulder, unknown to her I caught the expression on her face — and found myself staring and smiling. She was sitting so still she scarcely seemed to breathe. Her left hand half-covered her paper from the intrusive eyes of her neighbors; her right hand held the pencil above the last line as if posing for a time exposure. Her eyes were directed at the top edge of her desk but seeing far down the hidden years ahead.

I used to see that look on the concentrated faces of my kids at Redington — Clara, Alicia, Carlota, Gareth, Ardell, Fidel; and Cayetano that time he wrote his own history, closing with the line: "I hope I have a good time before I die."

E. H

The Year Is Ended

A COOL WIND here in my garden at my homestead is playing with the green leaves of my cherished trees and spicing the air with the fragrance from the thick bed of yerba buena. I sit in the canopied swing, my bare legs outstretched to the sun, the hose turned on the little walnut tree, the water pulsing to the welcome beat of the gasoline engine over the well down in the canyon, and, with sweet sadness, turn my thoughts back to Poso Nuevo.

A few weeks ago I gave the annual prizes, made the final reports, and helped print the May issue of *Little Cowpuncher*. Communication between my kids and me is broken. We're no longer a school — a unit. We're individuals going our separate courses outside the *esprit de corps* that has been the finest thing about our association. Something good in our lives has ended. Our relations, though always warm in friendship, will never be the same. Another year will bring other pupils (and those who remain will be older, different) and experiences. Our best year is now but a memory, but a powerful memory which will hold us tight like bonds of steel as long as we live.

Our "commencement" party was seven weeks ago tonight. I am trying to see it with detachment, to charm away the painful memories. It was fun for the kids because we worked our level best and they had a marvelous time anticipating it. As for me, I think of it as I imagine General Lee remembered Gettysburg. Time and again he had flung his indomitable troops against odds and they had done the impossible. Once more he threw his gallant men against overwhelming odds — and they did not do the impossible.

Among our trials were three of grave importance. Our audience was slow to gather. Some came fifty miles, some over a hundred miles, after a day's work. There were long waits for the first comers. Then we were attempting to give an outdoor program with phonograph music without any system of amplification. And worst of all the weather — that monstrous destroyer of human plans, health, safety, and wellbeing — turned against us.

My hopes were based on the bright success of the Redington dance pageant (also held outdoors in May), our Christmas performance at Poso Nuevo eighteen months ago, and our last Halloween festival — all done to phonograph music; but under mild clear skies!

Discounting the weather, we had the right ingredients for a hit. People came — lots of people. The kids knew their dances and songs and looked beautiful in their brilliant costumes. Our script, entirely original, was all right. But the hour struck and we made no magic.

If we could have had a dress rehearsal for all that changing of costumes! The children lived too far away. If we hadn't had to wait so long for the official guests! And, above all, if it hadn't turned so freezing cold! I never remember a May night in Southern Arizona so chilly.

The dancers in their wispy costumes did not complain. They burned with excitement. I hoped their gay swift movements would keep their blood moving fast enough to ward off congestion, although visions of pneumonia haunted me as they danced barefoot on the cold ground we had thoroughly dampened to lay the dust. The audience caused the greatest anxiety. Having come many miles at no little trouble and expense, nobody could enjoy sitting still in icy temperatures for two hours to see a school show. Nobody but kids. The children on both sides of the footlights had a wonderful time.

My own blue sheer was ample as I was in a lather of worry over the ladies in spring clothes out there in the dark freezing. The sudden cold was so unexpected that no one came prepared; many begged for wraps at the first intermission. I longed to pass out buckets of hot coals for foot-warmers.

Eleanor and Ernestina, old pupils of mine, finally arrived with the twelve dozen tamales after taking the wrong road, breaking an axle, and drafting a total stranger — whom they routed out of bed — to get his little truck and bring them and their guests to the fiesta. I despaired of repaying all this trouble with tamales and dancing little cowpunchers. And I couldn't forget that twelve car loads of people had long trips ahead of them as soon as my darlings graduated.

Now that time has passed and the belated summer heat is on, I can think of the audience as wishing for a whiff of that cold wind that roared in that night from the Arctic like an angry uninvited fairy. I can remember how beautiful my children looked and how proud they were to go through their songs and dances. For that little hour (so ill-timed, as it turned out!) they were stage folks, probably the happiest mortals on earth in the performance of their work.

Bill was in charge of make-up and his artistry showed best in the first act which called for "Old Fashion" costumes and characters. Arturo, as *Pa,* was his masterpiece and drew a salvo of applause as he strode out into the lights from two cars, dressed in high boots, suspenders, vest, and chin whiskers. Teddy was exquisite in curls, long tight bodice and fluffy paniers. Ysidra was a hit in her poke-bonnet, long calico with frilled pantlettes showing above her shoes. Herlinda was a prize. She has fair skin and typically Spanish features dominated by a long nose. Her dress was a cream-colored cashmere heirloom with stayed basque and sixteen-gored skirt that had been worn by her grandmother in her youth.

Mary and Socorro, our stars, were most beautiful in the final act as they danced in their softly flowing voiles. Sally, "electrician" in her car, told me afterwards that the car lights were so powerful that they pierced the thin costumes and showed the girls' figures. But are not figures part of a dance? That's why we were so careful about foundation garments. The girls have beautiful bodies. I hadn't realized that they were so shapely until I took them to my room to measure them for costumes and discovered how many undergarments their mothers make them wear. For once they were free and lovely as Greek maidens. As for the twenty or so roughnecks from the roundup who looked on, perhaps a little artistic education won't do them any harm. I hope the mothers got the same delight I did when they danced so joyously. The wild wind seemed to hold its breath for this loveliness.

Another surprising beauty that night was Inez Jane. Her slenderness made her look tall in the long clinging rainbow-colored mist Alicia had worn at Redington. The little blonde girl danced with her whole heart. She will not be with us next year. And in a city or suburban school where there are hundreds of girls she will be overlooked. But those of us who saw her in the glory of her Rainbow Dance will not forget her.

I am glad now that Mary talked back to me that night for the first time in two years. At the second intermission, crazily jerking costumes off and on boys and girls in my cubbyhole of a room, yanking squirming youngsters none too gently, yelling at those pestering me for safety pins and other properties, I lost my nerve.

"It's getting too late!" I cried desperately. "Entirely too late! We've got to leave out some dances. These interpretive dances —" I stopped and stared into space.

The girls looked up startled.

"Mrs. Bourne!" Mary cried sharply, fixing me with her big luminous eyes. "After all we've done! Practicing so hard! Getting our costumes ready! And this is the prettiest part! We'll NOT leave it out!"

Now I'm glad she insisted. The kind people in the audience will forget the cold discomfort. They will not soon forget how lovely my young dancers were that night. I'll keep those victrola records always. Years from now I'll play them. That quadrille will remind me of Herlinda, patrician in her grandmother's cashmere, a carried-away look on her face, swinging and promanading with her happy companions. Other pictures that won't fade from my memory are of Teddy and Pili, tiny and cute in their old-time schottische. Edward and Ramón as lean, painted savages leaping so gracefully. And later, jigging in their heavy cowboy outfits, marking rhythms vigorously with jingling spurs. And the four teenagers waltzing theatrically to *Cielito Lindo*. Those two boys and girls — Edward, Ramón, Mary, and Socorro — will not forget the excitement of that night — a fitting triumph to close eight years or more of attending a remote country school.

Of course we could not possibly have known it at the time, thankfully, but the dances in which dear little Teddy sparkled were to be her last performance. Only yesterday I sat in the quiet garden with Edward's letter in my hand, staring at the zinnias and the quivering leaves of the cottonwood, unable to believe the mournful message:

... Here in our house our hearts are broken. Teddy died at the hospital Thursday morning with pneumonia. She was only sick five days. We just can't content ourselves —

Teddy, the least "little cowpuncher." She used to forget sometimes and call me *Mamá*. It embarrassed her. She ducked her head, hiding her face while her companions laughed. It was purely accidental, but it pleased me.

Teddy loved school. Some children like school. Some pretend to like it. But Teddy really loved it. She wasn't quite five when she entered, but she cried every morning to come, so Pascual brought her. I accepted her, but I thought that she was going to be a bother; that she was too young to learn. I was wrong. She never had any trouble amusing herself and she learned quickly, easily keeping up with children a year or two older. At recess and noon she liked to play school, standing in front of the big chart with a pointer and making the other little children sit in the kindergarten chairs and say the words.

She learned to read and write, and dance and sing. We praised her and helped her and loved her, all of us, so that she had no feeling of constraint. Happily she moved about at will and spoke whenever she felt the urge — bothering nobody. Reading was fun for her. She always wanted to begin the lesson. When flash cards or word drills were given, she considered it a game and became very excited.

"*I*, Mrs. Bo'ne! *I! I!*" she cried in her high baby voice, bouncing in her chair in anticipation.

She liked to sing and soon memorized all the Spanish songs and some of the English ones the big children sang. The first time L. (a neighboring cattle buyer) came down I asked the kids to sing *Home On The Range* for him. Right away he picked out Teddy for special notice. When he caught my eye he grinned and slyly pointed to her — short, and plump as a cherub — as she stood in the aisle, one shoe untied, her stockings twisted, her little red sweater wrong side out, singing with all her might. When he left, Arturo went out to open the gates for him and came running back with a dime in his hand. "The visitor sent this to Teddy," he said.

She skipped for joy as she came up to get it and ran back flashing triumphant looks at her brother and sisters.

After that every time he came he brought something for her. Her mother told me that some of the little girls on the bus accused Teddy of asking for treats.

"She said," Amadita (her mother) told me, "'No, Mamá. I never ask him for anything. *El me quiere mucho!*'"

Above everything else, she liked to dance. It was not that she was especially talented. She was so young that movement and music appealed to her intensely. She was perfectly at ease, and danced naturally, with such true happiness that watchers had to smile. She and Chelo often danced together, round and round the room, marking the rhythm, never losing step. In my mind is an indelible picture of her and Pili dancing the schottische at our May festival. In her long yellow dress with tight white bodice and fluffy panniers, her hair piled high on her large head in Shirley-Temple-curls, she looked so cute! When Mrs. Smith went into the schoolroom where I was herding the costumed performers until the audience arrived, at sight of Teddy she cried to her companions — Helen Benedict and Mrs. Beach — "Look at this, will you!"

And when they danced, she and Pili, the half-frozen audience could not keep from laughing with pleasure at sight of those little feet going high in emphatic and well-timed kicks — and the little ones so serious about it!

Edward, the flower lover, was proud of how sweet she looked dressed as a rose in the scant costume he and his mother made for her.

Her baby arms and legs were dimpled and chubby. She had light ash blonde hair and a fair complexion. Usually she appeared to be heavier than she was. When I undressed her in my room that day to try on her costumes, I peeled off a sweater, a dress, another sweater, and two slips leaving her a little undershirt and panties. Her mother was always afraid that she would get pneumonia because she had had it when she was an infant.

I can't imagine her not in motion. When she came to class or went down the aisle to ask Mary a word, she skipped instead of walking. When she was sent to the board for writing or numbers, she ran. This excessive activity never annoyed me. I rejoiced in her energy, her eagerness for what came next.

She rushed through her lessons to cut out paper dolls, make wonderful water color daubs, valentines, lacy paper mats, or sets of doll dishes out of our pottery clay. She broke her crayolas, forgot to put the top on the paste jar, lost her scissors, used up her pencil which she loved to take to the pencil sharpener, and her desk was littered with papers, cut-outs, cardboard boxes, pieces of broken pottery, odds and ends of beads and colored pieces of glass. It would have been no use to scold her.

The bus usually left before she was ready to go, so there wasn't time for thorough clearing up.

"Teddy, put away your things."

"Aw right," she answered cheerfully, and shoved things out of sight before she dashed for the door. But when Socorro or Eloísa, the janitors, went to move her desk there was an avalanche.

She was too interested, too free-spirited, to be self-conscious. Somebody had to be fixing her clothes, or her hair, constantly. But when her mother curled her bright "crown of glory" and took off her cumbersome underwear and dressed her in a short blue silk dress, she was a doll — as beautiful as alive.

With infectious enthusiasm she went into everything — work, play, dancing, picnics, parades, public entertainments, with bubbling joy. She cried only when somebody shoved her out of her place in the cocoa line, or when the school doctor came. Doctors and nurses terrified her.

Yes, the year is over. I must try to stop thinking about Teddy and recall instead the final event in our grand May 8 fiesta. For if there *is* something for the future in the recollection of our wonderful past year, it lies somewhere in remembering the graduation exercises — the springboard for Mary, Socorro, Edward, and Ramón, to whatever comes next.

*   *   *

In consideration for our audience we did forego the grand march and national anthem, and we went indoors for the actual ceremony of graduation. The classroom had been prepared for inspection. With great gusto the children had made wall plaques of native clay to hold candles. We had a frieze of these soft lights around the room above the blackboards which were filled with "exhibits."

The graduation was impressive even if the clock was approaching eleven post meridian. Socorro and Mary were sweet in their simple white voiles with wreaths of white flowers on their new permanents. Under the spell of Mrs. Smith's address and Bill's proud sendoff, Ramón, poor boy, decided that he, too, was going to go to high school as Mary and Edward planned to do. The Aroses told me about his decision the next day, as if that made the whole thing possible! Of course he can't go! But the urge born in that big moment may be of benefit to the next generation.

The last hour of the day was spent in serving tamales, and dispatching friends. J. took Eleanor and her crowd back to town in my car, and I had a little visit with my Redington kids and Bill and Rosa who had crowned my pleasure by coming all that distance as a surprise.

When the company had gone, and some of the confusion cleared out of my den, I went back into the schoolroom and saw my two pretty girls dancing with the "greasy sack" fellows from the roundup. The backs of their lovely new dresses were crumpled and soiled.

As for our final issue of *Little Cowpuncher,* in the big rush after the party, of finishing lessons, hunting up and turning in books, making reports, and finishing other projects, it had to be anti-climatic. For the children, school was done for another year. They were still very interested in their report cards and promotion certificates. But their minds were on the big free outdoors, and the sooner they got there the better. Only the big girls felt responsibility yet.

A REPORT OF THE DANCES

In our drama on May 8, which we had on the outside stage Mr. Hernández and the boys made, we gave many different dances. There were folk dances such as flings, jigs, schottische, quadrille. In the second act we played as Indians, giving interpretative dances; and the little children danced as butterflies and roses in beautiful crepe paper costumes that Edward helped us make. In the third act we had the main dance festival and we had to change our costumes which took longer than we had imagined.

Some of our victrola music was classic and near-classic played by concert orchestras, and some was just popular. We had Swedish, Irish, and English folk dances and one Mexican dance. We made up our dances at school and they would have been better if our little victrola had played louder. Mary and I danced the most. We had five different costumes. I think I shall never forget our lovely dances I have them too clear in my mind.   — S. A.

THE COSTUMES

We had nice costumes. Many costumes. Some of them Mrs. Bourne borrowed from some University girls. Some she had from Redington School. Some she bought and our mothers made them and some of them our mothers bought too. In the first act we had old-fashioned clothes and they were nice and very wide. I had my grandmother's dress. It is very old. All the people liked it. It was so long and wide I had to hold it when I was dancing. The boys had nice costumes too. Our big girls looked beautiful. Their mothers had sewed very nice to make them.   — Herlinda Badilla

THE ART EXHIBIT

At the May 8 Festival we had a large and some distinguished audience. Twelve cars of people came besides our community and the roundup men. With the little time we had that day we also tried to arrange an art and pottery exhibit and I was in charge of it. There were pictures from the first to the eighth grade on the boards. They looked nice. All the audience admired them. There were four water color paintings from Mary, four from Socorro, one landscape from Ramón, and seven tempera and water color landscapes from Edward.

The pottery, made by several pupils, looked very pretty. There was not much as we had given away many of our best pieces and we had not finished some we started for the exhibit. Socorro is the prize potter. She had some beautiful pots to show. Mrs. Smith gave us many compliments. — E. H.

FUNNY THINGS THAT HAPPENED

In the afternoon Ysidra did not want to do her part in the play and Mrs. Bourne and all of us worried. But that night she did it just perfectly.

When we were having the show some more girls and I ran on the stage to untie our streamers for the Maypole too soon. There was still another dance to do first.

In E. B.'s room there was clothes all over the place on the bed and tables and chairs. When we changed our clothes they were thrown in a great pile on top of the little bed. And we lost some things. But we found them at school Monday — Inez Jane

A GIFT FROM MRS. AND MR. FRED RONSTADT

Friday afternoon of the party Mr. and Mrs. Ronstadt, Bill's father and mother, came out to leave us a nice present. They brought us some ice cream which we were very proud of. And we were happy to see them come 50 miles away from Tucson to see us. The whole school is sending millions of thanks. — S. A.

VISITORS FROM REDINGTON

We were surprised and awfully glad to have as our guests our half-brothers and half-sisters (they were Mrs. Bourne's kids too on the *Little Cowpuncher* paper) from far over the mountains on the San Pedro River at Redington. Clara, Carlota, Berta, Fidel, Manuel, Ruben, and Frank, and Mrs. Rosa and her husband came to our dance drama. I think it was really kind of them to come so far. Mrs. Rhodes is a very nice lady. It was fun to talk to them for they feel relation to us. We talked about the little paper. They were the first ones to start it and it seemed to me I had known them for a long time for I had read many stories they had written.

— Mary Hernández

PILI SAVES THE BIGGEST DANCE

Little Pili Aros, six years old, saved us from a mix-up in the intricate May-pole winding. The two second grade girls, unnoticed by the older pupils we had depended on, placed wrong. This imperiled the weaving as each boy had to do eight steps with his partner who was the fourth girl behind him at the beginning. Just as the music started Pili screamed loudly: "Chelo!" He had seen that she was the sixth, instead of the fourth, girl behind him. The quick change was made and the dance was saved. — M. H.

THE ROUNDUP COWBOYS CAME

This year the roundup lasted about two months. They came to Poso Nuevo Saturday before we had our dance on a Friday. And we had an awful time practicing for our dance on the outside stage because the cowboys had the *rodeo* (holdup) near the school and the dust was flying on our faces and we couldn't practice or sing very much.

We had more audience that I had thought we were going to have. We had all the vaqueros — they were eighteen. Lots of them were celebrating because some of them went to town in a little truck to get something for them to have a good time. But they didn't give us much trouble.   — R. A.

OUR HONOR ASSEMBLY

On the last day of school for this year Mrs. Bourne gave us prizes for the term. These are the ones who got prizes for perfect attendance which was a one dollar bill —

Ramón Aros, Socorro Aros, Víctor Aros, Pancho Aros, Arturo Aros, Ysidra Aros, Frank Aros, Consuelo Aros, Pedro Aros, Marcela Hernández, Edward Hernández.

For perfect sanitation charts:

Luis Badilla, Herlinda Badilla, Pancho Aros, Socorro Aros, Mary Hernández, Edward Hernández.

The biggest prizes were given for the Library Books:

First prize, Socorro Aros, who read 104 books.

Second prize to Mary Hernández, who read 81 books.

Third prize to Chelo Aros (1st grade), who read 23 books.

Souvenirs from E. B. were given to all the four eighth graders: Socorro, Mary, Ramón, Edward.

All of us had ice cream. The ice cream was Strawberry Frosties which Mrs. Bourne brought packed in dry ice and it was very good on a hot day when we were so busy trying to get all the books found and put away and the last issue of our *Little Cowpuncher.* Our paper closes today for the summer.   — Inez Jane Emery, *5th Grade*

MY HONOR I WILL NEVER FORGET
FROM MY DEAR COUNTRY SCHOOL

I feel so proud and high-chested for having received my Eighth Grade Diploma. And especially that our dear Mrs. Smith, and nearly all her office, came fifty miles to give an address. And our beloved clerk of the board Bill Ronstadt handed us our diplomas and gave us a few words. I am glad that all felt I had earned my honor.

I was really used to our school and my dear, dear, E. B. and I surely hate to leave her. But I am glad she felt proud of us the last time, for we tried to have her feel proud. I guess she regrets it as much as we do that we are going away, for she gave us education and fame.

I was also proud to have my dear former teacher Mrs. Campbell to see us graduate. I was in the sixth grade with her.

I had a white voile dress. Afterwards the vaqueros dancing with us ruined it with dirty hands on my back.

I regret to leave the little cowpunchers and my cowpuncher teacher. To all, I now say goodby. — Mary Hernández

SOCORRO'S TRIBUTE

Since my school term is ending I might as well say how much I appreciate E. B., and also how much I have enjoyed myself having her for my teacher. First, I must mention that this year of school has been to me like a whirl of wind over the Baboquívari Mountains. I have enjoyed it so much. And I will never forget that E. B. has made us all famous with her friends.

I am pleased with her for teaching us different kinds of dances, and stories, art, cleanness, good manners, and she has taught us how to give programs which I think most of the people who have come to our programs seem to go away and talk about nothing else for a couple of weeks.

I have been happy all the year through. She has taken us four eighth-graders to shows, parties, visits, rides, picnics, trips, and the Tucson Rodeo of Mr. Jack Kinney... I appreciate to have finished school with her and I am grateful for her name on my diploma. I hate school to end for I know I'll never have a loving teacher like E. B.

These words are my true thoughts and my thanks to my teacher for my Eighth Grade Education. Good luck for her coming years.
— Socorro Aros

While cutting the stencil for this "Tribute," I was reminded of a little second-grade girl's composition. When her teacher told the class to practice writing "Thank-you" notes, she gave them several examples on

the board, then asked them all to write an original
— each to someone of her choice. This little girl chose
to write to her teacher, saying:

Dear Mrs. B.
  Thank you for teaching us all that you know.
                                        María Elena

*   *   *

Seven weeks from day after tomorrow I will get up
early and drive down to Poso Nuevo to open school
again. And I will have to face nine empty desks. The
four eighth graders, the three Emery children, Frances,
and my little Teddy will not be there to greet me. Mary
and Edward will be in high school, proudly carrying the
banner of Little Cowpuncher School. Socorro and Ramón
will be learning in practical ways beyond school training.
The Emerys will be in Tucson, presumably with their
father. Frances will be in some migrant camp with her
mother. And Teddy — busy, happy, sweet little Teddy —
will be beyond pain or pity or the joys of human love
and learning.